**LETS GO United States of America!**

# The US Immigration Fix
# The Trump Way

FINALLY, A LONG-TERM IMMIGRATION FIX THAT PUTS
AMERICA & AMERICANS FIRST!

Donald Trump's signature issue is immigration reform because he loves America and Americans. As difficult as it is for good, hard-working Americans to believe, our government is working to keep us poor. They are lying and they are passing legislation that can only help somebody from another country beat out an American for the few jobs that exist in America. Then, these poor souls languish in misery and a lifetime of poverty. Trump knows that his plans help Americans first but it also helps illegal foreign nationals who will no longer be hurt by greedy corporations looking for slave-wage labor.

The US Immigration Fix takes interlopers out of the shadows and gives them the opportunity, **if well behaved**, to stay and work in America for a lifetime. No amnesty, no citizenship, no freebies is a demand Americans have made and it is satisfied in this plan. Those who sign up for the program must be vetted every year and must pay a fee each year or be deported. You're going to like this plan. Any questions?

BY
# Brian W. Kelly

Let's Go Publish, Publishers! PO Box 612 Wilkes-Barre PA, 18703
Copyright Brian W. Kelly 2016

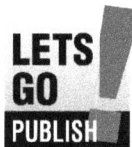

LETS
GO
PUBLISH

**Published by**:      LETS GO PUBLISH!
**Editor**             Brian P. Kelly
**Email:**             info@letsgopublish.com
**Web site**           www.letsgopublish.com

Library of Congress Copyright Information Pending

**Book Cover Design**      **Brian W. Kelly**
**Publisher**              **Brian P. Kelly**

**ISBN Information:** The International Standard Book Number (ISBN) is a unique machine-readable identification number, which marks any book unmistakably. The ISBN is the clear standard in the book industry. 159 countries and territories are officially ISBN members. The Official ISBN For this book  978-0-9980848-4-8

The price for this work is:                    **$16.95 USD**

10     9     8     7     6     5     4     3     2     1

Release Date:                          September 2016

LETS GO PUBLISH!

# Dedication

*Each & Every day when I go to work in the front office, and sometimes even before I arrive, my two co-workers on every book project are there to greet me and work with me all day—other than for extremely necessary biobreaks.*

*And, so this, back in 2015 was my 60th book and now as I tune it up without substantial changes, it is still dedicated to*
*these two fine individuals*

**Ben** & Dad

**Buddy**, Ben & Mom

# Acknowledgments:

*I appreciate all the help that I have received in putting this book together as well as all of the other 70 books from the past.*

*My acknowledgments were so large at one time that readers complained that they had to go through too many pages to get to page one.*

*And, so I put my acknowledgment list online, and it continues to grow. Believe it or not, it costs about a dollar less to print my books. No kidding!*

*Thank you and God bless you all for your help. Please check out www.letsgopublish.com to read the latest version of my heartfelt acknowledgments updated for this book.*

*Thank you all!*

# Preface:

The Annual Guest Plan, is the secret sauce of the US Immigration Fix The Trump Way. It is the perfect recipe for Donald Trump's solution to the problem of 60 million foreign interlopers (illegal aliens) residing in America today.

The Plan is the result of a ten year process from when Brian wrote his first patriotic book in 2006 titled Taxation without Representation. Version three is now current. The Annual Guest Plan was formalized in 2013. It was originally released as The Kelly Plan and for many weeks, each chapter of the plan was featured at the once very popular Conservative Action Alerts web site. Most of Kelly's articles are available for reading at www.brianwkelly.com.

At the time, Brian had examined the gang of eight plan, existing law, and other notions about how anybody might possibly solve the nation's concerns about illegal residents. Like Donald Trump, at first look, Kelly found no solutions other than amnesty and deportation. Both of these solutions directly addressed the issues that having 20 million to 60 million illegal foreign nationals in residence have brought on America.

When Kelly carefully read the gang of eight plan in 2013, he noticed that it smelled a lot like it was purposely designed to kill America. No jobs would be left for Americans; newly unemployed Americans would have to pay for newly minted citizens getting a lifetime of freebies; see them voting in national elections; and watch their numbers grow until there were 33 million more foreign nationals looking for jobs that Americans cannot even find.

According to Heritage.org, the cost for the 33 million brought in by reunification provisions was estimated at well over $6 trillion. It was a terrible deal for the country. Kelly was hunting for a real immigration fix.

Kelly looked at all of the things that Americans wanted in a real plan—things they liked and things they did not like. He also examined what interlopers liked about America. In his first cut in 2013 at solving the problem, Brian figured out a way to permit well-behaved interlopers to stay in America one year at a time with a hefty annual renewal fee, while giving Americans priority in all ways. It was a good plan but not as perfect as he had hoped. The biggest problem with the plan was that it was difficult to explain in clear concise terms.

Kelly was convinced that the plan actually would work and that it would solve the problem for the long haul and take a huge financial burden off the backs of Americans. And, so he kept at it, continually improving it until it was perfected. Every plan requires fine tuning and we would expect this to be the case with the Annual Guest Plan. By implementing the current iteration of the plan, the long-sought solution to illegal immigration is around the corner.

To see what US officials on the pro-American side of the issue would think about such a plan for America, Kelly contacted Pennsylvania Congressman, Lou Barletta. Many know Lou Barletta as a tireless advocate for fighting illegal immigration and amnesty. Mr. Kelly presented a detailed PowerPoint of his ideas in late January 2015 to the Congressman and his chief aid, Joseph Gerdes.

During the construction of the PowerPoint presentation, Brian was able to logically rearrange facets of the 2013 plan in such a way that they could be discussed point by point in a cohesive fashion and in a logical sequence. To give an idea of the completeness of the presentation facts, the first cut was about 160 slides. Before Brian gave the presentation, he further reduced the slide set so it could be completed in a reasonable amount of time.

The Congressman was most pleased with the presentation and the detail that backed up each and every point of the presentation. When the presentation was completed, the Congressman had another constituent waiting to see him, and he was advised by his aid that it would be best to wrap up the lively discussion.

However, the Congressman and Brian Kelly continued to engage in a lengthy dialogue on these issues until there was a logical break point. The Congressman spoke about the difficulties in getting immigration legislation for Americans through the House and the Senate, and he updated your author as to where the Congress was with some new initiatives.

During this interchange, the Congressman helped your author understand what was really happening in Washington, while your author helped the Congressman to fully understand the benefits of this immigration fix as a long-term solution to the problem of 60 million foreign nationals residing in America illegally.

If we could add this immigration fix to the "Beautiful Wall" and the Bills and the Amendments on Border Security, this would be the best anybody could do to solve the problem of interlopers in America once and for all. This would be the first comprehensive and comprehensible immigration plan ever put forward that favored America and Americans over foreign nationals.

Kelly promised the Congressman a text version of the presentation with its new logical flow so that he could take it, read it, and share it without having to figure out the hidden messages within the bullets of a PowerPoint.

As your author examined the document he produced, he realized that it was much more complete than the original Kelly Plan; its sequencing was much better; and the additions from the Barletta presentation / interview added a lot of missing pieces to the package. And, so, Mr. Kelly decided to re-work the text document to make it even better.

The result of course was his sixtieth book, which he called the Annual Guest Plan. Over time, after the book was out for about three years, Brian realized that a plan with an annual renewal built-in still might be misconstrued by Americans if it were called The Annual Guest Plan. Legalization for a lifetime implies a form of amnesty and the Kelly Plan was not amnesty and Donald Trump wants no amnesty. Each year the clock resets on foreign nationals who are permitted here under the Annual Guest Plan.

This book, Kelly's eightieth published book, focuses on the Annual Guest Plan as *the* tool to accomplish the goal of an American First solution to 60 million interlopers. This book offers many other notions besides the Annual Guest Plan such as a solution for green card holders not becoming citizens and for birthright citizenship, and for sanctuary cities and most of the issues in immigration that have gained the attention of Donald Trump and his followers. This immigration fix is the solution.

You won't believe how easy the problem is to solve if we can get our legislators and the current POTUS to cooperate. However, being a realist, I do not see this plan coming into being until Donald Trump is the 45th President of the United States.

In summary, this book presents the plan as the fix and then offers many other points on why this is the one and only immigration fix for our country.

**Who is Brian W. Kelly?**

Brian Kelly is the leading conservative author in America with this his 80th published book. Kelly is an outspoken and eloquent expert on immigration solutions. Though a Democrat, he is a JFK Democrat, and finds many Democrats are more like him as they have not bought in to the far left agenda and the propaganda of the current Administration.

Kelly has been writing patriotic books for more than ten years and he has many great books to his credit. He is the author of *Saving America The Trump Way*; *Taxation without Representation*; *Americans Need Not Apply*; *No Amnesty! No Way!*; *Jobs! Jobs! Jobs! The Trump Way*; *The Constitution 4 Dummmies!*; *America 4 Dummmies!* and many other patriotic books. Like many Americans, Brian is fed up with a stifling agenda in Washington that places the needs of foreign nationals in front of the needs of Americans.

He wrote this book to help Americans know what we can do to force our government to regain control of our borders, ensure our national security, keep our culture, enforce our laws, protect American jobs, make our language the language of the nation, and keep all Americans from being overwhelmed by illegal foreign nationals who offer few benefits and no allegiance to America. In addition to showing why amnesty is not the right medicine, Brian Kelly explains the best plan for America to again become a sovereign state with America-loving Americans in charge.

You are going to love this book as well as plan itself. All interlopers immediately are registered and accountable. You will see that The Annual Guest Plan (AGP) is designed by an American for Americans. Additionally, illegal foreign nationals will be very pleased because the plan uses deportation as a last resort and it immediately gets illegal foreign nationals out of the shadows. Few books are a must-read but The US Immigration Fix will quickly appear at the top of America's most read list.

Sincerely,

Brian P. Kelly, Editor

# Table of Contents

# About the Author

Brian W. Kelly retired as an Assistant Professor in the Business Information Technology (BIT) program at Marywood University, where he also served as the IBM i and midrange systems technical advisor to the IT Faculty. Kelly has designed, developed, and taught many college and professional courses. He is also a contributing technical editor to a number of IT industry magazines, including "The Four Hundred" and "Four Hundred Guru" published by IT Jungle.

Kelly is a former IBM Senior Systems Engineer and he was a candidate for US Congress from Pennsylvania. He has an active information technology consultancy. He is the author of 71 books and numerous articles. Kelly has been a frequent speaker at many US conferences.

When Kelly ran for Congress as a Democrat against a 13-term Democrat in 2010, he took no campaign contributions, spent just enough to buy signs and T-shirts, and as a virtual unknown, he captured 17% of the vote. Kelly says: "Writing books is lots easier than running for public office!"

# Prologue   Donald Trump's Formal Campaign Immigration Position

Before we begin to discuss the inclusive immigration fix in this book, let's look at the clear official position statement from the Trump web site. This brief position paper sets the stage and shows how serious Donald Trump is about solving America's problem with border jumpers, visa over-stayers, and otherwise illegal interlopers residing in the US.

## IMMIGRATION REFORM THAT WILL MAKE AMERICA GREAT AGAIN

### The three core principles of Donald J. Trump's immigration plan

When politicians talk about "immigration reform" they mean: amnesty, cheap labor and open borders. The Schumer-Rubio immigration bill was nothing more than a giveaway to the corporate patrons who run both parties.

Real immigration reform puts the needs of working people first – not wealthy globetrotting donors. We are the only country in the world whose immigration system puts the needs of other nations ahead of our own. That must change. Here are the three core principles of real immigration reform:

1. A nation without borders is not a nation. There must be a wall across the southern border.

2. A nation without laws is not a nation. Laws passed in accordance with our Constitutional system of government must be enforced.

3. A nation that does not serve its own citizens is not a nation. Any immigration plan must improve jobs, wages and security for all Americans.

## Make Mexico Pay for the Wall

For many years, Mexico's leaders have been taking advantage of the United States by using illegal immigration to export the crime and poverty in their own country (as well as in other Latin American countries). They have even published pamphlets on how to illegally immigrate to the United States. The costs for the United States have been extraordinary: U.S. taxpayers have been asked to pick up hundreds of billions in healthcare costs, housing costs, education costs, welfare costs, etc. Indeed, the annual cost of free tax credits alone paid to illegal immigrants quadrupled to $4.2 billion in 2011. The effects on jobseekers have also been disastrous, and black Americans have been particularly harmed.

The impact in terms of crime has been tragic. In recent weeks, the headlines have been covered with cases of criminals who crossed our border illegally only to go on to commit horrific crimes against Americans. Most recently, an illegal immigrant from Mexico, with a long arrest record, is charged with breaking into a 64 year-old woman's home, crushing her skull and eye sockets with a hammer, raping her, and murdering her. The Police Chief in Santa Maria says the "blood trail" leads straight to Washington.

In 2011, the Government Accountability Office found that there were a shocking 3 million arrests attached to the incarcerated alien population, including tens of thousands of violent beatings, rapes and murders.

Meanwhile, Mexico continues to make billions on not only our bad trade deals but also relies heavily on the billions of dollars in remittances sent from illegal immigrants in the United States back to Mexico ($22 billion in 2013 alone). In short, the Mexican government has taken the United States to the cleaners. They are responsible for this problem, and they must help pay to clean it up.

The cost of building a permanent border wall pales mightily in comparison to what American taxpayers spend every single year on dealing with the fallout of illegal immigration on their communities, schools and unemployment offices.

Mexico must pay for the wall and, until they do, the United States will, among other things: impound all remittance payments derived from illegal wages; increase fees on all temporary visas issued to Mexican CEOs and diplomats (and if necessary cancel them); increase fees on all border crossing cards – of which we issue about 1 million to Mexican nationals each year (a major source of visa overstays); increase fees on all NAFTA worker visas from Mexico (another major source of overstays); and increase fees at ports of entry to the United States from Mexico [Tariffs and foreign aid cuts are also options]. We will not be taken advantage of anymore.

# Defend the Laws And Constitution Of The United States

America will only be great as long as America remains a nation of laws that lives according to the Constitution. No one is above the law. The following steps will return to the American people the safety of their laws, which politicians have stolen from them:

# Triple the number of ICE officers.

As the President of the ICE Officers' Council explained in Congressional testimony: "Only approximately 5,000 officers and agents within ICE perform the lion's share of ICE's immigration mission...Compare that to the Los Angeles Police Department at approximately 10,000 officers. Approximately 5,000 officers in ICE cover 50 states, Puerto Rico and Guam, and are attempting to enforce immigration law against 11 million illegal aliens already in the interior of the United States. Since 9-11, the U.S. Border Patrol has tripled in size, while ICE's immigration enforcement arm, Enforcement and Removal Operations (ERO), has remained at relatively the same size." This will be funded by accepting the recommendation of the Inspector General for Tax Administration and eliminating tax credit payments to illegal immigrants.

# Nationwide e-verify.

This simple measure will protect jobs for unemployed Americans.

# Mandatory return of all criminal aliens.

The Obama Administration has released 76,000 aliens from its custody with criminal convictions since 2013 alone. All criminal aliens must be returned to their home countries, a process which can be aided by canceling any visas to foreign countries which will not accept their own criminals, and making it a separate and additional crime to commit an offense while here illegally.

# Detention—not catch-and-release.

Illegal aliens apprehended crossing the border must be detained until they are sent home, no more catch-and-release.

# Defund sanctuary cities.

Cut-off federal grants to any city which refuses to cooperate with federal law enforcement.

# Enhanced penalties for overstaying a visa.

Millions of people come to the United States on temporary visas but refuse to leave, without consequence. This is a threat to national security. Individuals who refuse to leave at the time their visa expires should be subject to criminal penalties; this will also help give local jurisdictions the power to hold visa overstays until federal authorities arrive. Completion of a visa tracking system – required by law but blocked by lobbyists – will be necessary as well.

# Cooperate with local gang task forces.

ICE officers should accompany local police departments conducting raids of violent street gangs like MS-13 and the 18th street gang, which have terrorized the country. All illegal aliens in gangs should be apprehended and deported. Again, quoting Chris Crane: "ICE Officers and Agents are forced to apply the Deferred Action for Childhood Arrivals (DACA) Directive, not to children in schools, but to adult inmates in jails. If an illegal-alien inmate simply claims eligibility, ICE is forced to release the alien back into the community. This includes serious criminals who have committed felonies, who have assaulted officers, and who prey on children…ICE officers should be required to place detainers on every illegal alien they encounter in jails and prisons, since these aliens not only violated immigration laws, but then went on to engage in activities that led to their arrest by police; ICE officers should be required to issue Notices to Appear to all illegal aliens with criminal convictions, DUI convictions, or a gang affiliation; ICE should be working with any state or local drug or gang task force that asks for such assistance."

# End birthright citizenship.

This remains the biggest magnet for illegal immigration. By a 2:1 margin, voters say it's the wrong policy, including Harry Reid who said "no sane country" would give automatic citizenship to the children of illegal immigrants.

# Put American Workers First

Decades of disastrous trade deals and immigration policies have destroyed our middle class. Today, nearly 40% of black teenagers are unemployed. Nearly 30% of Hispanic teenagers are unemployed. For black Americans without high school diplomas, the bottom has fallen out: more than 70% were employed in 1960, compared to less than 40% in 2000. Across the economy, the percentage of adults in the labor force has collapsed to a level not experienced in generations. As CBS news wrote in a piece entitled "America's incredible shrinking middle class": "If the middle-class is the economic backbone of America, then the country is developing osteoporosis."

The influx of foreign workers holds down salaries, keeps unemployment high, and makes it difficult for poor and working class Americans – including immigrants themselves and their children – to earn a middle class wage. Nearly half of all immigrants and their US-born children currently live in or near poverty, including more than 60 percent of Hispanic immigrants. Every year, we voluntarily admit another 2 million new immigrants, guest workers, refugees, and dependents, growing our existing all-time historic record population of 42 million immigrants. We need to control the admission of new low-earning workers in order to: help wages grow, get teenagers back to work, aid minorities' rise into the middle class, help schools and communities falling behind, and to ensure our immigrant members of the national family become part of the American dream.

Additionally, we need to stop giving legal immigrant visas to people bent on causing us harm. From the 9/11 hijackers, to the Boston Bombers, and many others, our immigration system is being used to attack us. The President of the immigration caseworkers union declared in a statement on ISIS: "We've become the visa clearinghouse for the world."

**Here are some additional specific policy proposals for long-term reform:**

# Increase prevailing wage for H-1Bs.

We graduate two times more Americans with STEM degrees each year than find STEM jobs, yet as much as two-thirds of entry-level hiring for IT jobs is accomplished through the H-1B program. More than half of H-1B visas are issued for the program's lowest allowable wage level, and more than eighty percent for its bottom two. Raising the prevailing wage paid to H-1Bs will force companies to give these coveted entry-level jobs to the existing domestic pool of unemployed native and immigrant workers in the U.S., instead of flying in cheaper workers from overseas. This will improve the number of black, Hispanic and female workers in Silicon Valley who have been passed over in favor of the H-1B program. Mark Zuckerberg's personal Senator, Marco Rubio, has a bill to triple H-1Bs that would decimate women and minorities.

## Requirement to hire American workers first.

Too many visas, like the H-1B, have no such requirement. In the year 2015, with 92 million Americans outside the workforce and incomes collapsing, we need companies to hire from the domestic pool of unemployed. Petitions for workers should be mailed to the unemployment office, not USCIS.

# End welfare abuse.

Applicants for entry to the United States should be required to certify that they can pay for their own housing, healthcare and other needs before coming to the U.S.

# Jobs program for inner city youth.

The J-1 visa jobs program for foreign youth will be terminated and replaced with a resume bank for inner city youth provided to all corporate subscribers to the J-1 visa program.

# Refugee program for American children.

Increase standards for the admission of refugees and asylum-seekers to crack down on abuses. Use the monies saved on expensive refugee programs to help place American children without parents in safer homes and communities, and to improve community safety in high crime neighborhoods in the United States.

# Immigration moderation.

Before any new green cards are issued to foreign workers abroad, there will be a pause where employers will have to hire from the domestic pool of unemployed immigrant and native workers. This will help reverse women's plummeting workplace participation rate, grow wages, and allow record immigration levels to subside to more moderate historical averages.

—end of Trump immigration position—

# Trump follow-up visit to Mexico with immigration speech in Phoenix

On Wednesday, August 31, 2016, accepting an invitation received by both the Republican presidential nominee and Hillary Clinton, Presidential candidate Donald Trump accepted the invitation and flew to Mexico City to meet with President Enrique Peña Nieto. The visit stimulated much interest, since stopping illegal immigration from Mexico by building a wall along the U.S.-Mexican border and conducting deportations of illegal immigrants have been key parts of Trump's campaign from the beginning

Trump began Wednesday's busy schedule in California where he held a fundraiser. He then flew to Mexico City and met with the Mexican President. Showing tremendous energy, after his meeting and remarks in Mexico, Mr. Trump flew to Phoenix Arizona Wednesday evening where he delivered his most extensive speech on the subject of illegal immigration since the onset of his campaign.

Fox News quoted Trump's post-meeting statement: "We had a very substantive, direct and constructive exchange of ideas." ABC News reported that Peña Nieto spoke first, speaking in Spanish through a translator, saying that Mexico will be a good neighbor to the United States and that the countries will work together as "strategic allies."

"We must always be open to talk about what has worked and what hasn't,' said Mexico's president, continuing by noting that his country and the United States will have a "relationship based on mutual respect." He said that during their private meeting he told Trump he would stand by Mexicans "wherever they are."

Peña Nieto said of Trump that "we may not be in agreement on a number of subjects," but the two countries are important to each other. He said the purpose of Trump's visit was to meet and talk about their views and described their meeting as "very open and constructive."

Illegal immigration is such a big issue in the United States that in addition to the campaign positions listed above in this chapter, and the newly expanded positions in his Phoenex speech, Mr. Trump needs a serious answer to the 60 million foreign interlopers who currently reside in the US and who have taken many American jobs. The chapters in this book are designed to address this aspect of the illegal immigration dilemma.

First, let's review the issues clarified by Donald Trump in his outstanding Phonix speech delivered August 31 in Phoenix, AZ.

# Donald Trump's immigration speech in Phoenix, Arizona:

*Thank you, Phoenix. I am so glad to be back in Arizona, a state that has a very special place in my heart.*

*I love the people of Arizona and, together, we are going to win the White House in November.*

*Tonight is not going to be a normal rally speech.*

*Instead, I am going to deliver a detailed policy address on one of the greatest challenges facing our country today: immigration.*

*I have just landed having returned from a very important and special meeting with the President of Mexico – a man I like and respect very much, and a man who truly loves his country. Just like I am a man who loves the United States.*

*We agreed on the importance of ending the illegal flow of drugs, cash, guns and people across our border, and to put the cartels out of business.*

*We also discussed the great contributions of Mexican-American citizens to our two countries, my love for the people of Mexico, and the close friendship between our two nations.*

*It was a thoughtful and substantive conversation. This is the first of what I expect will be many conversations in a Trump Administration about creating a new relationship between our two countries.*

*But to fix our immigration system, we must change our leadership in Washington. There is no other way.*

*The truth is, our immigration system is worse than anyone realizes. But the facts aren't known because the media won't report on them, the politicians won't talk about them, and the special interests spend a lot of money trying to cover them up.*

*Today you will get the truth.*

*The fundamental problem with the immigration system in our country is that it serves the needs of wealthy donors, political activists and powerful politicians. Let me tell you who it doesn't serve: it doesn't serve you, the American people.*

*When politicians talk about immigration reform, they usually mean the following: amnesty, open borders, and lower wages.*

*Immigration reform should mean something else entirely: it should mean improvements to our laws and policies to make life better for American citizens.*

*But if we are going to make our immigration system work, then we have to be prepared to talk honestly and without fear about these important and sensitive issues.*

*For instance, we have to listen to the concerns that working people have over the record pace of immigration and its impact on their jobs, wages, housing, schools, tax bills, and living conditions. These are valid concerns, expressed by decent and patriotic citizens from all backgrounds.*

*We also have to be honest about the fact that not everyone who seeks to join our country will be able to successfully assimilate. It is our right as a sovereign nation to choose immigrants that we think are the likeliest to thrive and flourish here.*

*Then there is the issue of security. Countless innocent American lives have been stolen because our politicians have failed in their duty to secure our borders and enforce our laws.*

*I have met with many of the parents who lost their children to Sanctuary Cities and open borders. They will be joining me on the stage later today.*

*Countless Americans who have died in recent years would be alive today if not for the open border policies of this*

*Administration. This includes incredible Americans like 21-year-old Sarah Root. The man who killed her arrived at the border, entered federal custody, and then was released into a U.S. community under the policies of this White House. He was released again after the crime, and is now at large.*

*Sarah had graduated from college with a 4.0, top of her class, the day before.*

*Also among the victims of the Obama-Clinton open borders policies was Grant Ronnebeck, a 21 year-old convenience store clerk in Mesa, Arizona. He was murdered by an illegal immigrant gang member previously convicted of burglary who had also been released from Federal Custody.*

*Another victim is Kate Steinle, gunned down in the Sanctuary City of San Francisco by an illegal immigrant deported five previous times.*

*Then there is the case of 90 year-old Earl Olander, who was brutally beaten and left to bleed to death in his home. The perpetrators were illegal immigrants with criminal records who did not meet the Obama Administration's priorities for removal.*

*In California, a 64 year-old Air Force Veteran, Marilyn Pharis, was sexually assaulted and beaten to death with a hammer. Her killer had been arrested on multiple occasions, but was never deported.*

*A 2011 report from the Government Accountability Office found that illegal immigrants and other non-citizens in our prisons and jails together had around 25,000 homicide arrests to their names.*

*On top of that, illegal immigration costs our country more than $113 billion dollars a year. For the money we are going to spend on illegal immigration over the next ten years, we* could provide one million at-risk students with a school voucher.

While there are many illegal immigrants in our country who are good people, this doesn't change the fact that most illegal immigrants are lower-skilled workers with less education who compete directly against vulnerable American workers, and that these illegal workers draw much more out from the system than they will ever pay in.

But these facts are never reported.

Instead, the media and my opponent discuss one thing, and only this one thing: the needs of people living here illegally.

The truth is, the central issue is not the needs of the 11 million illegal immigrants – or however many there may be.

That has never been the central issue. It will never be the central issue.
 Anyone who tells you that the core issue is the needs of those living here illegally has simply spent too much time in Washington.

Only out of touch media elites think the biggest problem facing American society today is that there are 11 million illegal immigrants who don't have legal status.

To all the politicians, donors and special interests, hear these words from me today: there is only one core issue in the immigration debate and it is this: the well-being of the American people. Nothing even comes a close second.

Hillary Clinton, for instance, talks constantly about her fears that families will be separated. But she's not talking about the American families who have been permanently separated from their loved ones because of a preventable death. No, she's only talking about families who came here in violation of the law.

*We will treat everyone living or residing in our country with dignity. We will be fair, just and compassionate to all. But our greatest compassion must be for American citizens.*

*President Obama and Hillary Clinton have engaged in gross dereliction of duty by surrendering the safety of the American people to open borders. President Obama and Hillary Clinton support Sanctuary Cities, they support catch-and-release on the border, they support visa overstays, they support the release of dangerous criminals from detention – and they support unconstitutional executive amnesty.*

*Hillary Clinton has pledged amnesty in her first 100 days, and her plan will provide Obamacare, Social Security and Medicare for illegal immigrants – breaking the federal budget. On top of that, she promises uncontrolled low-skilled immigration that continues to reduce jobs and wages for American workers, especially African-American and Hispanic workers. This includes her plan to bring in 620,000 new refugees in a four-year term.*

*Now that you've heard about Hillary Clinton's plan – about which she has not answered a single substantive question – let me tell you about my plan.*

*While Hillary Clinton meets only with donors and lobbyists, my plan was crafted with the input from federal immigration officers, along with top immigration experts who represent workers, not corporations. I also worked with lawmakers who've led on this issue on behalf of American citizens for many years, and most importantly, I've met with the people directly impacted by these policies.*

***Number One: We will build a wall along the Southern Border.***

*On day one, we will begin working on an impenetrable physical wall on the southern border. We will use the best technology, including above-and below-ground sensors, towers, aerial surveillance and manpower to supplement the wall, find and dislocate tunnels, and keep out the criminal cartels, and Mexico will pay for the wall.*

### *Number Two: End Catch-And-Release*

*Under my Administration, anyone who illegally crosses the border will be detained until they are removed out of our country.*

### *Number Three: Zero tolerance for criminal aliens.*

*According to federal data, there are at least 2 million criminal aliens now inside the country. We will begin moving them out day one, in joint operations with local, state and federal law enforcement.*

*Beyond the 2 million, there are a vast number of additional criminal illegal immigrants who have fled or evaded justice. But their days on the run will soon be over. They go out, and they go out fast.*

*Moving forward, we will issue detainers for all illegal immigrants who are arrested for any crime whatsoever, and they will be placed into immediate removal proceedings. We will terminate the Obama Administration's deadly non-enforcement policies that allow thousands of criminal aliens to freely roam our streets.*

*Since 2013 alone, the Obama Administration has allowed 300,000 criminal aliens to return back into U.S. communities – these are individuals encountered or identified by ICE but who not detained or processed for deportation.*

*My plan also includes cooperating closely with local jurisdictions to remove criminal aliens.*

*We will restore the highly successful Secure Communities*

*program. We will expand and revitalize the popular 287(g) partnerships, which will help to identify hundreds of thousands of deportable aliens in local jails. Both of these programs have been recklessly gutted by this Administration. This is yet one more area where we are headed in a totally opposite direction.*

*On my first day in office, I am also going to ask Congress to pass "Kate's Law" – named for Kate Steinle – to ensure that criminal aliens convicted of illegal reentry face receive strong mandatory minimum sentences.*

*Another reform I am proposing is the passage of legislation named for Detective Michael Davis and Deputy Sheriff Danny Oliver, two law enforcement officers recently killed by a previously-deported illegal immigrant. The Davis-Oliver bill will enhance cooperation with state and local authorities to ensure that criminal immigrants and terrorists are swiftly identified and removed.*

*We are going to triple the number of ICE deportation officers. Within ICE, I am going to create a new special Deportation Task Force, focused on identifying and removing quickly the most dangerous criminal illegal immigrants in America who have evaded justice.*

*The local police know who every one of these criminals are. There's no great mystery to it, they've put up with it for years. And now, finally, we will turn the tables and law enforcement will be allowed to clear up this dangerous and threatening mess.*

*We're also going to hire 5,000 more Border Patrol agents, and put more of them on the border, instead of behind desks. We will expand the number of Border Patrol Stations.*

*I've had a chance to spend time with these incredible law enforcement officers, and I want to take a moment to thank them. The endorsement I've received from the Border Patrol officers means more to me than I can say.*

### Number Four: Block Funding For Sanctuary Cities

*We will end the Sanctuary Cities that have resulted in so many needless deaths. Cities that refuse to cooperate with federal authorities will not receive taxpayer dollars, and we will work with Congress to pass legislation to protect those jurisdictions that do assist federal authorities.*

### Number Five: Cancel Unconstitutional Executive Orders & Enforce All Immigration Laws

*We will immediately terminate President Obama's two illegal executive amnesties, in which he defied federal law and the constitution to give amnesty to approximately 5 million illegal immigrants.*

*Hillary Clinton has pledged to keep both of these illegal amnesty programs – including the 2014 amnesty which has been blocked by the Supreme Court. Clinton has also pledged to add a third executive amnesty.*

*Clinton's plan would trigger a Constitutional Crisis unlike almost anything we have ever seen before. In effect, she would be abolishing the lawmaking powers of Congress in order to write her own laws from the Oval Office.*

*In a Trump Administration, all immigration laws will be enforced. As with any law enforcement activity, we will set priorities. But, unlike this Administration, no one will be immune or exempt from enforcement – and ICE and Border Patrol officers will be allowed to do their jobs. Anyone who has entered the United States illegally is subject to deportation – that is what it means to have laws and to have a country.*

*Our enforcement priorities will include removing criminals, gang members, security threats, visa overstays, public charges – that is, those relying on public welfare or straining the safety net, along with millions of recent illegal arrivals and overstays who've come here under the current Administration.*

**Number Six: We Are Going To Suspend The Issuance Of Visas To Any Place Where Adequate Screening Cannot Occur**

*According to data provided to the Senate Subcommittee on Immigration and the National Interest, between 9/11 and the end of 2014, at least 380 foreign-born individuals were convicted in terror cases inside the United States. The number is likely higher, but the Administration refuses to provide this information to Congress.*

*As soon as I enter office, I am going to ask the Department of State, Homeland Security and the Department of Justice to begin a comprehensive review of these cases in order to develop a list of regions and countries from which immigration must be suspended until proven and effective vetting mechanisms can be put into place.*

*Countries from which immigration will be suspended would include places like Syria and Libya.*

*For the price of resettling 1 refugee in the United States, 12 could be resettled in a safe zone in their home region.*

*Another reform involves new screening tests for all applicants that include an ideological certification to make sure that those we are admitting to our country share our values and love our people.*

*For instance, in the last five years, we've admitted nearly 100,000 immigrants from Iraq and Afghanistan – in these*

*two countries, according to Pew research, a majority of
residents say that the barbaric practice of honor killings
against women are often or sometimes justified.*

*Applicants will be asked for their views about honor killings,
about respect for women and gays and minorities, attitudes
on Radical Islam, and many other topics as part of the
vetting procedure.*

**Number Seven: We will ensure that other countries take
their people back when we order them deported**

*There are at least 23 countries that refuse to take their
people back after they have been ordered to leave the
United States, including large numbers of violent criminals.
Due to a Supreme Court decision, if these violent offenders
cannot be sent home, our law enforcement officers have to
release them into U.S. communities. There are often terrible
consequences, such as Casey Chadwick's tragic death in
Connecticut just last year. Yet, despite the existence of a
law that commands the Secretary of State to stop issuing
visas to these countries, Secretary Hillary Clinton ignored
this law and refused to use this powerful tool to bring
nations into compliance.*

*The result of her misconduct was the release of thousands
of dangerous criminal aliens who should have been sent
home.*

*According to a report from the Boston Globe, from the year
2008 through 2014, nearly 13,000 criminal aliens were
released back into U.S. communities because their home
countries would not take them back. Many of these 13,000
releases occurred on Hillary Clinton's watch – she had the
power and the duty to stop it cold and she didn't do it.*

*Those released include individuals convicted of killings,
sexual assault and some of the most heinous crimes
imaginable, who went on to reoffend at a very high rate.*

### Number Eight: We will finally complete the biometric entry-exit visa tracking system.

*For years, Congress has required a biometric entry-exit visa tracking system, but it has never been completed.*

*In my Administration, we will ensure that this system is in place at all land, air, and sea ports. Approximately half of new illegal immigrants came on temporary visas and then never left. Beyond violating our laws, visa overstays pose a substantial threat to national security. The 9/11 Commission said that this tracking system should be a high priority and "would have assisted law enforcement and intelligence officials in August and September 2001 in conducting a search for two of the 9/11 hijackers that were in the U.S. on expired visas."*

*Last year alone, nearly a half a million individuals overstayed their temporary visas. Removing visa overstays will be a top priority of my Administration. If people around the world believe they can just come on a temporary visa and never leave – the Obama-Clinton policy – then we have a completely open border. We must send the message that visa expiration dates will be strongly enforced.*

### Number Nine: We will turn off the jobs and benefits magnet.

*We will ensure that E-Verify is used to the fullest extent possible under existing law, and will work with Congress to strengthen and expand its use across the country.*

*Immigration law doesn't exist just for the purpose of keeping out criminals. It exists to protect all aspects of American life – the worksite, the welfare office, the education system and much else. That is why immigration limits are established in the first place. If we only enforce the laws against crime, then we have an open border to the entire world.*

*I will enforce all of our immigration laws.*

*The same goes for government benefits. The Center for Immigration Studies estimates that 62 percent of households headed by illegal immigrants used some form of cash or non-cash welfare programs, like food stamps or housing assistance. This directly violates the federal public charge law designed to protect the U.S. treasury.*

*Those who abuse our welfare system will be priorities for removal.*

**Number 10: We will reform legal immigration to serve the best interests of America and its workers**

*We've admitted 59 million immigrants to the United States between 1965 and 2015.*

*Many of these arrivals have greatly enriched our country. But we now have an obligation to them, and to their children, to control future immigration – as we have following previous immigration waves – to ensure assimilation, integration and upward mobility.*

*Within just a few years immigration as a share of national population is set to break all historical records.*

*The time has come for a new immigration commission to develop a new set of reforms to our legal immigration system in order to achieve the following goals:*

*To keep immigration levels, measured by population share, within historical norms*

*To select immigrants based on their likelihood of success in U.S. society, and their ability to be financially self-sufficient. We need a system that serves our needs – remember, it's America First.*

*To choose immigrants based on merit, skill and proficiency*

*And to establish new immigration controls to boost wages and to ensure that open jobs are offered to American workers first.*
*We want people to come into our country, but they have to come in legally and properly-vetted, and in a manner that serves the national interest.*

*We've been living under outdated immigration rules from decades ago. To avoid this happening in the future, I believe we should sunset our visa laws so that Congress is forced to periodically revise and revisit them. We wouldn't put our entire federal budget on autopilot for decades, so why should we do the same for immigration?*

*Let's talk about the big picture*

*These ten steps, if rigorously followed and enforced, will accomplish more in a matter of months than our politicians have accomplished on this issue in the last fifty years.*

*Because I am not a politician, because I am not beholden to any special interest, I will get this done for you and your family.*

*We will accomplish all of the steps outlined above, and when we do, peace and law and justice and prosperity will prevail. Crime will go down, border crossings will plummet, gangs will disappear, and welfare use will decrease. We will have a peace dividend to spend on rebuilding America, beginning with our inner cities.*

*For those here today illegally who are seeking legal status, they will have one route and only one route: to return home and apply for re-entry under the rules of the new legal immigration system that I have outlined above. Those who have left to seek entry under this new system will not be awarded surplus visas, but will have to enter under the immigration caps or limits that will be established.*

*We will break the cycle of amnesty and illegal immigration. There will be no amnesty.*

*Our message to the world will be this: you cannot obtain legal status, or become a citizen of the United States, by illegally entering our country.*

*This declaration alone will help stop the crisis of illegal crossings and illegal overstays.*

*People will know that you can't just smuggle in, hunker down, and wait to be legalized. Those days are over.*

*In several years, when we have accomplished all of our enforcement goals – and truly ended illegal immigration for good, including the construction of a great wall, and the establishment of our new lawful immigration system – then and only then will we be in a position to consider the appropriate disposition of those who remain. That discussion can only take place in an atmosphere in which illegal immigration is a memory of the past, allowing us to weigh the different options available based on the new circumstances at the time.*

*Right now, however, we are in the middle of a jobs crisis, a border crisis, and a terrorism crisis. All energies of the federal government and the legislative process must now be focused on immigration security. That is the only conversation we should be having at this time.*

*Whether it's dangerous materials being smuggled across the border, terrorists entering on visas, or Americans losing their jobs to foreign workers, these are the problems we must now focus on fixing – and the media needs to begin demanding to hear Hillary Clinton's answer on how her policies will affect Americans and their security.*

*These are matters of life-and-death for our country and its people, and we deserve answers from Hillary Clinton.*

*What we do know, despite the total lack of media curiosity, is that Hillary Clinton promises a radical amnesty combined with a radical reduction in immigration enforcement. The result will be millions more illegal immigrants, thousands more violent crimes, and total chaos and lawlessness.*

*This election is our last chance to secure the border, stop illegal immigration, and reform our laws to make your life better.*

*This is it. We won't get another opportunity – it will be too late.*

*So I want to remind everyone what we are fighting for – and who we are fighting for.*

*So I am going to ask all the Angel Moms to come join me on the stage right now.*

*[[PAUSE FOR ANGEL MOMS – EACH SAYS THE NAME OF THEIR CHILD INTO THE MICROPHONE]]*

*Now is the time for these voices to be heard.*

*Now is the time for the media to begin asking questions on their behalf.*

*Now is the time for all of us, as one country, Democrat and Republican, liberal and conservative, to band together to deliver justice and safety and security for all Americans.*

*Let's fix this problem.*

*Let's secure our border.*

*Let's stop the drugs and the crime.*

*Let's protect our Social Security and Medicare.*

*And let's get unemployed Americans off of welfare and back to work in their own country.*

*Together, we can save American lives, American jobs, and American futures.*

*Together, we can save America itself.*

*Join me in this mission to Make America Great Again.*

*Thank you, and God Bless you all!*

# Chapter 1 The Fix Is In!

## The Fix Satisfies Americans First

The US immigration fix is in and it is very comprehensive, comprehensible, and All-American. If you are one of the Americans who is sick and tired of having your lunch eaten and your job taken by a foreign interloper, using your tax money, then you are going to like this fix. The fix addresses each of your pet peeves about immigration and it outlines solutions that benefit America and American citizens. It can work because while making American citizens #1 again after years of a poor governmental response to our needs, this solution should also be very popular with the underground illegal alien community. It is win-win.

If you are an illegal foreign national, this is your opportunity to be out of the shadows living like all other humans in America. You are going to like this fix. If you are an anchor citizen, or the mom or dad of an anchor citizen, you are going to like this fix. If you are on a temporary visa and your plan is to stay in this country with a green card, or illegally if you cannot get one, you are going to like this fix. The bottom line is that this fix is in and it is designed to help all constituencies. Isn't it about time?

Of course no fix would be needed if there were no problem. All Americans are all too aware that there are way too many problems with our immigration system, most of which are because the laws that are in place today are being ignored by Congress and the POTUS. Some may be skeptical and ask what good is another law? That is a great question.

This is the answer and it is simple. If the Congress will not propose the fix and the POTUS won't sign the fix if proposed, then Houston, we do have a big problem. The people cannot stand for this. Therefore, the representatives of those parties offering no real solutions will lose their reelection bids. The people will vote them out. Once the people are able to bring the corrupt representatives back home, the government will be able to change for the better.

If the fix is in, and the Congress and POTUS enact it into law, and the new POTUS will not enforce it, this time we will have a people's Congress that will be able impeach the new President post haste. This important matter must be solved before America has a higher illegal population than legal. When states with majority of illegal foreign nationals begin to petition the US government for the right to secede from the union, we will then see how far this problem will have taken us. Let's not let that happen. We never have to go there. We will prevail. We have the fix. The fix is in. Donald Trump as President will assure the fix.

Have you ever asked yourself what problems are we trying to solve with an immigration fix? What are the basic objectives we hope to achieve? Let's look there first. Since it is tough to find proof of an objective or a goal, we will synthesize our own with some help from some already written and/or codified material. Overall those we have deduced are the objectives for most Americans looking for the US Immigration Fix:

Looking for already existing documentation from US immigration law or from US agencies, as you will see in the Graham article discussed below is hopeless. It is non-existent. So, I decided that I would first look at what we tell our newly minted citizens so they understand what they must do to be good citizens. There are a number of immigration objectives for America right here in the immigration oath. It is thing of beauty:

*"I hereby declare, on oath, that I absolutely and entirely renounce and abjure all allegiance and fidelity to any foreign prince, potentate, state, or sovereignty, of whom or which I have heretofore been a subject or citizen; that I will support and defend the Constitution and laws of the United States of America against all enemies, foreign and domestic; that I will bear true faith and allegiance to the same; that I will bear arms on behalf of the United States when required by the law; that I will perform noncombatant service in the Armed Forces of the United States when required by the law; that I will perform work of national importance under civilian direction when required by the law; and that I take this obligation freely, without any mental reservation or purpose of evasion; so help me God."*

The principles embodied in the *"Oath"* are codified in Section 337 of the Immigration and Nationality Act (INA), which provides that all applicants shall take an oath that incorporates the substance of the following:

1. America first, last, and always
2. Support the Constitution;
3. Renounce and abjure absolutely and entirely all allegiance and fidelity to any foreign prince, potentate, state, or sovereignty of whom or which the applicant was before a subject or citizen;
4. Support and defend the Constitution and laws of the United States against all enemies, foreign and domestic;
5. Bear true faith and allegiance to the same; and
6. Bear arms on behalf of the United States when required by the law; or
7. Perform noncombatant service in the Armed Forces of the United States when required by the law; or
8. Perform work of national importance under civilian direction when required by the law.

# State Department Mission Statement

*Here it is:*

*Create a more secure, democratic, and prosperous world for the benefit of the American people and the international community*

Quite frankly, the State department could have done better. I am not pleased with the State Department's Mission Statement because America's mission is not to serve the world but to serve Americans. And, so I would change this as follows:

*Create a more secure, democratic, and prosperous world for the benefit of the American people and by benefitting Americans, so also will the world we create benefit the international community.*

# Mission Statement of the USA

The United States has a Mission Statement which basically provides the objectives for the nation in mission language. We all recognize the first sentence of the Constitution:

"We the people of the United States, in order to form a more perfect *union*." Notice the word *union*. That is key. The objective is to have a *union* of peoples, not an unrelated collection of diverse elements. That union of people over the 240 years of US history has melted into a people known the world over as the citizens of the United States.

Right below you will find a bulletized US Mission statement according to the founders. This in essence is the purpose of the US government brought forth in the Constitution:

- Establish justice
- Ensure domestic tranquility
- Provide for the common defense
- Promote the general welfare

- Secure the blessings of liberty to ourselves and our posterity
- All rights are granted to the people; none to government
- National government is bound by the Constitution
- People's inalienable rights come from God
- Bill of Rights are explicit notions of specific freedoms and liberties already granted in the constitution

# USCIS Mission

As an aside, the official term for illegal interloper in US law and jargon is *illegal alien*. This is the way immigration law describes the term *illegal alien— "an alien who has entered the United States illegally and is deportable if apprehended, or an alien who entered the United States legally but who has fallen "out of status" and is deportable."*

The most important part of the mission statement of the U.S. Citizenship and Immigration Services (USCIS), the government agency that oversees lawful immigration to the United States is listed under the category of *Vigilance*.

"In this era of increased global threats and national security challenges, we will remain mindful of our obligation to provide immigration service in a manner that strengthens and fortifies the nation. We will exercise a holistic approach to Vigilance as we perform our mission. We will carefully administer every aspect of our immigration mission so that new immigrants and citizens can hold in high regard the privileges and advantages of lawful presence in the United States."

From this objective, we can see the major defined purpose of this important Immigration Agency:

- Strengthen the nation
- Fortify / protect the nation

- Maintain a lawful presence
- Be careful who we let into the country (global threats)
- Privilege of citizenship is for citizens

To look at the role even more objectively, it helps to point out that the USCIS mission does not include the following:

- Reunification
- Providing gifts of any kind to illegal foreign nationals
- Admitting terrorists into the US
- Changing the demographics of the US
- Permitting illegal aliens to reside and work in America
- Assuring welfare/healthcare is granted to illegal aliens
- Providing any advantages to illegal aliens over citizens

And so, having read the terrific Graham article summarized below and from examining the preceding mission statements and from living in the US all my life, I have created a list of the objectives for immigration law which is reasonably complete. It is the list from which we designed The US Immigration Fix.

The following is a healthy collection of beliefs, objectives and goals from which an effective immigration policy can be built. In fact, the plan US immigration fix is in the building.

- Assure America and Americans citizens are always #1
- Minimize the tax burden to zero to support immigration policy
- Enforce Immigration Law or Change it
- Secure our borders to protect Americans
- Assure that illegal aliens are not granted amnesty
- Do not permit illegal aliens to reside or work in America
- Assure that applicants for citizenship follow US laws

- Assure that foreign visitors are vetted through a legitimate process
- Assure than Illegal aliens do not vote in any US election
- Assure that Americans have priority for all new jobs
- Assure no path to citizenship for illegal aliens
- Assure welfare benefits go only to us citizen (no freebies)
  - Includes cash, education, healthcare etc.
- Eliminate Birthright Citizenship (Anchor Babies)
- Subsidize Self-Deportation for illegal aliens
- Encourage through large stipends self-deportation for anchor citizens
- Adopt English as America's language
- Collect Back Taxes
- Employer fines for illegal workers
- Provide accountability so America gets paid back for any services

# Is illegal immigration a crime?

Before we look at the Graham article let's answer this simple question. The fact is I should not be trying to figure out a solution for illegal immigration with 60,000,000 interlopers living in the US when the law says this should never have happened. FAIR.US is a group on the side of American Citizens in this issue. The following is from their web site. it is their perception on the notion that illegal immigration is a crime. It was written in 2013 and certainly still applies:

# Illegal Immigration is a Crime (2013)
by FAIR.US

Each year the Border Patrol apprehends hundreds of thousands of aliens who flagrantly violate our nation's laws by unlawfully crossing U.S. borders. Such illegal entry is a misdemeanor, and, if repeated after being deported, becomes punishable as a felony.

The illegal alien population is composed of those who illegally enter the country (referred to as "entry without inspection — EWI") in violation of the immigration law, and others enter legally and then sty illegally (referred to as overstayers). The immigration authorities currently estimate that two-thirds to three-fifths of all illegal immigrants are EWIs and the remainder is overstayers.

Both types of illegal immigrants are deportable under Immigration and Nationality Act Section 237 (a)(1)(B) which says: "Any alien who is present in the United States in violation of this Act or any other law of the United States is deportable."

**Illegal Immigration Is Not a Victimless Crime**

Apologists for illegal immigration try to paint it as a victimless crime, but the fact is that illegal immigration causes substantial harm to American citizens and legal immigrants, particularly those in the most vulnerable sectors of our population — the poor, minorities, and children.

Illegal immigration causes an enormous drain on public funds. The seminal study of the costs of immigration by the National Academy of Sciences found that the taxes paid by immigrants do not begin to cover the cost of services received by them.1 The quality of education, health care and other services for Americans are undermined by the needs of endless numbers of poor, unskilled illegal entrants.

Additionally, job competition by waves of illegal immigrants desperate for any job unfairly depresses the wages and working conditions offered to American workers, hitting hardest at minority workers and those without high school degrees.

## Illegal Immigration and Population Growth

Illegal immigration also contributes to the dramatic population growth overwhelming communities across America — crowding school classrooms, consuming already limited affordable housing, and increasing the strain on precious natural resources like water, energy, and forestland. Until the recent economic recession and high unemployment, the immigration authorities estimated that the population of illegal aliens was increasing by an estimated half million people annually.

## Illegal Immigration Undermines National Security

While most illegal immigrants may come only to seek work and a better economic opportunity, their presence outside the law furnishes an opportunity for terrorists to blend into the same shadows while they target the American public for their terrorist crimes. Some people advocate giving illegal aliens legal status to bring them out of the shadows, but, if we accommodate illegal immigration by offering legal status, this will be seen abroad as a message that we condone illegal immigration, and we will forever be faced with the problem.

## Border Patrol: Necessary But Not Sufficient

The Border Patrol plays a crucial role in combating illegal immigration, but illegal immigration cannot be controlled solely at the border. The overstayers as well as the EWIs who get past the Border Patrol must be identified and removed by the interior immigration inspectors of Immigration and Customs Enforcement (ICE). Today, the policies of the Obama administration are working at cross purposes to this objective. ICE is constrained from detaining and deporting most illegal aliens they encounter with the exception of those with criminal convictions or threats to the national security.

## What Can Be Done?

There must be a comprehensive effort to end illegal immigration. That requires ensuring that illegal aliens will not be able to obtain employment, public assistance benefits, public education, public housing, or any other taxpayer-funded benefit without detection.

The three major components of immigration control — deterrence, apprehension and removal — need to be strengthened by Congress and the Executive Branch if effective control is ever to be reestablished. Controlling illegal immigration requires a balanced approach with a full range of enforcement improvements that go far beyond the border. These include many procedural reforms, beefed up investigation capacity, asylum reform, documents improvements, major improvements in detention and deportation procedures, limitations on judicial review, improved intelligence capacity, greatly improved state/federal cooperation, and added resources.

## What about The Costs?

Effective control and management of the laws against illegal immigration require adequate resources. But those costs will be more than offset by savings to states, counties, communities, and school districts across the nation.

**-End of FAIR description of illegal immigration as a crime-**

The US Immigration fix as we discuss in the chapters of this book is a cost-neutral plan to solve the problem of illegal immigration in the US for good. It includes all aspects of the immigration issue, addresses all concerns, and provides a framework that can be used to incorporate new ideas and new programs as they are deemed necessary. Components of the plan as dictated by the objectives defined for US immigration include:

- General Requirements
- Enhanced Border Security
- The Annual Guest Plan
- Registration and Guest System
- Visa System
- Birthright Citizenship / Stipend system
- Accountability / Collection System
- Revenue System
- Employer System
- Technology Deployment

# What are the Objectives of Current Immigration Law

The notion of wanting an objective for this fix that will become our immigration policy leads us immediately to a conundrum. In these United States, I am not the person who should be deriving, qualifying and quantifying our current objectives.

My thought was that I would only need to find the long-term objectives of current policy and assure that the fix which is proposed accomplishes the objective. That is where the problem lies today and why it would be so difficult to accept a fix to a procedure, the objective of which has never been stated. And so the set of objectives above was partially derived from this analysis by Otis L Graham in 1991.

In May 1991, Otis L. Graham--Center for Immigration Studies (CIS) looked at the immigration world as it existed at that time, and tried to tackle the formulation of an objective a posteriori from the operational results of the past. Graham wrote an outstanding analysis of how our immigration objectives have been formed or *not formed* by the agencies that administer immigration law. His article is titled *Rethinking*

*Purposes of Immigration Policy.* It is a perfect title for a groundbreaking work.

Much of the data and some opinion in this section of the book are attributable to the information I have gleaned from reading this lengthy article. It is far too big to include in its entirety in this work. Besides, it would be inappropriate in its entirety as the times have changed since 1991 and ideologies play a much deeper role in the immigration policy divide of today than in 1991.

As hard as it may be for John Q. Public to believe, U.S. immigration policy, as set forth in law and regulation, has long lacked explicit and precisely stated objectives or even goals. Immigration law, until recently however, despite no written objectives, has produced results that were in sync with the laws as written. In the absence of explicit goals these results can be seen as the operative or "revealed goals" of the immigration policy.

Predominant among these revealed goals is that of *family reunification* preferential admission of immediate and extended family members of citizens and legal residents. This was formalized in 1995 after this article was written when the Congress passed The Immigration Act of 1965. This eliminated the national origin quota system that had favored immigrants from Europe to the exclusion of those from other parts of the world.

That system was replaced by a "family preference" quota framework that systematized the sponsorship of relatives by legal immigrants. According to the League of Women voters, "Clearly, the current family reunification system is not working well for many legal permanent residents and their immediate family members." Despite its having messed up our demographics, it still isn't good enough for those that wanted the working system changed in 1995.

The Utopian goal of family reunification is goal has been an axiom of Congress in nearly four decades of immigration legislation (including the Immigration Law of 1990 and the 1995 revision). It made kinship the determinant of the bulk of our immigrant selection. While you are reading, ask yourself if that is really good.

There is no God-given right for anybody to be permitted into America. And, so the notion that one person from a family can automatically reunify with the many left behind is absurd. If reunification is the goal, then the one person in America should go back to the home country. The USA cannot solve all problems by putting its citizens at a disadvantage.

If Americans were aware in the 1990's that the demographics of America from mostly European would change dramatically because of Congress's action, would we have stood for the erosion of the melting pot society and the substitution of the idea that diversity and division should replace unity of purpose. Even a country as generous as America can give up the advantages of controlling its own destiny when unscrupulous reunifications for example have found as many as 100 family members literally pulled into America by just one relative. When we talk about immigrant selection of course we are talking about selection for citizenship and all of the associated benefits thereof.

Ranking second as a revealed objective according to Graham's analysis is the admission of refugees. He notes that underlying our generous refugee policy is an array of psychic motives: "affirmations" of American-ness, expressions of national generosity, acclamations of freedom, and votes of confidence in growth and change. We like to feel good about doing good things.

These emotional underpinnings are expressed internationally as the need to vindicate particular foreign policies, to "embarrass" an adversary, or to celebrate America's status as the winning model of what a society should be." Until the notion of terrorism snuck into the equation, America was as good as it gets in terms of refugee acceptance even though in many cases citizen groups felt that too much was unhealthy.

In 2016, it no longer can be seen as a badge of honor for a country to admit refugees in large numbers without careful vetting. In fact it is nothing less than a nation permitting itself to commit suicide. The fact is that in this terrorist-filled world, refugees from regions sponsoring terror may not be who we think they are and they may not be who they say they are. What compelling reason is there for taking that chance and having a terrorist who hates Americans living next door?

Donald Trump pulls no punches in taking a totally pro-American stance on the issue. Americans must be protected from disease and from terrorism. Trump is against allowing Syrian refugees for example, into the U.S until they can be cleared and verified. Right now, since there are no valid records in Syria, this is actually not possible.

Trump has warned since his rise to prominence as a presidential candidate that it could be a way for terrorists to easily sneak into the country. How many terrorists does it take to kill 50 people in a nightclub in Florida? Would more terrorists than one be needed to kill in other cities?

Trump is 100% correct that there is no US administrative process to determine who these people are..."we are the worst when it comes to paperwork...this could be one of the great Trojan horses." There is an old adage about better to be safe than sorry.

A third revealed goal from Graham's analysis of examining the operations impact of immigration, though distant in importance behind either family reunification or the admission of refugees, is to meet labor force needs. Although the 1990 Immigration Law more than doubles the numbers of skills-based immigrants, they will still constitute less than ten percent of the total.

**Graham's conclusions and some explanations follow:**

"Another unstated but important result of immigration policy is our long-standing acquiescence in large-scale illegal immigration, effectively an intent to fill the perceived needs of some employers for cheap and docile labor and to avoid offending neighboring countries or domestic ethnic constituencies."

In other words, when this was written, just five years after Reagan's wholesale 1986 amnesty, in which there was much family reunification abuse, government officials had acquiesced to lightly enforce immigration laws instead of doing the job in a robust, meaningful fashion.

In other words, bureaucrats gave themselves permission to not do their jobs according to the law. If the US government—let's be like Trump and call these entrenched politicians the Elite Establishment—had enforced our laws at the border and in the workplace, we would not be suffering the ills of over 60 million foreign interlopers taking from our shrinking bounty today.

The conclusion that Graham makes is that US policy objectives were overtly permitting this to happen.

"Though the stated purposes of immigration policy are few and vague, taken together the revealed purposes are powerfully evident. One purpose since 1965, has been the alteration of our demographic future and the delay of population stability. Immigration, and the much higher fertility rates of immigrants, could produce a doubling of the population, to half a billion, by the year 2080. The demographic transformation of American society is occurring without the consultation or consent of the American electorate."

Did Americans authorize our government to replace people of European descent with those of other nationalities? Would the pre-1965 system, which took into consideration the balanced ethnicity of the current population in determining the proportions of immigrants not have been a better way? How did this happen?

Was there an agenda item to change the makeup of the US demography? Why in anyone's objectives, written or otherwise, would there have been a requirement to bring in tons of people from Micksnokoland, even though there were no citizens in the US who were from Micksnokoland? How in a fair system of ethnic balancing could white people in the US have become an endangered and let me add—a highly disrespected species? Somebody had an ideological agenda that was not shared with the American people or it would have been cut off at the pass. Now, these same people, now exposed, expect Americans to stand by and do nothing. I don't think so.

When he signed Congress's act into law in October 1965, President Lyndon B. Johnson stated that the act "is not a revolutionary bill. It does not affect the lives of millions....It will not reshape the structure of our daily lives or add importantly to either our wealth or our power." Americans know now that Lyndon B. Johnson was as wrong on that point as wrong could be.

"Historically, immigration policy was seen as part of "nation-building" to populate a relatively empty land. Are large numbers of immigrants now needed for a land that is built, or even as many believe overbuilt? For some, "nation building," now implies the creation of a more "diverse" nation, energized by a greater mix of ethnic, racial, and national origins. For them, the U.S. constantly faces enervation and stagnation, saved only by steady enrichment of its population from abroad. The idea is odd in a multi-racial, multi-ethnic society of 250 million people."

In other words, the idea of multiculturalism and diversity is like telling all the tribes to maintain their own national identity rather than joining the melting pot of a unified country. This typically does not result in harmony as we find today. This is not good and it is not building our nation in a way in which it can survive and grow and thrive. It is literally killing us.

"The anachronistic and unintended purposes and goals of our policies demand a fundamental reassessment and reform. The guiding criteria in that renewal must be that immigration policy above all should do no harm: should not harm the conditions or opportunities of the U.S. labor force, should not confound sound national population objectives, should not burden social services, and should not exceed the assimilative capacities of American society."

In other words, letting whoever wants to come with unrestricted access into this country as has happened by hook or crook since 1986, does not mean that the country can assimilate them well—especially if those selected want to maintain their separate identity. America should be for Americans. Let me repeat. America should be for Americans. After all, we built it.

"If immigration policy is to contribute to the demographic future we want, the government must encourage national debate on demographic goals and then select them. Population stabilization, as stated by the 1972 Rockefeller Commission, remains the most cogent and defensible objective, with immigration ultimately set to match emigration."

The 1972 Rockefeller Commission was clear in its objectives for population growth—zero.

" *In the brief history of this nation, we have always assumed that progress and "the good life" are connected with population growth. In fact, population growth has frequently been regarded as a measure of our progress. If that were ever the case, it is not now. There is hardly any social problem confronting this nation whose solution would be easier if our population were larger. Even now, the dreams of too many Americans are not being realized; others are being fulfilled at too high a cost. Accordingly, this Commission has concluded that our country can no longer afford the uncritical acceptance of the population growth ethic that "more is better." And beyond that, after two years of concentrated effort, we have concluded that no substantial benefits would result from continued growth of the nation's population.*

"Current emphasis on immigration as an entitlement of kinship must be recognized as an historical aberration. Labor force needs should once again become the prime determinant of immigration policy, but balancing with greater rigor the desire of employers for cheap, flexible labor with the protection of conditions of U.S. domestic workers. Immigration policy should supplement the domestic labor market with well-targeted, short-term infusions of specialized labor, but without undermining the high standards or incentives that should inform the domestic labor market."

Graham suggests that jobs for Americans are paramount and bringing in cheap labor will help a few Democrat and Republican elitists, but not help the American population at large. .

"The U.S. can either evolve towards a high-technology economy with a labor force of constantly advancing productivity, wage levels, and skills, or it can drift towards a low technology, low-skill, and low-wage economy, marked by widespread job instability and growing income disparity. Immigration policy will be important to the outcome."

Today those at the lowest ladder of the economic spectrum wait for nobody. They hop on a train or get into an inner tube or figure some way to get to America. Then, they go on welfare. How is that good for America? Democrats think it is good for their long term ability to hold the important offices in the country. Republicans in the elite establishment want to legalize all illegals and not permit them to make a minimum wage. Better yet, keep the illegal population illegal and in the shadows. Continue the status quo if not enforcing immigration law and keep expensive American employees from finding jobs. Meanwhile conservatives want to take back our country and we see Donald Trump as the only politician in America with a chance of doing exactly that.

## Forming Immigration Objectives & Goals

Rather than suggest that you wait for all the buildup to see the goals we would produce for the Fix that we are about to explain, as you know we outlined them all in the eralier part of this chapter.

And so, now that we all have been through all of the back up work and we have read the terrific Graham article, we can again the list of objectives. This list is summarized from having examined the many mission statements shown, from the Graham article, and of course from living in the US all my life, This list of the objectives for immigration law is reasonably complete. It is the list from which we designed The U.S. Immigration Fix.

The following is a healthy collection of beliefs, objectives and goals from which an effective immigration policy can be built. In fact, the plan US immigration fix is in the building.

- Assure America and Americans citizens are always #1
- Minimize the tax burden to zero to support immigration policy
- Enforce Immigration Law or Change it
- Secure our borders to protect Americans
- Assure that illegal aliens are not granted amnesty
- Do not permit illegal aliens to reside or work in America
- Assure that applicants for citizenship follow US laws
- Assure that foreign visitors are vetted through a legitimate process
- Assure than Illegal aliens do not vote in any US election
- Assure that Americans have priority for all new jobs
- Assure no path to citizenship for illegal aliens
- Assure welfare benefits go only to us citizen (no freebies)
  - Includes cash, education, healthcare etc.

- Eliminate Birthright Citizenship (Anchor Babies)
- Subsidize Self-Deportation for illegal aliens
- Encourage through large stipends self-deportation for anchor citizens
- Adopt English as America's language
- Collect Back Taxes
- Employer fines for illegal workers
- Provide accountability so America gets paid back for any services

Now, let's move forward into the next chapters in explaining the fix which includes the following. The solution framework addresses each of these notions of a US Immigration Fix:

- General Requirements
- Enhanced Border Security
- The Annual Guest Plan
- Registration and Guest System
- Blue Card System
- Birthright Citizenship / Stipend system
- Accountability / Collection System
- Revenue System
- Employer System
- Technology Deployment

# Chapter 2   Anybody Ready for the Big Immigration Fix?

## The Fix is Definitely In

The US Immigration Fix is in. Unfortunately few want to hear about it. Those who do seem to be unable to wrap their arms around a plan that is not too harsh or too mellow—a plan that lies in between the extremes. I am sorry to say to those who want the immigration battle to go on in the US that I have a fix for the problem and it is right in between amnesty and deportation except for one thing. It is designed to be America-first. Who wants it? I think everybody does; but first they must find out about it and that is why I wrote this book.

This is not my first book on the subject of immigration. When I was trying to convince my fellow patriots that we had a big problem that government was ignoring, I wrote a gentle book called Taxation wWithout Representation, which touched on the issue but its focus was on taxation. I was not happy with my treatment of the 60,000,000 illegals in the country. All the book did at the time was warn of consequences and show that illegal border jumping was a high cost item for American Taxpayers.  Most of us already knew what I had outlined. I got to write it formally.

As I saw more and more corporations taking jobs offshore, I also saw those corporations that could not leave the country leaving their American workforces behind and with impunity bringing in replacement workers for the Americans who lost their jobs. I was very upset. This prompted me to write another one of my classics, Americans Need Not Apply!  By the way, this book is still available and it still can teach some lessons for those that think unfettered illegal immigration is win-win. Actually nobody wins. I felt my job in both books was to inform the public of what it was that was actually hurting them.

Then, I kept hearing about Democrats (I am a JFK Democrat) wanting to open the borders up fully; let anybody in without vetting or inspection; and quickly grant them amnesty and soon citizenship so they could vote Democrat and the US would never ever see another Republican in the nation's highest office. Again, I was outraged, so I wrote a book about what was happening so all my fellow Americans would know and then we could let our Congressmen know that we wanted all this stuff stopped. This book was titled: No Amnesty! No Way! Again, I did my job and those who chose to know now could know what the shylocks in Congress had in store for the American people.

This was before the President decided that he could make laws of the ilk that Congress would never approve, and a fully Republican Congress cowered at the thought that this President might not like them and if they acted against him, he would ruin their chances of being reelected seventy more times. Selfish Congressman, no representation, and a president who had a big agenda were about to defeat America.

This time, instead of warning Americans as I had thought I was doing in the past, I figured everybody already knew but were rendered helpless by a wimp Republican Establishment and a determined Democratic Party. Democrats were determined to put American employees out of work, replace them with foreigners, and then while the Americans were drinking beer at the VFW, they would slip in all these now semi-citizens with documentation that would enable them to vote. The Republican dominated Congress had already showed the President he could do anything so why not?

Since everybody already knew about the chicanery, it would not help to say it again. But, it would be a good idea to talk about a solution for the underlying problem of interlopers destroying America with our POTUS and Congress's permission. Everybody could see the massive illegal immigrations with nobody seeming to be able to speak the American language at K-Mart, Walmart, and all my favorite stores. Everybody already knew!

In my many years with IBM, I was a problem solver. The correct and Constitutional and the simplest answer was to enforce US immigration laws and deport the 60,000,000 back to their home countries. Despite paying through the nose in taxes and despite many hospitals and other organizations going out of business because of EMTALA laws and many others favoring illegal residents above citizens, Americans had not faced real hardship that was supported by the media since WWII.

The media this time around is a branch of the Democratic Party though they will not admit it. Lying is the in-thing today. Good hearted mostly Christian Americans were duped into thinking it was not right to send these people home. So, many, even those who had lost their jobs could not stomach the idea of deporting 60,000,000 resident simply because they were living in the US in an unauthorized illegal state against the written US immigration laws. So, what could I do?

Well, I ran for Congress and the US Senate but I had little money and even my peers would not give me enough votes to win as I could not make myself known to the voters and I refused to campaign like a suck-up looking for a favor. Yet, even when I was on the ballot, the electorate voted for the favored politician du jour. Sometimes, one feels like giving up but then what? Not me!

I decided to solve the problem logically instead of simply warning the people about it. Having the media and the leadership of both political parties against me did not help me to spread my message very quickly. But, I knew I needed a real message that outlined a solution to the problem of 60,000,000 illegal foreign nationals residing in the US in the shadows. And, so, as a poet who writes prose, I resorted to writing down a plan that would solve the problem. Every problem solution needs a name and so I called my solution to the illegal immigrant problem in the US, The Annual Guest Plan. I wrote a book in 2015 with that exact name and it is still selling.

I got the attention of Congress and of Donald Trump's campaign team but not enough to make my efforts meaningful. I knew that I had the right message but I was afraid and still am than nobody will ever hear it.

I am convinced the plan that I outlined as the Annual Guest Plan is the right plan but its release as a "guest plan" hurt its opportunities for acceptance. I reached back a few months ago and I decided that this was not a potential implementation problem, this was a marketing issue. The name Annual Guest Plan conjured for American the thought of a free ride for illegals as part of an expanded welfare scheme.

This is as far from the truth as possible. And so, now, as I am looking at how to actually fix the problem in 2016, I decided to use language that all Americans would understand and that is why the book you are reading the US Immigration Fix Is In! For those who read this book, you will get the message. Much of the Annual Guest Plan is included in the Fix but this book is built with the intention of showing how this solution can work rather than describing the solution and ending it right there.

Every Congressional solution to the occupation of the US by 60 million illegal foreign nationals is trumped by the idea that border security must come first. Yet, as perhaps this is merely a ruse by Congressmen in the pockets of lobbyists and donors, border security never comes. If it were to come when promised umpteen years ago, it would be here today.

Since 1986 from the Reagan amnesty to today, at a clip of about 3 million per year, interlopers have chosen to cross the southern border or simply overstay their visas in order to gain residence in the US. Calculate 3 million per year from 1986 to 2016 and write down the result. I challenge anybody to show proof that there are less than 60 million interlopers living and working in the US today. They are not simply doing farm labor. More and more are taking white collar jobs.

Over time, because Democrats like the idea that the new dependent foreign class will vote Democrat one day, and Republican political elites want so much to please their donor class, who employ these "residents" at sub-minimum wage rates; our government has again intentionally chosen to ignore the wishes of the American people to serve its own massive greed.

The Donald Trump and Ted Cruz plans would definitely stop the new potential illegal foreign nationals at the border. However, nobody seems to focus on those illegal residents who are beginning to think they own significant parts of America. I am hearing more and more talk about La Rasa, who have a Radical 'Reconquista' Agenda. Their goal is to one day reoccupy California, Arizona, and New Mexico. So far by illegally entering these states, their percentage of occupancy os dangerously high to a takeover number. We need to acknowledge what is going on and address the 60,000,000 who today live in America, and not the groups who want to take over parts of the US. Somebody else can deal with those.

My solution addresses the 60,000,000. It is the product of a lot of research and thinking. It is called the Annual Guest Plan and it should be put into legislation and passed and implemented ASAP. *The US Immigration Fix* adds to the compelling arguments of The Annual Guest Plan for the good of America. .

As I noted in the beginning of this chapter but which I wish to repeat, over the last six years, I wrote two books about the problem with resident illegal foreign nationals. The books are titled Americans Need Not Apply, and No Amnesty! No Way!

These books capture the essence of the problem of 60,000,000 foreign interlopers living in America. Initially I had no solution so I kept researching and thinking and researching and thinking and finally it came to me. What if we made a deal with the interlopers and the American people within which both parts of the puzzle could be solved and be OK! This is the essence of the Annual Guest Plan but there is lots more.

As long as an interloper who chooses to be a "annual guest" is well behaved, and we citizens get to define what that means, they will have a right to live in America and hold a job for which an American citizen is not competing. Annual Guests will be 100% out of the shadows and will live like you and I within our neighborhoods, paying for housing as we do. Their kids will go to school and they will pay school taxes like you and I. As part of becoming an annual guest, the former interloper agrees that there will be no more freebies.

Thus, in order to gain their status, they must promise not to be a burden (defined as costing taxpayers) or they promise to voluntarily deport. The government will help in their deportation and in fact may offer a substantial stipend of $5,000 to $10,000 or more (to-be-determined) for those who agree to go and not come back without paying back their to-date burden.

Americans will not pay a dime for Annual Guests for education, healthcare or general living. Iron clad identification databases will be built and ID cards with biometrics will be issued and those without such identification will be deported immediately once the program is in full implementation. EMTALA (what some call free emergency care) will be provided but the annual guest receiver must immediately self deport if the cost of service is not quickly paid. An electronic accountability database (EAR) will also be built to keep track of any costs that are not immediately paid by the "annual guest." Unapproved balances mean automatic deportation.

Annual Guests (AGP) must begin their freedom in the US by registering at no charge at one of many facilities. US officials will know all illegal foreign nationals at that point as their status will be legal. Sixty million people must be registered within six months. This is clearly do-able as our national elections are accomplished with many people in just one day. After registering, the former interloper must apply in-person for an annual guest visa and be approved or agree to be deported if they do not apply or do not gain annual guest status. Since registration is the first act, any interloper who decides to skip the rest of the process will be easy to locate.

Americans believe the influx of illegal foreign nationals hurts them and from my own observations, we Americans are 100% correct. With the Annual Guest Plan, Americans are back in charge. The table is turned in this program with the citizen now holding all the TRUMP cards.  AGP's will have no welfare or health benefits other than those provided by their employers. If they seek US benefits, in their application they will have agreed to be summarily deported.

They will not be able to vote in any election in the US for any office local, municipality, state, or federal. Unless they return to their home country, and begin a process like all others from that country, they can never become a citizen of the US. Under no circumstances as an annual guest, can they ever vote... ever!

Registration will be free for a period until it is obvious all interlopers should be registered (perhaps 3 months and maybe 6 months) at which time registration will have a charge of say $50.00. At some point new registrations will be closed and the unregistered will be deported. Those deported will have decided not to accept the olive branch and would do so at their own peril.

All registrants must pay $100.00 to apply for annual guest status and go through a vetting process. Renewal will also be $100.00 or a fee that recoups administrative expense.

Those granted annual guest status merely have to be well behaved in order to stay in the US for a lifetime. In year two, each annual guest must appear in front of US officials to be vetted again and pay their annual guest fee of $100. The fee is $100 per year every year unless it costs more to process them. Each year until the plan is proven, each guest must appear before US officials and pay. To repeat, AGP's must make personal appearances once a year to renew and pay their $100.00 and be vetted each year to get their ID cards refreshed.

The key point is that these folks are guests of American citizens. They began as uninvited visitors (interlopers) but this AGP process changes their status. They are not American Citizens or citizens. They are guests. Once registered and approved, they have a special right granted by the citizens of the US to remain in the US as long as they are well-behaved, and no longer.

They have no special privileges. American Citizens have all the privileges of citizens in our own country / state.

More facts about *The US Immigration Fix* are noted in this book in its many chapters. Additionally, many different perspectives are brought forth so Americans can see that this is a pro-American approach to solving a big problem. There are other advanced notions about immigration in the overall plan that may help US officials deal better with the ongoing issue of people wanting to crash into America uninvited for various purposes.

For example, *The US Immigration Fix* should never cost the US more than if the plan were not in force. Yearly fees would be adjusted as needed to assure there is no taxpayer burden. Illegal foreign nationals who chose to be Annual Guests when granted permission would never be permitted to ever become a burden, financial or otherwise on the citizenry of the USA.

You have read a very light introduction to a very detailed plan which is explained in many chapters in this book. This fix is intended for the benefit of Americans. These plans to help America take into account the fact that 60,000,000 people slipped into America or stayed unlawfully. This book accommodates over 60,000,000 foreign interlopers but the bottom-line is that Americans come first

It would be a proper question to ask "Why should America choose to do this?" Simply because America is a kind nation, and Americans have big hearts. Americans will be the winners in this plan, and former interlopers will also gain. Of course the fact that Americans do not want to summarily deport 60,000,000 illegal residents overnight is a prime motivator. Americans do not have the stomach to execute, or deport 60,000,000 illegal foreign nationals. Additionally, Americans are sick of paying and will no longer pay.

Taking a look at the costs of not having an Annual Guest Plan v having such a plan; it is obvious that there are some special things that can be done to help keep families together, and these too can cost Americans less; not more.

For example, suppose an anchor baby through his or her parents could choose to take a $50,000 stipend to give up anchor baby citizen status and go to his or her home country unimpeded -- with his or her parents. What if the US also provided a large stipend for the mother and father to be resettled in a safe area of their home country?

They could start anew with a bankroll and become entrepreneurs in their home country. There may be families who could gain a grub stake of as little as $70,000 to several hundred thousand dollars, depending on the # of children, to start fresh in their home country with their families intact.

Why would they want to stay in America when they have an opportunity to become somebodies in their home countries?

The idea of the *Annual Guest Plan* is to help those stuck in America doing meaningless labor for peanuts. It is also a plan to help Americans subjugated to the effects of a new but clandestine wage scale that comes before all minimum wages, for which they cannot compete. The cost of interloper services is in the hundreds of billions. We have more than enough reserves to pay for any program that reduces the lifetime burden of an interloper on American taxpayers.
Food for Thought

Frosty Woolridge has a deep perspective on the problem. This quote is from Frosty. It helps all of us get a sense of the reality of the perpetration being played on US taxpayers by our government:

*As shown on CBS with Katie Couric this past week, 300,000 pregnant Mexican women cross the border to birth their babies, known as 'anchor babies', in American hospitals at an average cost of $6,000.00 per birth with no complications. If the child suffers heart defects, Downs Syndrome, Autism or any other problems, the costs jump to $500,000.00 with long term care into the millions of dollars. All footed by the America taxpayer!*

*Not mentioned in Couric's report, that child enjoys free breakfasts and lunches through 13 years of publicly funded education at an average cost of $7,000.00 per year. Additionally, American taxpayers foot the bill for all medical and housing assistance for the child and mother. More hidden costs add up with ESL classes to teach the child English. Connecticut alone suffers 120 languages in their schools while Colorado suffers over 40 foreign languages that cripple their classrooms.*

*The list of expenses paid for by American taxpayer soars with time and numbers of illegal aliens. Additionally, legal immigrants sponsor their relatives in chain migration and family reunification at US taxpayer expense.*

*These immigrants take American jobs while they burn American taxpayer funds for immigrant welfare. This all happens while the US national debt approaches $10 trillion. Immigrants flood into this country while jobs cascade out to China where we owe $1 trillion in T-bills as of 2008. Additionally, we suffer a $700 billion annual trade deficit.*

*In summary, the Annual Guest Plan* (AGP) was developed by Brian Kelly in 2013 and released as *The Kelly Plan*. Brian examined the gang of eight plan, existing law, and other notions about how to solve the nation's problem with illegal residents. He found none of the solutions addressed all of the issues that having 20 million to 60 million illegal foreign nationals in residence brought to America. He read the gang of eight plan in 2013, and noticed that it smelled a lot like it was purposely designed to kill America.

No jobs would be left for Americans; newly unemployed Americans would have to pay for newly minted citizens; voting in national elections was not ruled out; 33 million more foreign nationals would be invited. It would cost over $6 trillion. It was a terrible deal for the country. Kelly looked at all of the things that Americans did not like and he looked at what the interlopers liked. He figured out a way to permit well-behaved interlopers to be able to stay in America while giving Americans priority in all ways. This plan actually will work and it will solve the problem and take a huge financial burden off the backs of Americans.

# Chapter 3    General Requirements

## Various systems are required for the Fix

The objective listed as General Requirements is to assure that a structure is created in the "Fix" project for its completion. The structure must include the following solutions and discuss the elements of the particular solution that solve particular problems or concerns.

Including this solution, General Requirements, as discussed in Chapter 1, there are nine other solutions which will be discussed in the sequence as shown below

1. General Requirements
2. Enhanced Border Security
3. The Annual Guest Plan
4. Registration and Guest System
5. Blue Card System
6. Birthright Citizenship / Stipend system
7. Accountability / Collection System
8. Revenue System
9. Employer System
10. Technology Deployment

## Enhanced Border Security

There are many considerations for how to secure the border and this section will address them and offer thoughts on each

# The Annual Guest Plan

The Annual Guest Plan is put forth as the solution for solving
the problem of already having 60 million illegal foreign
interlopers residing in the US with many of them holding
American jobs.

# Registration and Guest System

This system will outline the processing requirements to register
all 60,000,000 illegal foreign national interlopers. It will also
outline the requirements of a guest system and the databases
necessary to support known "Annual Guests."

# Blue Card System

This system will define an innovative new way to process those
individuals who are annual guest card holders, visa holders,
and green card holders. It will define a means of consolidating
the card systems and it will offer the US a way for the various
cardholders to be cost free for the US.

# Birthright Citizenship / Stipend System

There are arguments going on today about the fourteenth
amendment and whether it was intended for those who enter
our country illegally. This area offers concrete suggestions for
how to solve this dilemma in favor of Americans.

The underlying objective for Americans is for the benefits
provided for illegal or legal guests or birthright citizens to no
longer be a cost burden for US taxpayers. You will see

analyses that prove that very generous stipends could be offered selectively for various classifications who are costing substantial sums to the taxpayers.  The analyses prove that such incentives for various classifications specified in this section to self-deport could be very lucrative for their financial future and still save the US taxpayer many dollars.

# The Accountability / Collection System.

The Accountability / Collection system is required by the Annual Guest Plan so that fees and fines can be appropriated and collected. There must be an advanced computerized system built system that adds accountability and collection records to the one time interloper's database.

Any cost that is directly attributable to the former interlopers will be collected and processed by the collection system and for those interlopers who cannot pay everything at once the accountability system will keep track of what is owed for say, an emergency hospital visit. All balances are due and payment plans may be in force to gain partial payments rather than force the former interlopers into deportation, the least desired but very necessary potentiality.

# The Revenue System

The Revenue System will be designed to use the same databases as the accountability / collection system. Annual fees and fines and other revenue items such as special USCIS services will be classified and will automatically be posted to the former interloper's records for collection purposes.

# The Employer System

This system will hold information about employers. There will
be various fees and fines that will be assessed on employers
who choose to use non-citizens or who have already used non-
citizens as employees. There will be a certain fee and/or fine
based on each employee who is a non-citizen, whether in
former illegal status, visa status or  a particular blue card
status.

# Technology Deployment

No solution for immigration with over 60million records can
be achieved without technology. The better technology the
better results. Smart cards, retina scans, bar coding, RFID or
whatever will be needed at various locations across the country
as well as the systems to process the transactions over
something like if not exactly the Internet.

# Chapter 4   Border Security

## Americans no longer trust government on immigration & border security

Border Security is a major focus of the Immigration Fix but the solutions are so well known that there is no attempt here to duplicate the work of others. The Barletta border plan discussed below is close to what US citizens want—100% border security with no excuses. What US citizens do not want is the extremely long time frames (2 to 7 years) for implementation. They need to be shortened appropriately. A better plan, perhaps is the Trump Plan to build a wall and a lot more. We examine that in this chapter

Citizens have given up on trusting the Executive Branch to execute the laws passed by the Congress and signed by the President at the time. The Executive Branch has a proven record of failure and in fact through executive orders and through bureaucratic memoranda, this branch of government, through the direct or indirect actions of the POTUS, is violating constitutional separation of powers by the de facto changing of immigration laws.

As a former Constitutional Law Professor as the President purports to be, he knows or he should know that writing and changing laws is the sole right of the Congress of the United States. Anything short of this is breaking the law.

Since the people cannot rely on this President to execute the laws of the nation faithfully according to his oath, this has created a constitutional crisis, and so far, with Congress not taking any definitive action, the people are losing.

The President as noted, is acting as dictator in chief, rather than as the chief executive in a democratic republic. Therefore, more and more citizens are looking to Congress to solve this problem. Unfortunately, the 114th Congress does not seem to be up to the task. Citizens must get fired up enough to contact these representatives. We must get our own pens and phones out to assure this lawless behavior stops immediately.

## The Border Security Americans Want!

In an America first plan, with the help of the Border States and the states with entry / exit ports, etc., the Congress would make the decision as to whether and when the border is secure. Governors and state legislators would provide major input. At any time if the border is not made secure, or is not on its way to being secure, the Congress may take action such as suspending or canceling items that are in play such as the Annual Guest Plan (discussed in subsequent chapters) or they may take other definitive actions to get things back on track.

Unfortunately, the reluctance of Congress to act swiftly may put former interlopers back into the shadows if they are ever permitted to leave. The Annual Guest Plan identifies all former interlopers so finding them after the registration process can make it substantially easier to deport them. That, of course is not the objective of the Big Immigration Fix but the Fix is nothing without the Congress's support.

Deportation is not a desirable outcome since deportation to so many is an unacceptable alternative. Therefore, the border must be quickly made secure. It simply must be done. So, we will have to wait for a Trump presidency or a major Obama change of heart for this to happen.

Besides the HR 399 Bill and the Barletta Amendment and the other amendments noted below, there are some major notions that would also go a long way to help citizens believe that the government is doing all it can regarding border security. Some of these from my own analyses include the following:

- Minimum 50% increase in # border patrol agents
- Biometrics--Fingerprint scans captured for all interlopers.
- Devices @ International airports & ports of entry
- Citizens provide smart ID / passport to get back
- Procedures developed by independent consultants, not executive branch
- Goal: Improve efficiency /effectiveness of agents & border security
- Multiple full, huge fences, moats, obstacle areas
  - We got a man on the moon first!
- Impenetrable fences built across entire S&N borders.
  - High tech solutions may work but a fence is a sure thing
  - Make solutions at the border from hard steel
  - We cannot afford not to protect our borders
  - Southern border is the big priority
- Need legislation to take away presidential discretion in border affairs.
  - May need Constitutional amendment!
- Full management of border in Congress's hands
  - Delegate enforcement to the individual states with funding
  - Can be achieved de-facto if not by law;
    - Feds must be prohibited from suing states over immigration
    - Make it a states' issue for border states
- Major fines & sanctions on employers
  - Those that continue to hire illegal foreign nationals
  - Those that use contracting groups -- rental illegal employees

# People do not trust the POTUS

The major point here is that there has been so much faith lost between this POTUS and the citizens on the immigration issue, the people would like Congress and the states to take charge of border security. Just as the President is ignoring Congress; if the President persists in his lawless behavior, Congress must ignore the President and institute executive committees to take actions. With the clear power of the purse, it must fund those actions. When Donald Trump becomes president, the Obama-type objections will disappear 100%.

A lawless first executive who finds no limits to his authority has proven unworthy of America's trust. Therefore, an alternative must be exercised. Since there is much more faith that the states affected and the Congress, together, would do the right thing, the majority of Americans want them in control of their own borders with the Congress in an administrative role.

Those interested in a real border solution know the President is failing us intentionally. Therefore, to repeat, the majority of Americans want Congress and the states, not the President to protect the borders. Moreover, we want them to signify that the border either is secure or is not secure, and to take remedial action. This may create another Constitutional crisis but it is one that would benefit the people, not just the Marxist progressives trying to undermine our country.

# The Senate forgot about real Americans

American citizens, as well as current and future immigrants to America, deserve better. When the US Senate in April 2013, introduced what they called the Border Security, Economic Opportunity, and Immigration Modernization Act, it was a sham, and the Senators knew it was a sham.

They cowered to President Obama, and they felt that with the immense power held by President Obama, the Democratic majority could ram this unjustifiable act upon the American people, who largely opposed it. Donald Trump's America will be administered for America and Americans first!

Thankfully, we have regular elections as more than ever we see both the Democrat and Republican leaders colluding to help foreigners at the expense of the citizens of this country. Regular Americans from both parties are waking up at election time to the fact that our leaders are not working on our behalf, and we have begun to vote them out of office by name.

## H.R. 399 contains the Barletta Amendment

Let's get back to what I like to call the new Barletta Bill—H.R. 399. The Bill also contains a Barletta amendment, adopted by the committee, which requires the Department of Homeland Security (DHS) to submit to Congress an evaluation of the biometric exit system within 90 days of the bill's passage, in order to establish a baseline against which the new systems will be measured.

The HR 399 Bill passed the in committee and now it is moving along through the House. Of course in the last month, House and Senate Republicans have already caved on the Homeland Security bill to stop Obama's illegal executive amnesty and the effect of Morton memos. I have yet to digest all of that but few conservatives are pleased.

"The most basic responsibility of the federal government is to protect the citizenry," Barletta said. "Unless and until we have complete control of our borders, it will remain impossible to fulfill that obligation. We should not even begin to discuss anything that approaches a pathway to citizenship until we secure our borders."

Let me tell you more about this bill, and then I will tell how Congressman Barletta and I are more in synch on methods than either of us knew before our meeting and interview that particular Friday morning. With my background as an IBM Systems Engineer, I have deep respect for technology and I know that merely having technology is not a panacea for bringing in any benefits to any program. But, the right technology deployed for the right purpose, designed and implemented effectively can provide huge benefits to the American people.

## Biometric exit

Rep. Barletta has long championed a system which keeps track of people who arrive in the United States on a visa, and also if and when they depart. More and more interlopers enter in this fashion and do not ever leave. Barletta loves the idea of tracking them with biometrics, including fingerprints. So do I.

This would enable federal authorities to know immediately when someone has remained inside the country after a visa has expired. The legislation requires the Secretary of Homeland Security to implement biometric exit protocols at all of the nation's air and sea ports within 5 years, and all land ports within 5 to 7 years.

You can never start unless you begin and vice versa. Sometimes you are forced to walk before you can run. Sometimes, bureaucracy and conditions warrant a slower approach. The big bang theory may have created the world, but the world it created was in chaos. And, so, a defined incremental approach is appropriate. Five to seven years, however, is way too long, and the Congressman shares my opinion on that.

I do not want to put words in the Representative's mind, but surely, he would like this done sooner than the prescribed time frame in the bill. And, so this is the beginning of something very good for America. As a former IBMer, I know that if the federal government were to decide that it wanted to get this done in six months, as Obama's amnesty and executive orders all have had short time horizons, technical consulting companies, such as IBM could be delivering results within the period using an incremental approach.

The situation at the border and in the homeland gets worse each day that we delay. Moreover, many Americans do not trust the intentions of the current president. They are concerned that we must construct our plans to operate and we must implement the plans within short time frames that do not permit a future president or congress to scuttle them before they are completed.

We all remember the border fence from many years ago that passed the Congress and then was never fully funded. The Barletta Bill addresses those in America by stopping the growth in the numbers of interlopers, and our current inability to track them.

"We know that about 40 percent of all people who are in this country illegally did not cross what we think of as a traditional border," Barletta said. "They arrive in this country on a visa, the visa expires, and they simply never go home. What this means is that if your state is home to an international airport, you effectively live in a border state."

The Annual Guest Plan covers those now in the country illegally. Therefore, the Barletta Bill and the plan covered in this book, are just about 100% in synch—a hand and glove approach.

## Operational control

The border security bill requires that DHS achieve operational control of high traffic areas of the southwest border in two years, and the entire southwest border in five years, and establishes a commission to independently verify that the border is secure. "Operational control" is defined in current law as "the prevention of all unlawful entries into the United States, including entries by terrorists, other unlawful aliens, and instruments of terrorism, narcotics, and other contraband." *(Secure Fence Act of 2006)*

## Using technology and infrastructure

The bill requires a deployment of nineteen specified technological capabilities in each Border Patrol sector along the southern border of the United States and adjacent maritime regions. As you would expect, the geography, threats, and challenges of each sector must be considered to ensure the most efficient and effective deployment of resources.

The legislation mandates specific fencing and infrastructure requirements, including the construction of 27 new miles of fence, the replacement of all landing mat fence (64 miles), and the construction of 415 miles of access roads, new boat ramps, and access gates. The bill requires Customs and Border Protection Air and Marine to fly a minimum of 130,000 annual flight hours and to operate Unmanned Aerial Vehicles, or drones, at least 16 hours per day, seven days per week.

Now we have to get this bill passed and signed and implemented. I would recommend several important amendments. They have previously been suggested by NumbersUSA. Without the changes (amendments) recommended by NumbersUSA, this bill may find itself in the history books as bluster going noplace.

But, again, it helps to get started. While working to make this bill even better, concurrently, we all should be working to get the Annual Guest Plan introduced and passed to solve our internal US problem with illegal foreign nationals.

# Objections to HR 399 by Numbers USA

On Monday, January 26th, NumbersUSA updated its position paper on HR 399, the Secure Our Borders First Act, in its current form.  They cannot support the bill in its current form.  There are several things that need to be fixed before this can really become the bill to go with to finally secure the borders.

NumbersUSA does not believe that HR 399, as it came out of the Homeland Security Committee last week, will actually secure our borders.

They cite the major shortcomings of the bill as the following:

"1) The majority of the deadlines in the bill, and certainly the majority of those carrying any sort of penalty for noncompliance, fall outside the term of the current administration. The Obama Administration is thus largely free to continue systematically dismantling our border security and enforcement system. Even worse, the next administration will face penalties early in its first term (two years from enactment) for failing to meet deadlines, even though the current administration is actually to blame.
At a minimum, deadlines need to be set so that the current administration has an incentive to comply."

"2) Seven years is far too long for our nation to wait for a biometric exit system that was first enacted in 1996. Moreover, since the deadlines for implementation, with the exception of a small pilot program, fall outside this administration's term, President Obama has no incentive whatsoever to even begin rolling out the system before he leaves office."

"At a minimum, the biometric exit system should be required at ALL airports, seaports and pedestrian crossings within two years, with a one year deadline for an exit system at 15 airports, 15 seaports, and 15 pedestrian crossings. An additional two to three years should be sufficient for the vehicular exit system."

"3) Despite the talking points put out by the Homeland Security Committee, HR 399 does NOT satisfy the requirements of the Secure Fence Act of 2006. The Secure Fence Act required 700 miles of double-layered, reinforced fencing. Existing miles of vehicle barriers and single-layered fencing do not satisfy this requirement, and should not be counted as part of the mandated 700 miles. It is only by counting this less effective fencing that HR 399 can pretend to meet the requirements of the Secure Fence Act by adding only 48 miles of new double-layered fencing...."At a minimum, the bill should require the construction of the full 700 miles of reinforced, double-layered fencing Congress mandated in 2006."

"4) The border simply cannot be secured as long as Border Patrol agents are forced to release the illegal aliens they apprehend, instead of rapidly removing them from the United States. Catch-and-release policies must end. Similarly, President Obama's unconstitutional amnesties must be stopped."

NumbersUSA fights Congress and the President on our behalf. They are urging House Republicans to insist on a robust amendment process to address the major deficiencies outlined above as well as some other shortcomings of HR 399.

This group ends their exhortation to Republican lawmakers with the following:

"Americans have been waiting since 1986 for a secure border and serious enforcement of our immigration laws. Congress must take the time to get this right because we cannot afford to wait another 30."

# The Donald Trump Border Security Plan

I have brought the Trump plan in from his web site. It is fully included in the Prologue to this book right before Chapter 1. To get us revved up again, I will repeat the beginning below:

## IMMIGRATION REFORM THAT WILL MAKE AMERICA GREAT AGAIN

The three core principles of Donald J. Trump's immigration plan

When politicians talk about "immigration reform" they mean: amnesty, cheap labor and open borders. The Schumer-Rubio immigration bill was nothing more than a giveaway to the corporate patrons who run both parties.

Real immigration reform puts the needs of working people first – not wealthy globetrotting donors. We are the only country in the world whose immigration system puts the needs of other nations ahead of our own. That must change. Here are the three core principles of real immigration reform:

1. A nation without borders is not a nation. There must be a wall across the southern border.

2. A nation without laws is not a nation. Laws passed in accordance with our Constitutional system of government must be enforced.

3. A nation that does not serve its own citizens is not a nation. Any immigration plan must improve jobs, wages and security for all Americans.

# Chapter 5    Gang of Eight Compared to Annual Guest Plan

## Gang of Eight not as citizen friendly as AGP

We have yet to explain the Annual Guest Plan in any Detail. One means of doing that in summary form is to compare it to the Senate's Gang of Eight debauchery which Marco Rubio and company tried to put down our throats in 2013.

You may recall that in 2013, many of us learned about the Gang of Eight Senators' plan for immigration amnesty for all interlopers. It would have made the Annual Guest Plan or the US Immigration Fix theoretically unnecessary but it would have gotten us into a deeper mess than we were already in. Those Americans who think, were not pleased. The Rubio Plan was extremely generous to interlopers and very costly to US taxpayers. It was not a fair deal for citizens of the US.

You are going t love the Annual Guest Plan as our solution to the problem of having 60 million illegal interlopers running around our country at night so they are not spotted by the gendarme. That is a lot of shadows. I

Why would the liberals, Democrat and Republican in the US Senate do something like this? First of all, it is what they wanted. It was not forced upon them. Secondly, I am convinced that Senators are so removed from the people at large, they are out of touch and have no idea what is happening in the country. All Senators should be fired.

Perhaps until Obama is replaced, both houses of Congress should be sent home until further notice.

We all know that more than any other nation in history, the United States has welcomed immigrants in search of a better life. That is how many citizens got here over the many years from our founding—and even before—while the colonies were being settled.

For their own reasons, the millions of people who regularly enter the US illegally intentionally choose to violate the core principle of the rule of law in the US, and in fact, they mock and belittle the legal naturalization process. They, as illegal guests make demands of our kind and generous host country as if they have an entitlement to free services.

Thus, there is continued large-scale immigration without an effective assimilation. In other words, the interlopers want America's benefits but they do not want to adapt in any way to America's culture. With only 40% of green card holders making the transition to citizenship, today's foreign nationals must find something wrong with America to not choose to make the final step to citizenship. Many others would love the opportunity.

It seems that they do not really want to be Americans. They do want to be treated as Americans for benefits and all good things with all due rights, but they are happy holding allegiance to their home countries. The American people are fed up with this.

## America, once a melting pot!

America long ago became known as the melting pot for people wanting a new place to live and raise a family. In the early days, immigrants left behind their old ways and they became Americans by choice; and they were proud to become Americans. As they say, they melted in.

My father, born 101 years ago in 1915 in America, from a pair of Irish immigrants, for example, would immediately get upset if and when I would wear an Irish Sweatshirt. He felt I was bragging about being Irish. He cautioned me, his middle son, that I was an American, not an Irishman. Today's illegal interlopers and many green card holders choose not to identify with America. Yet, in many cases, we provide for their every need.

Unfortunately, for Americans, many interlopers and foreign nationals carry resentment and disdain for our country once they get here. Their negative feelings are exacerbated by an unkind press that would rather be typing up the news in Soviet Russia than in America.

All of these negatives threaten social cohesion and America's civic culture and our sense of common identity. We are not a diverse country. We are a country of diverse peoples with a common purpose and union. An especially annoying aspect of today's distortion of immigration is when immigrants, in legal or illegal status are assimilated into the welfare state rather than into a society of opportunity.

## Meaningful reform v charade of eight.

2016 has been another bloodbath, as conservatives are fed up with those who have been shown to be RINOS, as well as Democrats whose votes move the country further left to Marxism than most Americans in both parties think is good for the country. Donald Trump kicked butt as he was the only Republican the people would trust to execute the conservative approach rather than liberal.

Instead of offering a meaningful reform, such as the US Immigration Fix, including the Annual Guest Plan, the subject of this book, the Gang of Eight offered a charade. The act did not address the intricacies of America's immigration challenges. Instead the Senators offered a magic wand approach trying to pretend they were solving everything in one colossal bill, with the Democratic Party [I am a Democrat] ready to take undeserved bows.

This bill, S. 744, would have granted immediate amnesty to the estimated 11 million illegal aliens (20 million to 60 million in my estimates) in the country and "promised" that in the future the border would be made secure. The Bill also granted broad new powers to the scandal-ridden Obama Administration and it would cost taxpayers an estimated $6.3 trillion. Who's got that kind of money?

Americans said "no" as quickly as the bill was passed in the US Senate. Yet, the Senators chose not to listen to the country. Instead they decided to convince us they were right. They fired off paid ads in the form of propaganda in attempts to sell the Bill to the people as something good for Americans, while the House leadership contemplated the Bill. Americans rejected it and the House unexpectedly held its ground. In the fall of 2014 the people went ahead and rejected many of the Bill's proponents and sent them packing. Marco Rubio survived to run for President but his betrayal is forever imprinted on the frontal lobes of conservatives.

# Congress now works for Congress; not the people

The Senate Bill imposed $trillions of additional exorbitant costs on the people, and it was filled with political trade-offs and misguided policies. It offered a continuation of benefits (freebies) to all immigrants; participation in social security; no priority of jobs for Americans; a path to voting and citizenship; and a number of other unsavory aspects. It was as if it were written by a foreign power hoping to overthrow the USA from within.

It seemed to many that the US government was trying to bribe the unwelcome interlopers into accepting a sweet deal that with enough chicanery would be welcomed by an ignorant majority of Americans. Americans, however, woke up, and rose to the front of the opposition and proved in this instance that we are not dumb!

And, so, this gang of eight bill has been rejected and with good cause. Beware however, as Americans that our Senators are not on our side in this battle. We must call them to task on their actions on immigration. They are not free agents. They are supposed to be representatives of the people of the US, accountable to us and not beholden to foreign entities.

**Initiative, Referendum, Recall, & Impeachment 'R Good!**

It sure would be nice if we were able to use Initiative, Referendum, and Recall at the National level to assure that the will of the people was the mission of our representatives. If they did not execute the peoples' will, we could then recall them from office.

Few conservatives would not agree that Democratic leadership in the last twenty years at the federal level has morphed into the Marxist Party. In this Party remake, individual initiative and survival of the fittest no longer matter.

At the municipal level, the people, Democrats and Republicans have not adopted this hard left Marxist philosophy and simply want our representatives to be trustworthy and do what is right for us.

In fact, unfortunately for the health of America, most people do not pay enough attention to government. However, never before in our history has vigilance to the actions of public servants ever been more necessary. Politicians of today will take your wallet from your front pocket, stare you in the face, and blame the guy next to you. Then, they will try to talk you into believing that you did not see what you clearly observed. There is little value for honesty or the truth.

## We get the government we deserve

We get the government we deserve. It is not the people; it is our leaders who have betrayed us on issue after issue. But, it is we the people who must hold the leaders accountable. We should not be asking them for special favors for it emboldens them. If we send them home for good, they cannot hurt us again.

The Marxist-leaning Democratic leadership of today would reject JFK if he appeared as a candidate against Hillary Clinton, the heir apparent in the Democrat Party to replace President Obama if he chooses to step down Hah!

That is because the Democratic Party, which claims to be the party of the people only when it is convenient, is no longer for the common American. They just have not told us yet. We are the John and Jane Doe's out here on the streets trying to live. Our important representatives have left us in their dust and they have moved on to better things than us.

The leaders of the Party take no blame for their antiquated Marxist policies, even as more and more of their citizen members have no jobs, and while the remainder are eking life out with depressed wages and little hope.

Democratic leaders are simply looking for votes from illegal foreign nationals. They do not put forth candidates who care about the people—the citizens of the United States of America. If you tell yourself the truth every day, you will agree.

# Is any of this good?

As a Democrat it disturbs me that my party is trying to dilute US culture and get the new foreign voters to include themselves as virtual Democrats in waiting. This movement is not designed to help America or Americans. And, so, we the people have little hope.

In lockstep with the Democrats, Republicans also want the vote of the interlopers more than they want to provide proper representation for their constituency.

Neither Party is fit for the people today. And, on the notion of illegal immigration, both major political parties are operating against the will of the people. This will happen until the people begin to pay attention more regularly to the actions of our *noble* officials.

In the below section, and accompanying chart, I contrast the Gang of Eight Bill with the Annual Guest Plan. It shows that our Senators have a different agenda than we do.

If you were not sure that the Annual Guest Plan was a good deal for you before, this analysis should open your eyes. if you were ambivalent on the Gang of Eight plan before, these facts should convince you that there was a sellout of Americans in play in 2013, spearheaded by the US Senate. A stodgy group of tired old tired men, who no longer care about America, turned against the people.

Thankfully, Americans stopped them this time. Unfortunately, President Obama, the Energizer Bunny, continues to reject the will of the people and he is now breaking the Constitution. Obama's goal is to give the interlopers the freebies they want without asking for congressional approval. This lawless behavior is leading to the ruination of our country

# The Gang of Eight didn't play it straight

Americans throughout 2013 heard the constant drumbeat about the Gang of Eight's Amnesty program. Before we go on in any more detail about the Annual Guest Plan, let's compare bullet by bullet, the Gang of Eight plan (G of 8) with the Annual Guest Plan (AGP).

## 2013 Gang of Eight v Annual Guest Plan

| | G of 8 | AGP |
|---|---|---|
| Border secure | No | Yes |
| Jobs | Favors Interloper | Favors Americans |
| Amnesty | Yes | No |
| Path to citizenship | Yes | No (same as today) |
| Permanent residents | Yes | Never, Only guests |
| Voting | Yes | No, Never |
| Welfare benefits | Yes | No, Never |
| Freebies | Yes | No, Never |
| Anchor babies | Yes | No, stipends |
| Employer fees/fines | No | Yes (just one employee) |
| Reunification | 33M in 10yrs | Not for Guests |
| Coerced-deportation | None | As needed |
| Self-deportation | No | Pay stipend |
| Must have healthcare | No | Yes |
| Must be employed | No | Yes |
| Must speak English? | No | Yes |
| Oath of allegiance | No | Yes, tailored for guest |
| Deported interloper returns | OK | $50K fine |
| Hire illegals now | OK | Fine / Sanctions |
| Cost/debt accountability | No | Yes |
| Taxpayer Costs | 100-500M | Zero |
| Payback plan | No | Yes |
| Accountability Database | No | Yes |
| Interloper fine | $2000 | $2000 |
| Fake ID fine | No | $500 |
| Employer fine | No | $2000 per worker |
| Back taxes | No | Yes (interview) |
| Tax interview | No | Yes |
| Tax Due for off books work | No | Yes |
| Additional Paybacks like medical & education costs | No | Yes |

# Chapter 6   Annual Guest Plan— the Best Fix

## How does Annual Guest Plan actually work?

The Annual Guest Plan! aka (AGP) is process driven. Nothing is by chance. The annual guest process begins by registering all interlopers and all visa holders, expired or otherwise. The current batch of visa holders will be permitted to become Annual Guests in this first round, but after this registration period, the spigot is closed.

In this one-time process, I expect that we will find about 60 million interlopers before we even get to signing them up for annual guest status. If there are less than we really expect then the program is not as attractive as we think it is; the shadows may be more lucrative for some interlopers; or we will simply have "guessed wrong." Regardless, we will have given them our best shot!

The short view of the process is that after registration, the new registrant signs on the dotted line and agrees to abide by the terms of the annual guest process, including no lawsuits. Post registration, they must then apply for annual guest status. After gaining a six month free pass from authorities for merely registering, giving their biometrics, and signing the registration document, the newly registered potential guest gets an ID card. They then have two choices.

1.  Register for the AGP Program over a six month period
2.  Apply for AGP Status in next 6 months or Self Deport

- Two interviews – re residency and finances
- Pay $100 per year (estimate) each year
- Renew guest status yearly in person

# Apply for AGP status or self-deport.

The AGP is very generous in its desire for unhappy illegal interlopers to go back to their home countries. As such, after registration, the US will provide a check for estimated self-deportation costs and provide each registered and self-deporting interloper with a minimum $5,000 stipend after deportation expenses paid by the US. Nonetheless, all interlopers who are not deemed to be bad guys can sign up and stay under the Annual Guest Plan.

If time expires, and the registrant has neglected the call and has simply chosen not to apply for annual guest status and this interloper has not chosen to self-deport with benefits, ICE will be tapped under the new law to deport the registered perpetrator with no assistance, and no funding (no stipend) from taxpayers. It is the registrant's call.

# Two interviews (double vetting)

Interlopers, who choose to be guests become guests through a process that includes several interviews to prove their worthiness in America. During the interviews, they agree to a number of stipulations to get out of the shadows permanently as there will be no more shadows once the AGP is in force.

They also agree to pay an annual renewal fee. In addition to other fines, fees, & taxes determined by US officials, they agree to be well behaved; to hold a job; to obtain their own healthcare insurance; to not vote, and they promise to take no freebies ever from the US, States, or Municipal governments. Most importantly they promise to stay clean and be good residents of America.

If all goes well as noted in the previous paragraph, and thus the former interloper qualifies to become an annual guest; the next step is celebratory as the former interlopers, who had earlier in the process become registrants are pronounced "Annual Guests." Of course the lifetime ends when the former interloper messes up or contracts a debt to the welfare or health system that they choose not to pay back. The collection system records all debt and the accountability system keeps track of it.

In this full process, besides fines taken on account if need be, the registrant pays a $100.00 annual fee for the first year and all subsequent years, and gets his or her Photo ID card. The ID includes biometric information, of which the interloper agrees may be a source of identification, as a requisite to the plan.

Their financial database record called an Electronic Accountability Record (EAR) and smart card information is also updated with their new status. As long as they keep their noses clean, and renew their status every year, they can live in the US forever, without fear of deportation. But, they must renew their application in person every year.

Otherwise, they have chosen to ignore our generous hand, and deportation is the only option available. It is a simple plan; a simple process; that is it. It solves the problem of as many as 60 million interlopers for good.

Perhaps you have noticed that there are more than ¾ of the pages left to read in this book. If so, then you know that there are lots of other details to make sure this plan works for Americans as intended, and that Americans understand that it is not even close to an amnesty. That is why we need a small book, such as this to explain its components. Don't let anybody kid you. As part of the Big pro-US Immigration Fix, the Annual Guest Plan is the real deal.

## Children of guests

Children under eighteen of adult guests must also become Annual Guests. They too must be registered and approved. Anybody 18 years of age or older is considered an adult.

Children of guests must be registered and interviewed at the same time as their custody parent. Their database records and ID cards are also linked to their custody parent.

The Annual Guest Plan registration fee for months one to three is zero for children and adults. Months four to six is $25.00 for children and $50.00 for adults. Months seven through twelve (a grace period) permits children to be registered for $100.00 and for adults—to encourage quick registrations, the fee is $500.00.

Remember, if $500.00 is too much for poor people, those who register in the first three months pay nothing. Laggards pay or are deported. Who wants laggards in the US anyway?

The custody parent and children must always live in the same country. All children must appear with the custody parent in all interviews. If both parents have US custody, then the whole family must be present at the same interviews.

In other words, if for some reason, a child or an adult does not register or commits a crime worthy of deportation, all children of the custody parent as well as the custody parent are deported to their home country at no charge to the United States Treasury. Deportation costs will be paid by the Treasury but there will be a balance due for such expenses on the custody parent's financial database record, known as an EAR, to be described in detail later in this book.

Clearly a better option if going down the road to coerced deportation is to register, take the minimum $5,000 per person stipend, plus expenses and then self deport with or without your family.

To review the fee amounts set to assure these processes do not cost the taxpayers over a five year period. The annual renewal fee is $100. The annual fee for a child of a custody parent is $25.00. If the custody parent is a legal child under 18 years of age, the fees are the same as for a child, and there are no fines.

Back taxes, however, will be assessed for anybody who once worked in the US. When a parent is approved as an annual guest, attending the same interviews, the children are also approved, even though each child will have their own AGP and ACCT database record (EAR) and their own ID card.

## Can I spend a lifetime as a guest?

In order to remain an annual guest throughout their lifetimes, former interlopers must be well behaved guests. This means that, among other things, as previously noted, they continue to stay away from all crimes and misdemeanors, or to which we can all relate: they keep their noses clean.

Additionally, they may not take any freebies from the US government. That means they may not use welfare and health services without paying for them. They also must renew their guest status annually and pay their fines, fees & debts as prescribed. They must pay for their children's education through the taxation system—school taxes etc., just as citizens must. There is no free lunch. The stick for violating AGP provisions is deportation.

Annual Guests must have health insurance. They may then reside and work in the US for a lifetime. Obamacare is not an option. They may collect unemployment compensation under the same terms as US citizens.

They can apply and pay for a special passport that gives them return rights if they visit other countries. Travel is not restricted other than the same restrictions which US citizens follow. There are a lot of benefits to the interloper for becoming an annual guest and lots of benefits to Americans. For example:

- No more shadows
- No more freebies
- No more cost to Taxpayers

## How does the plan work?

Starting from the top again, the plan begins with the registration of all 20 million to 60 million interlopers who have been in the US since January 1, 2017. This date may change based on when the law is passed. The politicians are now suggesting there are only 11 million interlopers in the US but we all know this is a farce. There are 60 million for sure. Prove me wrong.

There is a six month registration period followed by a six month grace period. At the end of year one, all interlopers must be registered and must have applied for annual guest status or the sheriff will be duly notified.

For the first three months after the program commences, to kick off the program properly with a jump start, there is no charge for registration. This one is on-us—but Americans will get this back many fold by having our guests register. In the second three months, there will be a $50.00 fee for adult registration. After six months, the registration period is technically over but there will be a six month grace period in which deportation notices are served and the adult registration fee is increased 10X to $500.00.

The message of course is to register quickly and enjoy being out of the shadows for at least six months while we all see this can work. Any time after registration, the registrant may apply for annual guest status; and must apply for annual guest status within the full one year of the registration program. AGP applicants in the first six months are desired.

The fee for the annual guest application and the renewal, provided there are no appeals, is $100.00. An aspirant for annual guest status must be interviewed by US Officials for suitability and a second interview is also required the first year of the program for the determination of debts, fees, and fines.

The yes or no decision is to be a programmed decision that is mostly automated based on interview responses and background information responses, and a set of evaluation questions of the interviewer based on their perceptions of what happened in the interview. All negative case determinations may be appealed; but appeal costs must be paid up front by the registrant / former interloper or deportation proceedings are scheduled.

The default for those who do not register or who, after six months of being registered do not apply for annual guest status, and do not appeal, is coerced deportation.

At the end of one year, the objective is to have all interlopers registered as Annual Guests. Nobody will try to deny those in good stead to become Annual Guests. If big, big mistakes were made during the initial interview process, the aspirant, once gaining annual guest status may appeal the costs with a small down payment. If the appeal is not approved, the fees for this appeal are payable immediately. This is not a joke. This is an opportunity for interlopers to gain a respectable status in the US, if that is what they want.

There are many advantages of the Annual Guest Plan (AGP) to interlopers and citizens alike. Many advantages come to the US simply via the registration process. In other words, if it were not hypocritical to register illegal foreign nationals and then set them free to go back into the shadows, it would be a good idea for the US to have every person currently in an illegal status registered.

It is the difference of knowing and not knowing. This would simply help US authorities know how many interlopers there are; where they came from; and where they live. It is dangerous to have foreigners in illegal status living in the shadows. Don't you think?

All interlopers become known during registration before they even apply for annual guest status. Whatever cost effective biometrics (fingerprints, facial scans, etc.) can be deployed at the processing centers should be applied. As noted, the first part of registration, the demographics and questions / answers can be done online or in special kiosks on-site without officials supervising the activity. During the registration on-site activity, a photo is taken and all appropriate biometrics are captured such as fingerprints, facial scans, retina scans.

To stay out of the shadows for the next six months, the registrant must carry the Photo / Biometric ID on their person at all times. Everybody who was once an interloper, including bad guys, except those who decide not to apply, will have registration ID's at this time. Those who do not apply will not be happy. They will be deported. This is the stick part of the Trump position. If a guest does not want to be well-behaved, they will be tapped on the shoulder, and we will know where to find them, and they will be asked to leave.

Since there will be a one year period in which not everybody will have ID's it will be difficult to determine who is eligible for services and who is not. In other words, registered and unregistered interlopers, who are currently getting freebies during this interim period, may choose to continue to use their fake IDs to get their stuff.

The use of "may" here is not to indicate permission; it is to indicate possibility. This is a crime, but admittedly, during this one year period, it will be difficult to enforce until the one year period is up, and biometrics then are permitted to back up the ID card. This is the end of fake IDs in America.

In summary, the major points in the AGP plan are as follows:

- Addresses all American concerns on America's side
- Annual Guests may reside in America and hold jobs
- No freebies; no voting; no citizenship; jobs citizens1$^{st}$
- Must be residents of US before Jan. 1, 2017
- Six month registration period w/ 6 month grace period
- 3 months no charge; next 3 mos. $50.00; then $500
- Lower children fees: 0, $25.00, and $100 respectively
- Capture demographics, biometrics; get photo ID
- Registration part online & part @ authorized venues
  o  Any Fed or State Building such as Post Office.
- Requires 2 onsite interviews; get ID; pay fees, fines.
- Interview 1 – demographics; Interview 2 – financial
- All interloper debt kept in Electronic Accountability Record (EAR); collectible over time.
- Must apply for annual guest status in 6 months
- AGP fee $100; Must pay fines, costs, back taxes
- Encourage special categories to downgrade or self-deport
- Special stipends or subsidies offered for 1. reunified citizens, 2. green card residents, and 3. anchor citizens to either become Annual Guests or self-deportees.
- Special stipend for registered guest who self-deports
- All applicants for registration accepted.
- Application methodology: Using computer intelligence
  o  Most decisions on the spot

- o May be granted additional time while application appealed
- o Appeal may be initiated by registrant or US official

# Annual Guest Plan is not a welfare system

an annual guest is just a guest. Americans are gracious to even consider granting those who broke our laws such a status. The master of the house always sets the rules and the guests may leave or stay at their own volition or at the pleasure of the master of the house.

This is the major tenet of the Annual Guest Plan. Guests have no rights other than those rights specifically granted by the master (we the people) and those rights may change at the whim of the master if the program or the guest's participation in the program does not work out well.

# an annual guest, a guest, not a benefit recipient

Before a guest signs on the dotted line, and such a signature is a requirement for the AGP during the acceptance interview, they must agree to a number of provisos. By signing, they accept each and every proviso. They cannot pick and choose. They are the guests. The taxpayers of the US as citizens are the masters. These provisos include the following:

- Learn to speak English in 5 years
- English test each renewal
- Incremental English improvement
- A guest is nothing but a guest
- A child of a guest is a guest, not a citizen
- No anchor babies can be produced by guests

- Program is at pleasure of Congress
- Must renew guest status once a year.
- Must permit Photo ID & databases to be updated
- Must pay annual fee & something towards debt.
- Zero amnesty as demanded by Americans.
- Debt is accountable and payable
- Does not require immediate deportation
- No US family reunification provisions as Reagan amnesty
- US stipends may be used for reunification in home country
- Parents of anchor babies & anchor citizens benefits
  - May choose stipends to demote to AGP status
  - May take stipends to self deport
- Guest never permitted to vote
- May hold current jobs at minimum wage or more
- For new jobs, Americans have preference
- AGP requires strict enforcement of all current laws
- Obama immigration amnesties repealed
- Other stipulations at the whim of the master (the people)

# Chapter 7   Interloper Registration Factors

## Advantages for Interlopers and Americans

We have covered many topics so far in this book. In order to better make certain points in this book, it helps to go back sometimes to previously covered material to discuss it further. In this way, we can get a clearer notion as to what The Annual Guest Plan is exactly all about.

First of all, we have learned that there are major advantages to Americans and to interlopers for the registration process alone. For interlopers, once registered, they get a six month pass from ICE. They are out of the shadows. For US citizens, and US officials, this will be the first time ever that we know for sure how many foreign nationals in illegal status are residing in this country. Knowing this, we can make sound decisions about the types of programs we can afford and those that we cannot afford.

Without a free-style registration process in a program such as The Annual Guest Plan, we would be flying blind. Knowing who is in America prior to this program, has been unachievable. In this process, which costs an interloper nothing to register in the first three months, Americans learn the names and addresses and we get to capture the biometrics of interlopers who are potential guests.

At the end of six months and no later than a year, Americans and our government will know exactly how many foreign nationals in an illegal status are in America plus we learn the following:

- Who they are;
- Where they live;
- What they look like;
- Indisputable biometric identification
    - Fingerprints, retina scans, facial scans etc.
    - Stored in Photo ID and in database
    - Photo also stored in database
- Interlopers can never hide again from authorities

Though no debt tracking occurs in the registration process itself, a separate EAR record is created in a huge accountability database (ACCT) on behalf of each interloper during the registration process. This will be used to track all interloper debt. Identification data will be stored in the ID card and in an AGP record in a Demographic database designed specifically for the Annual Guest Plan.

The biometric data will also be kept on file in this database. The file will have multiple keys and thus it can be accessed by ID# as well as any biometric. As an aside, capturing whatever types of biometric data is achievable and cost effective.

A big advantage to both interlopers and Americans alike is that the terms illegal / legal and documented / undocumented, are about to disappear from our vocabulary. There is no reason why everybody should not register as the first part of becoming a lifetime, legal guest. Anybody unregistered is an illegal alien.

# The AGP approval process in review

Once somebody is approved in a two-interview process after registration and they become an annual guest, they pay fees and fines and back taxes determined from the acceptance interview. If the new guest cannot pay all that is due, it is recorded in the EAR and the debt accumulates in the ACCT database. As noted, this is an accountability database set up to store amounts due to the government for fines and back taxes, etc. An AGP agent schedules a payment plan if necessary, though the desired result is payment during the Aspirant interview for annual guest status.

In addition to being able to live in the US without harassment, an interloper can work legally in America. They may keep their jobs and they may compete with Americans for advertised jobs with Americans having a clear priority. More than likely, the wages of former interlopers will increase as they can no longer be paid under the table once they are legal entities in the US.

## Americans are first for new jobs

For Americans, we do not get the jobs now held by interlopers. I would not even agree to that if I were an interloper. I would not sign up without being able to continue working. Americans may choose to keep our current jobs of course and we may apply for any new job formerly held by an interloper who is either deported or who does not make guest status. The difference from the past is that any new job opening goes to a qualified American before any guest or visa holder of any kind.

The no-cost Registration in the Annual Guest Plan for the first three months is a big gift from Americans to interlopers. During this period, interlopers can avoid rapid deportation. Those who, after six months, are not actively trying to become part of the program and who are not registered, may be deported, or they may attempt to gain approval for a six month grace period by paying a $500.00 fee instead of zero for the first here months and $50.00 for the second three months. No interloper may apply for annual guest status without first becoming a registrant.

The process will be designed to be low cost in its implementation so that there is not a huge administrative nightmare associated with the program. My career in IBM involved designing first of a kind, innovative, and complex systems so nobody can tell me this cannot be done with a proper plan and great execution.

It will be an efficient bureaucratic process that incorporates online offsite data collection and efficient pre-programmed interviews with federal agents or designated officials at another level. Any extra costs associated with this process will be paid for by the aspirant and added to the EAR. EARs with balances of course are collectible.'

There is no such thing as a citizenship path for Annual Guests. In other words, a short transitional path to citizenship is not available. However, an annual guest has no less stature than a foreign national in his or her home country and thus may use the same process as exists today for everybody else to go for citizenship.

For the home countries, this program provides assurances that somebody in the US who has been in an illegal status cannot jump ahead of those waiting at home. To say differently, all existing home country citizenship candidates are ahead of a new annual guest.

Likewise, there is no path to a green card from annual guest, period. There is no line jumping. All candidates ahead of a registrant / aspirant / guest in the same category for citizenship or green card stay ahead. In other words, nothing is changed regarding citizenship or green card status. The candidate or guest must wait in line as all others for citizenship or green card status. Yet, if willing to accept annual guest status, the shadows are 100% gone.

There is no annual guest voting – ever. This option is simply not available. Only citizens can vote in any US election at any level. This eliminates the possibility of foreign nationals taking over the government of small towns or even large towns.

New interlopers after January 1, 2017 or another agreed upon date, are not eligible for the program and will be deported immediately. These are not part of the 20 million to 60 million today but might be deemed as opportunists to get in on the Annual Guest Plan by crossing into the country illegally after hard deadlines are established. This program is not designed to encourage additional interlopers.

## Assurances in the workplace

Employers & various service providers such as hospitals, doctor's offices and schools need scanners and readers and a means (software) of updating the databases with pertinent information. Without being prepared in the workplace or where services are provided, we would quickly fall back into the situation where everything is free, and there is no tracking.

All of this capability does not have to be in place to begin the Annual Guest Plan but it must come on line quickly to preserve the integrity of the program. As capabilities come on line, the program will be strengthened. Such devices are inexpensive & readily available and can work over secure Internet connections that are already in place. With a major American contracting firm that an independent such as myself trusts, such as IBM, in charge of implementation, the prospects of success are substantially higher.

When the Annual Guest Plan passes Congress and is implemented, all other immigration laws, other than those specifically modified by the legislation are still in effect. The AGP will require some laws to be modified to accommodate features of the plan. And so existing law must become more favorable to accommodate necessary changes for Annual Guests, Aspirants, & Registrants.

# Intelligent Q&A to gain information

Using an intelligent Q & A methodology, requests for data from registrants and aspirants can be prompted and collected by computers quite readily, most approvals will be decided immediately by the computer based on programmed decision blocks. Aspirants can be notified at their AGP interview if they are approved rather than the system creating delays in the process.

As a rule, there will be no judges or lawyers or major hoops to jump through. Artificial intelligence and the administrative interview will be the method that helps assure that we get good people into the program and the bad guys are left behind intentionally.

All expenses are paid by the interloper. If the fees are not set high enough to pay for the systems, the fees will have to be raised.

# Appeals for those rejected

An interloper / registrant, who is not approved may appeal online for a set fee. They may also request an appeal interview, the cost of which will be known ahead of time, and paid by the aspirant / appellant.

In the approval process and later as yearly renewals kick-in, and periodically via email and or USPS notices, requests for payment of fines and back taxes will be made. Those, who ignore all requests to pay anything will be aggressively deported. The financial well-being of the program will be taken seriously.

Such deportation actions will not include stipends or subsidies and all costs for deportation in such instances will be borne by the interloper. Those not paid will be added to the EAR record. American taxpayers will not pay for coerced deportations but as noted, will provide stipends for those in various categories to encourage self-deportation. These stipends are discussed in later chapters.

These scenarios shall be defined in general terms along with a schedule of categories for which stipends will be offered. In some cases, these stipends / subsidies would be for those who otherwise would be accepted into the program but who, for their own reasons, opt for gaining the stipend while self-deporting. The stipend itself is collectible as the payment goes on the accountability record for any deportee that for any reason is permitted back into the country.

Of course America wants all debts to be paid immediately. But, when the AGP begins, there will be many debts, such as unpaid taxes owed that appear at first to be too large to be collectible. When agents deem payments difficult to collect, at a minimum, all charges that cannot be paid immediately are added to the debt record (EAR). They are stored in the interloper accountability database ACCT and are available for collection any time in the future.

Interloper debts incurred and charged to the EAR endure until paid. American debts are always payable and the government at various levels even forecloses on homes to assure payment. I would recommend against this unless the annual guest has simply decided to not pay at all. No special privileges will be extended to guests.

# Registration venues

A good part of the registration can be done online from the interloper's PC or from a Public Library or any place in which access to the Internet is available. Nearly all of America's 16,604 Public Library buildings offer free public access to computers, to the Internet and to trained staff equipped to help library users gain technology skills and find the information they need for school, work and more.

These venues can help interlopers begin the process of registration. Public access Internet terminals are available also in many cities. New York City for example is switching its 7000 pay phone kiosks to Internet Kiosks. By the time an interloper comes in for the photo and biometric capture for the registration, most of the front-end "paperwork," should already be completed online, and thus the interview process can be swift and not costly. The small $100 annual renewal fee reflects an optimism about controlling costs.

The primary venue to begin the registration process and the application for annual guest approval would therefore be the interloper's own PC for text work. Data input work that can readily be done at home is done at home. For the interviews and for Photo ID and biometric scans, federal and state offices can be made available.

For example, drivers' license photo centers would be ideal. Across the country these service all US citizens so there is more than enough capacity if the states consent. Additionally, there are 31,272 retail post offices in the US as well as thousands of federal buildings. In Pa for example. Approximately 70 Photo ID centers in the state handle the whole state (7 million). It is estimated that there are 2000 Driver Centers in all 50 states.

So, the interloper would complete the registration process at one of these staffed venues and his or her biometrics including fingerprints and a photo are captured. Demographic data is either entered and/or verified. Interlopers who do not know the language may bring somebody who does (a family member or friends) with them to the centers.

# Rapid process registration and sign-up

The objective is for registration to be a swift, cut and dried process to reduce processing expenses. Substantial information is collected at registration but no determination of acceptance for the interloper / registrant is given. There is no risk to register. Everybody who attempts to register will be registered and will receive a photo ID good for six months during which they are expected to apply for annual guest status.

The ID is given to the registrant when the registration process is complete. The first three months of the registration period are no charge. In the second three months the cost is $50.00, and the next six months is a special grace period as the process is expected to take just six months. The grace period fee is $500.00 payable up-front. The message of course is register once and early.

Though bureaucratic and perhaps some technical snares can be expected, they should be easily overcome with a proper implementation plan. I would recommend building this system even before the legislation is approved.

My own personal experience with passport photos taken in post offices is that they are done efficiently. Each approved site would have to have the equipment to take the photo, capture the fingerprints at least, and whatever biometrics are possible. The site would then issue the ID card and complete the aspirant data for the AGP approval in the AGP master database. Additionally, the EAR would be built in the ACCT database shortly thereafter in the second interview.

ID card coding and marking can provide changes in status. For example, registrant would be the first status, followed by aspirant, followed by annual guest, or unapproved / appeal status. The status is encoded in the database and in the ID card. Periodically the photo id card pictures and status information would need to be refreshed.

# Appeals!

When a guest is not approved, they may appeal. An estimate of the cost of appeal is given to the aspirant and it must be paid before the appeal is accepted. No appeal cost is borne by American taxpayers. An aspirant may appeal unlimited times with new grounds. Each time, the aspirant must pay estimated fees up front. Aspirants also must pay any estimated court costs / attorney fees that are involved in the process before proceedings. Taxpayers pay nothing.

Sometimes, the USCIS agents, in hardship circumstances, may approve of charges being added to the Accountability database to cover costs when cash cannot be paid up front. This cannot be the normal methodology as it defeats the purpose of paying up front. USCIS discretion would be based on hardship case by case with a goal of less than 1% of appeals to be granted this exception. Any extra attention required during the aspirant interviews may result in an additional cost being assessed in addition to the $100.00 annual guest initial and annual fees.

## Annual guest renewal process

According to long-time immigration law, green card permanent resident status must be renewed every ten years even though the green card holders are called permanent residents. The process for renewal is swift and rarely is renewal not granted.

Likewise annual guest status must be renewed in person annually at a fee of $100. The process should not be cumbersome or time consuming. Throughout the year, background workers can follow the flow of activity that requires the ID card, and can also cull other databases in audits to assure that Annual Guests are well-behaved.

At the annual brief interview, all demographic changes are updated. In fact, the annual guest may make demographic changes throughout the year over the Internet. Archives of the prior data must be kept for verification. In the renewal session, the annual guest will also be asked to pay any fines and any other debt on their EAR record in the ACCT database.

Based on strict guidelines, those who make no attempt or a less than minimum attempt to pay their debt, may be asked to self deport. Those who make no payment and/or are belligerent about it will be sent through a coerced deportation scenario. Demographic changes not reported annually may result in a $200.00 fine. This renewal process is integral to program working for all Americans

# Why implement Annual Guest Plan?

From the very first page of this book, we have been explaining the answer to this question. In a nutshell, it is a merciful way to handle interlopers legally without requiring coerced deportation. The process helps Americans and interlopers and does not harm either. Nobody in the US, including the interlopers gain by having them living in the shadows. Many interlopers may choose self-deportation—with or without stipends. Some may qualify for deportation loans / stipends. During the registration period, it may be a good idea for the US to pay for much of the deportation expense of an interloper. Of course the expense must be captured in an EAR.

Without a fix, the existing mess created by the president has the potential to create revolution in this country as the citizens are sick and tired of being pushed around by a government that favors foreigners over Americans.

Even conservatives do not have the stomach for mass deportations. But, the media's constant message of unfairness helps promote this feeling. We have already demonstrated that the cost of deportation is more than offset by the savings to the US taxpayer. In fact it is a substantial net plus for Americans. With the AGP, deportation is mostly voluntary and encouraged. It is not often coerced.

## Smart card technology

Since smart cards can deploy many different technologies simultaneously, the best technology at the best price must be selected for the ID card material. For example, certain homeland and port and employer stations may not have certain technologies such as barcode, mag stripe, RFID, or smart sequencing readers, etc.

But, the card itself may have all technologies so it would be universally readable. I would grant no forgiveness for not having readers where they are needed, despite the potential difficulty. I see this as a red herring as all of these ports etc. can be readily equipped by a good contractor, such as IBM with proper equipment to assure all is well, and America wins, when the program is ready.

## Data collection / processing is key to plan

There will be two different databases associated with each registrant / annual guest. One, which we will call the Annual Guest Plan (AGP) database. It will store demographic and biometric information and it will be linked to a second database. This database is called the Accountability Database (ACCT) and it will contain the former interloper's Electronic Accountability Record. This database will be the basis for storing data and collecting data for any services that are not immediately paid. It will also be used for financial accountability to assure a "guest" is not abusing the system.

During the registration process, the interloper's personal internet machine as well as onsite scanners and data input devices will be connected to large systems of computers over Secure Internet or over the government's private network. These will create and link to the proper records in both databases. The data captured will fill those records as it is scanned or keyed and made available.

Thus, during the registration process, both the AGP and the ACCT databases will be created and/or maintained, and all necessary data will also be loaded on the card. The real database goodies will come from new input as well as verification of registration input, during both interview processes.

# Nothing happens overnight in Scranton

Nothing happens overnight just about anywhere else in the universe, also. And, so, as we discuss how to implement The Annual Guest Plan, just because it all cannot be done at once is no reason to not begin as much as possible right away. Life and IT infrastructures happen incrementally. Some are planned and some just happen. Each day, after you plan and begin action, things move a little bit closer to your goal.

Eventually, all known technology features will be deployed and they will help make the Annual Guest Plan and any plan for immigration change that uses technology or requires trained people, much more effective. There is no reason for anybody to be lost in the system.

Once AGP is implemented, all the shadows should be well lit. A country that dreamed, formed the ideas, made the detailed plans and finally put a man on the moon with limited technology in the 1960's, can do anything it wants. It first must decide that it wants to do it.

And, so, it should be easy to locate those who overstay visas as well as other interlopers, such as those who arrive on an airplane or a ship or who cross one of our borders. We must decide to start one day, rather than always putting it off.

When interlopers show up for services with their fake ID's, somehow they receive free services. Once biometrics are part of the system, this will end. Lou Barletta calls this the one fingerprint and out method of protecting American interests. You get to use your finger once for services and never again, because we know who you are.

If our leaders wanted to stop this abuse as a nation, we could do so right away but not overnight. If we wanted to solve it a year ago, it would be solved already. We start with dreams which help us with ideas, and then we make plans and then we take action, and that is how we get things done.

When representatives sit around wringing their hands because their donors are not willing to give if they do the right thing or because it may not work well immediately; they simply don't get it. Until they get it or it is certain that they will never get it, Americans must keep hammering and be demanding that everything be done overnight. Eventually, bad representatives will be unelected, and good representatives will begin to respect the people again.

# Chapter 8   Barletta Bill & Annual Guest Plan Working Together

## America and Americans First!

On February 6, 2015, I presented the Annual Guest Plan to Congressman Lou Barletta and his District 11 Director, Joseph H. Gerdes, in the Hazleton Congressional Office. Congressman Barletta and I had a great conversation about our nation and its problems with illegal immigration and the millions of people living in the shadows in the US. They recognized Jeff Sessions' contributions and though in tune with the Annual Guest Plan, they needed time to fully commit. Hopefully next year or sooner!

The Congressman is focusing on Border Security to stop the flow, where my emphasis is how to deal with the people already here. Lou Barletta is a real tough American who is doing what is right for America first, rather than being concerned about reelection.

Just before our meeting, House Speaker John Boehner named Barletta to the Counterterrorism and Intelligence Subcommittee of the House Homeland Security Committee. Now, the Congressman from Northeastern PA will have a major voice on immigration security.

Even before he was given this opportunity to be on the select committee, Rep. Lou Barletta has always been on the side of Americans in the immigration battle. His voice has been heard in the Halls of Congress. Since last year, for example, he has been pushing a bill that would use fingerprint technology to keep track of foreign visitors who overstay their visas as well as many other initiatives.

January 21, 2015 was another eventful day for the Congressman as he was able to lend his support to the *Secure Our Borders First Act* as it passed in the House Homeland Security Committee. The Bill was introduced by Rep. Michael McCaul, R-Texas, Chairman of the Committee on Homeland Security. This legislation enables the United States to gain and maintain control of the country's land and maritime borders. The bill, known in the House as H.R. 399, contains my Congressman, Lou Barletta's amendment to implementing a biometric exit system to track visa over-stayers, and report to Congress its success.

# Bias taught by media and schools hurts Americans

Let me pause here momentarily as I feed you something, about which Congressman Barletta and all decent conservatives face every day, from this untruthful administration, their sycophants in the media, and their accomplices in teaching our youth. Just look at this picture on the next page and ask yourself what is the message?

We see two bricklayers, one with a *D* on his chest, with obviously darker skin, and another with an *R* on his chest, and lighter skin. The latter is feverishly undoing whatever the former does to build the path to citizenship. This is part of a grade school quiz. Look at the answers one child gives. Where do kids get such knowledge?

This scene is all about an un-promised path to citizenship, which the same people who want Obama's illegal amnesty to become the law of the land, claim is not their intentions. But, we, who know how the slippery slope works, also intuitively know, despite their denials, that the next step is instant citizenship.

### Dear Kids: Democrats are good! Republicans are bad!

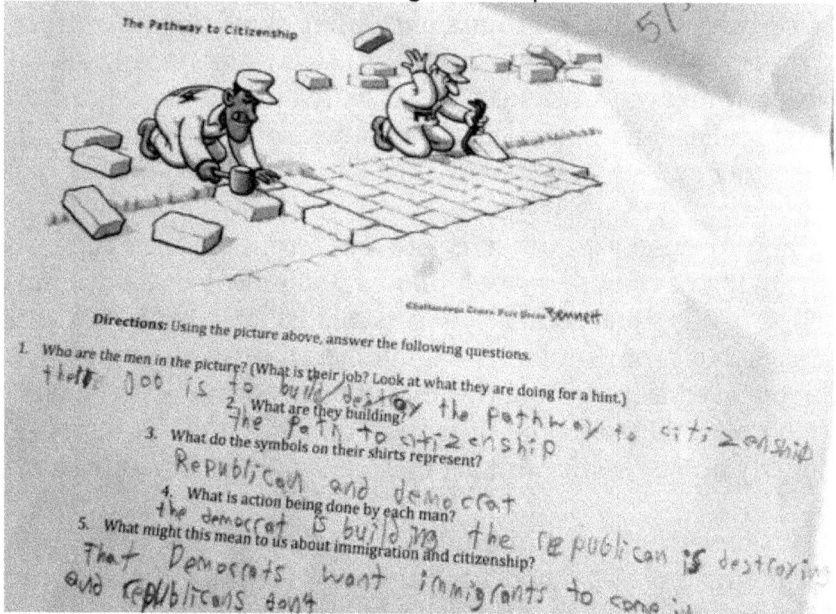

The Pathway to Citizenship

Directions: Using the picture above, answer the following questions.

1. Who are the men in the picture? (What is their job? Look at what they are doing for a hint.)
   their job is to build the... The Path to citizenship

2. What are they building? the pathway to citizenship

3. What do the symbols on their shirts represent? Republican and democrat

4. What is action being done by each man? the democrat is building the republican is destroying

5. What might this mean to us about immigration and citizenship? That Democrats want immigrants to come in and republicans don't

Citizenship in this scenario means a Democratic dynasty forever made up of people who, on their own, often would choose to be green card holders, and not citizens. One might conclude that these folks simply do not want to pledge allegiance to the USA.

Meanwhile on the right of this disturbing picture, they depict a light colored guy as the nasty Republican assailant, working feverishly to undo the great work of the foreign interloper trying to carve out a path to citizenship. They do not capture that the interloper is living in the shadows after having busted into the country in violation of American law, and that he is stealing benefits using fake ID from American taxpayers, including the school child's parents.

There is great power in caricatures, and without an explanation, a student in grade school would conclude that

Democrats are good, good, good, and Republicans are bad, bad, bad. That is, until they have to go find a job and there are none available for long-time Americans—meaning them.

Congressman Barletta thinks citizenship should come with responsibilities such as respect for the Constitution, and all American laws, and a deep desire on the part of the aspirant to swear allegiance to the US and melt within the pot along with all other citizens.

This propagandist cartoon is intended to put all Americans, who do not want their votes diluted, their incomes diluted, and their family's prospects for success diluted, on a big guilt trip. Instead of caring for their own families, they should think about everything from the foreigner's perspective—foreigners who want their jobs and their spots on main street, and their family home—if they can get it. That is not the American way.

This propaganda comes from the Obama Administration's tight grip on K-12 schools and the controversial "Core Curriculum." This was a classroom quiz about who's who in America—bad Republicans stopping people from doing well in life or good Democrats willing to give Republican's assets to those in need—as long as their origin is a foreign country.

As noted, many interlopers from foreign lands would be pleased to take American places at the home table for the benefits provided, but they do not really want to be American citizens.

Thankfully, the teacher in this case was disciplined by supervisors for not showing that there are two sides to every story. Why would they not show the American side of the story if just one side were permitted to be told? There should be no ambivalence about what is good for America and Americans. That is what should be taught so that teacher or school bias cannot mess with our children's minds.

When our own government, our schools, and the media mock Americans who try to put Americans first in America, we are definitely in trouble as a country.

## Annual guest program adoption helps immediately

Instead of waiting several years for HR 399, to gain the biometrics of would-be interlopers, when they are entering the country legally on a visa, the Annual Guest Plan can be implemented three months after the law goes into effect. As a tech, I know how to do this so I am sure, IBM or a company that is as good as IBM would be able to get the job done. When Donald Trump is president; almost all things will be possible for America and Americans.

This is not Obamacare, which is anti-American and so cronies of the administration should not be the implementers. Therefore, a robust schedule and an implementation by seasoned professionals can dramatically cut the time frames as put forth in HR 399 for biometrics.

I would have been fired long before retirement if the work I did along with other Systems Engineers was not successful. And, so, you go with what you know. I would recommend IBM 100% or another top consulting / IT contracting firm to be chosen for the job. No matter who, they must be monitored closely.

The specs must first be drawn up in detail and in readable format, and from there, somebody like me can monitor the process for the government. The Private sector can get this system up in six months after passage. They know how to get things done without government waste and bureaucracy. Without being trite; I have actually been there and done that.

When you see the number of places in which technology can be deployed, you too will believe that this can be done. There are over thirty-thousand post offices and other spots where interlopers can be registered swiftly and smoothly.

# Chapter 9   What To Do about Stragglers?

## Stragglers are those who do not sign up?

What happens to new illegal entrants who were not here by the residency date that is chosen? Well, every great plan needs rules. The AGP applies only to those interlopers who are residing in the country as of say, May 30, 2015. We will need a way of enforcing this rule but let us remember that under all circumstances, it will be better than it is with today's plan which we might call *ad hoc Obama.*

For any sincere plan to work, the border needs to be vigorously enforced in the ways that Congressman Barletta and his committee suggest. Additionally, all Obama ad hoc directives and the Morton Memos need to be repealed so that we can do our best to stem the flow of bad guys, and plain old interlopers into America, and then we can deal with those illegally here.

In other words, new interlopers must be deported immediately once the program begins. After all, they will have been here for just a short while. It will be more like going home after a little vacation in America. They will pay their own deportation expenses and receive no stipends. However, on their way out, we will register them and capture their biometrics, and start them in our system with a status of rejected and deported.

Additionally, if an interloper happens to be enjoying a junket in his or her home country and are not in residence in the US when the AGP begins, they are not welcome to return to be registered.

## Possible option-- new interlopers during signup period

I am wrestling with the idea that perhaps during the Registration and AGP signup period of one year, we might let new interlopers into the country and register them on the spot. But, this would be a costly notion for any illegal foreign national who takes the option. It must be very expensive in order to deter their arrival. I am thinking of an option for a new interloper to pay a $10,000 to $50,000 fine to be eligible for registration and a guest interview. What do you think? This is not part of the plan. It is just a thought.

In this case, the potential guest would have to pay the fine first, and then go through the same process as all registrants and aspirants for annual guest status. They must prove their worthiness in their AGP approval interview; otherwise, just like any others in the system who do not make the grade, officials would use coerced deportation without a return ticket

When the one year registration period is completed, the registration system would still be live but only for stragglers deemed worthy by USCIS. It will be shut down very soon after the last qualified registrant is registered and has applied for AGP status. Rules would need to be codified to define exactly what a straggler actually is besides those who are embroiled in lengthy appeal processes.

After a year, in essence, we would expect all to have been processed through registration and be just short of being approved as aspirants to become Annual Guests. That means all others, who have not already become Annual Guests, would be declared to be in an illegal status and their next stop when located, would be deportation. As noted, there is the possible option of them being rescued in the short term by paying a huge fine, such as $50,000.

## Huge fines for laggards and no credit

For well-behaved former interlopers, there may be times that certain services such as Emergency Medical Treatment Active Labor Act (EMTALA) or doctor services or pharmaceutical services may help save a life or stop a big issue before it becomes life threatening. In such instances, an annual guest in the short term might not be able to pay what is due. The ACCT Database will be programmed so that health or welfare service providers can submit charges for approval and the charges will be carried until a payment plan can be arranged for the annual guest. The services would be added to the EAR in the financial accountability database (ACCT) and be tracked until paid.

There will be no cash benefits to registered guests, period. For those who wait until the last minute and are beyond the time limits of the plan, no credit will be given for an assessed fine. Deportation is the only option in this case unless they pay the fine in cash immediately, and promise to abide by the terms of the Annual Guest Plan. Again, AGP is not a welfare program.

# Chapter 10    Mandatory Personal Interviews

## Two interviews required for annual guest status

Two different onsite interviews shall be conducted for each aspirant to annual guest status. The preferred AGP path is from interloper to registrant to annual guest aspirant to annual guest. No interview will be held for registrants but they will meet with a screener to assure their data is completed and correct before receiving their card.

Lots of data will be collected during the registration process in which the interloper does face a screener / agent. Americans would not want it any other way. Thus, technically we could say there are three interviews but the first is merely to assure the registration records are built properly.

The first major interview to become an annual guest is called the *Acceptance Interview.* This is the most important interview for an aspirant to annual guest status. It determines whether the aspirant is approved or not approved.

The other interview does not really matter for approval, but it certainly does matter to assure that Americans get a fair shake financially, period. This other interview is called the IRS / Debt & Taxes Interview. Its purpose is to determine how much the aspirant owes for fines and logical violations of US law, and for unpaid taxes.

# Preparing for the Interview

Aspirants will receive a set of instructions at their registration screening so they can prepare for their two interviews. by the time they have their first interview, they will have completed a number of questions online at home or in a designated facility. They may have friends and/or family help them in this process and these same people may come with them to their interviews to assist.

Aspirants will arrive for their interview at the proper time carrying the documents that are required such as any identification cards they possess, birth certificates, marriage licenses, note from landlord verifying address, references from churches and work, documentation from charitable agencies and volunteer agencies such as Little Leagues, etc. Additionally, any police records, medical receipts, W-2's, 1099's etc., and tax returns should be brought to the interview. These will be all spelled out to registrants as they leave their registration venues.

Sample forms and instructions will be created for downloading to further aid in this verification data collection process. A task force in USCIS will need to create these forms as quickly as possible, and the programming team will need to work this into the interview Q & A process.

The shell documents need to be in a form to enable the aspirant to present them to the proper people in their lives for completion, rather than have these folks start off with blank sheets of paper. The objective is to have as much proof as to the authenticity and worthiness of the aspirant and proof of background information as possible..

Americans want good people to live in America. And so, Americans want good people to be accepted into the Annual Guest Plan.  The objective of both interviews is to permit good people into the country.

Nobody wants shylocks who want a free ride.  In fact, if during the debt interview, the aspirant exhibits poor behavior such that they mock attempts to collect debt and taxes, they may have their acceptance reset and be asked to go back to endure another acceptance interview. The second time, depending on their attitude, they may not be accepted.

## The Acceptance Interview

The Acceptance Interview is thus the key to the program. In this interview a programmed set of questions will attempt to determine the background of the aspirant in terms that an evaluation can be made.  Based on responses to simple questions, background programs will guide the interviewer to be even more thorough and professional than they could be without the AI-aided immediate interaction they will have at their fingertips.

Criminals are not wanted as guests. This interview cannot be a full background check as interlopers have been hiding their existence for many, many years. There are few record entrails left from people cleaning up their tracks as they go.

And, so Annual Guests, who are approved and who live in the USA based on that approval, will continue to have background checks performed in the *background*, at least for the first year after they have become Annual Guests. This is a way in which the bulk of aspirants can be approved even if all the data is not in. It is a good thing, not a bad thing.

The Acceptance Interview would consist of a series of questions, mostly yes or no and the computer would be preprogrammed using the same standards / guidelines for all applicants. Lying in this interview will cause eventual deportation as the full background checks are completed.

Aspirants may be granted annual guest status, and should be granted such status when the preponderance of evidence as analyzed by the A-I system, tells the acceptance interviewer that all is well with a particular aspirant.

## A bad past means non-acceptance

Criminal activity, drug use, gang membership etc. are queried and responses provide data in the form of a programmable point system in which the aspirant is approved or disapproved. Having an agent spend hours, days, or weeks laboring over an approval would be unaffordable to the citizenry and it would result in a failure of the program.

By pre-programing the expert agent's questions, and enabling different interactions depending on responses, (using programmed actions) the data will influence the yes / no decision and the machine will provide a way for the interviewer to make an on-the spot recommendation.

The award of annual guest status is the default, unless the bad data is so entrenched in the aspirant's past, that the computer system provides an immediate negative response with the reasons.

And, so a quick decision can be made with available facts. Additional facts will be gained as background checkers delve more into the responses. Blatant errors in judgment will be corrected and approval may be rescinded if absolutely necessary after the fact.

All-in-all we must remember that these people, who would be looking for freedom in guest status, today, operate in the shadows, and they theoretically roam free doing whatever they do. Making a mistake in the initial approval of their application is not any more deadly than them never having applied. Bringing them into daylight is a major plus for

America. They are already here. Approving their status even if questionable for a short while, is not a bad thing. It is a good thing. It eliminates the shadows, and it makes the process achievable.

# First year is formal probation

The first year after approval for the annual guest is designated as the probation period. Actually, all years are uncertain as violating the rules may result in a fine or deportation. Again, expectations are that the aspirant, now turned annual guest is going to make it through this last hoop. The interloper has registered, and has applied and so far, so good! Let's let American officials who never dealt with these folks before person to person or record to record, check things out, and make some better determinations over the first year period.

Additionally, in the first year after approval, the guest is required to gain a medical certification at their own expense or their first renewal will be denied. Health insurance is not something Annual Guests are qualified to receive from the government. They are guests; not permanent residents, and not citizens. In order to renew, a head of household must have a job and health insurance.

The objective of the aspirant data collection process and the interviews is to accept better than 99% of the aspirants for annual guest status, and it should do a pretty good job of it considering the massiveness of the effort. The bottom line is that acceptance is not automatic.

All aspirants must pass the acceptance interview process in order to become an annual guest. And any further reviews in the first year must also prove that the initial approval was valid and proper.

If the aspirant is accepted as an annual guest, they must pay a $2000 fine by the next annual AGP renewal. During the first year, in addition to other first year activity, the objective would be to collect the fine up front. However, for some, the fine may be charged to the guest's ACCT EAR 9debt) record. If the number of agents is not sufficient to complete the first year's background verifications, USCIS may extend these for no more than two more years.

# IRS / Debt & Taxes Interview

An IRS / Debt & Taxes Interview follows the Acceptance Interview but has minimal bearing on acceptance as an annual guest other than attitudinal as noted above. In other words, an aspirant can become an annual guest without the IRS / Debt Interview being fully completed based on backlogs.

The objective is to conduct both interviews on the same day so that the aspirant does not have to return. After registration, potential aspirants upon initial indication / application, will be advised about what materials they need to bring in for these two interviews.

The agent conducting the interview will be trained to use demographic factors – age, jobs, etc. – all of which can be prompted via a computer questionnaire. The end result is that, based on the responses, the computer program will estimate the taxes, fees & any other fines owed. For example, unauthorized driving, using fake ID, counterfeiting, etc. will add fines to the ACCT databases. Agents will also use estimates of earnings and gain acceptance of the amounts so that the tax amount may be determined.

The summary of the IRS / Debt & Taxes Interview is shown below in bullet form:

- Documentation must be provided
- Yes or no questions
- # of years is a key component
- Computer determines amount due
- Aspirant agrees or appeals
- Aspirant pays appeal costs before appeal
- Total amount added to ACCTDB if accepted
- No appeal after acceptance
- All databases updated including ID card
- to reflect status & amt. due
- ACCT record updated with agreed amount due
- No future disputes on amount due permitted

# Accountability Database?

The accountability database, ACCT, will contain an Electronic Accountability Record (EAR), similar to an Electronic Health Record (HER), or an Electronic Medical Record (EMR). This is a unique idea for a government that likes to give one person's dollars to another without ever keeping track of how much was given to whom. Today, regardless of the service, there is never a request for a payback of taxpayer dollars. Why is this?

## Payback is a b—tch

Politicians like to gain favor by spending Mary's dollars to give five different Joe's a break. They buy votes with all of our dollars. They rarely have sympathy for those they help. They hold them accountable for no payback just a lifelong commitment to keep the villain politicians in office for having provided the favors.

This corrupt system kills us domestically as it is the norm in our welfare system and it is killing us on the immigration front. It not only costs taxpayers as much as $500 billion per year, it serves as a huge magnet for the world to ignore our borders, and simply "come on down!"

Once the incentive for freebies is gone, only the productive members of society will try to come to America. The quality of our new citizens and our guests will increase.

## Valid in Health Information Technology Systems Also!

Today in the Health Information Technology realm, computerized database systems already can accommodate EMRs and EHRs. Even in the domestic health industry with so many payments coming from government in the form of welfare for health purposes and EMTALA, I would propose a new record type called the EAR. But that is not the focus of this book.

Let's define the three databases which we just introduced. Two are currently used in all Health Management Software in doctors' offices and in hospitals, clinics and pharmacies. The third is being proposed in this book to accommodate those guests who simply cannot pay off a huge debt in a short period of time.

- EMR Electronic Medical Record – Doctors or health services provider's local database patient record
- EHR Electronic Health Record – Doctors or providers sharable database patient record kept in a national database [in the sky!]
- EAR Electronic Accountability Record— Doctors or providers sharable database and/or an immigration database of financial data used to capture and store all paid and unpaid charges & payments [in the sky!]

There is no EAR record today, called the ACCT database in the Annual Guest Plan. The US medical system has no such database; but it should. Before we implement a system for Annual Guests, rather than deport everybody that owes the US a dime, and never collect anything, we must assure that we can capture the amounts due to the US Treasury or other government treasuries such as those in states, counties, and municipalities.

The best example to show the value of a financial accountability notion being built into all government systems is the case of a lottery winner who has been on government care and cash all their lives. With no accountability, even Uncle Sam has no idea how much was spent on the care and feeding of such individuals. I bet there are many of them.

## How many dollars or in-kind welfare are received?

And so, when their ship comes in, they know there is no need to pay back anything to the taxpayers that helped get them through the tough times in their lives. They know that the taxpayers did not keep track of anything, and there is never a need to pay anything back, even at 3% per year.

You may have read about cases in which the converse is true however. What about a massive lottery winner, who continues to collect their government benefits and they never look back and they never pay anything back. Worse than that, they never think of telling the government to shut off their benefits because they are now OK!

Intrinsically, we all know this is wrong. However, I would never suggest that when a positive life changing event occurs that government step in and ruin the parade completely. Does the lottery win make the new millionaire an elite? Possibly, but so what? I see no problem in raining on say half of the parade for big lottery winners, who owe society for their personal care over many years.

Why should a future lottery winner not have to pay back what he or she has received in benefits? They will not be inclined to ever pay them back unless we, the givers keep track of our "gifts." Lottery winners are not the only ones who should pay back. All receivers should pay back something for what they received when they needed help the most.

By the way, to repeat, in this instance, I would limit the government's take to 50% of lottery winnings to pay back lifestyles paid by taxpayers even if the winner owed more. Who would ever play the lottery, theoretically beneficial to Americans, if all the proceeds went to our wasteful government officials?

Additionally, people recover from disabilities that put them on the dole. As they recover, and as their fortunes change, it would not be bad for them to be asked to pay back something—let's say on a yearly basis to ease the strain on taxpayers.

So, the bottom line is that the ACCT / EAR database whatever you choose to label it, will be built to track unpaid taxes, expenses—all debts owed in the annual guest process. It does not matter if it was OK or not OK debt; earned or unearned; paid or unpaid.

The AGP yearly guest renewal on-site appearance can be used to assure that all debt is paid. The fee each year must be paid with no excuses. Either the guest makes full payment or an approved partial payment of their EAR balance, or they may be put on a USCIS approved payment plan.

If former interlopers refuse to pay what the agents think is a proper amount or if they refuse to pay anything at all towards their fines, and back taxes, they are candidates for a deportation that will happen. It must be a risky proposition for the former interloper in order to assure payment.

Additional charges may be assessed by the interviewers based on the behavior of the AGP interviewee.

For example, if the aspirant gives a hard-working USCIS agent or a stand-in from the Post Office a hard time when calculating debt, taxes, etc.? The cost for any extra interview time should be paid by the aspirant at an appropriate cost rate. The computer program may advise the interviewer that an additional fee needs to be collected right then and there.

In every instance in which an aspirant or a guest indiscriminately and inappropriately takes more interviewer time than deemed appropriate, their EAR should absorb an extra charge or they should pay the charge immediately. These records are kept to assure payback over time, and so in the long run, there are no costs to the US taxpayer.

The database records of registrants should "never" be deleted. I would think that a record deletion should need proof of death for at least 50 years in the grave. The US objective is to collect for all debts from the debtor or the beneficiary of the debts.

# Chapter 11   Jobs for Americans First

## Americans don't benefit when jobs are taken

The "Citizens for Laws" group notes that "For every 100 illegal aliens who find jobs in the US, 65 American workers are displaced." Just this February, 2015, in the news, they announced that for each job that has been created since 2008, two jobs have gone to illegal foreign nationals.

Somebody, who is supposed to be representing Americans, is not doing their job. Any idea who that may be?—Congress and the President. There are precious few jobs and those that are advertised are quickly taken by illegal foreign nationals. Quite frankly, Americans are sick of foreigners taking American jobs.

Why are foreigners able to take American jobs so easily? Are Americans bad employees? No! It is pure economics. Since there is no workplace enforcement of the immigration laws by the Obama Administration, employers can pay illegal workers illegal wages or whatever they want, and there is no retribution.

Moreover, employers further protect themselves from possible arrest by hiring contractors who then hire illegal foreign nationals as employees. Thus, companies can appear to have no employees on the books when and if the government comes checking.

# Businesses benefit with illegal employees

Why are businesses so anxious to hire foreigners? That too is easy to answer. Illegal foreign nationals, as well as those here legally on special work visas will work for peanuts rather than go back to their home countries for work. This drives wages down for all Americans in all industries where this practice is permitted and immigration is not enforced.

When the price of everything is going up, it makes little sense that median family income is dropping rapidly. It ought to be rising with the price of food, clothing, and all goods and services upon which Americans depend.

Of course there are great plaudits for the successes of the fracking industry and all the employees being hired in this industry. But, it is the last successful industry in America.

Guess what? The Obama administration would shut it down in an instant if it could. Worse than that, instead of opposing Obama in destroying these great jobs, which assure oil and natural gas independence, your Democratic Senator would support him 100%.

With fracking and actually with our poor economy, gas and oil prices are almost back to where they were when President Obama took office. Ironically, though he is against drilling anywhere in the US, and he hates fossil fuels, the President has taken credit for the recent lowering of gas prices. He is one of the few humans alive who actually does get to have it both ways.

There are many statistics to prove that taxpayers are paying for illegal aliens to live here to the tune of $100 billion to $500 billion per year. It is all illegal but with no enforcement, anything goes.

Taxpayers are not only paying for those taking their jobs, they are suffering suppressed wages to the tune of another $200 billion per year as a result of interlopers taking our jobs at substantially lower wages, thereby lowering the wage amount hiring threshold.

## Taxation without Representation!

In 2008 when I wrote the first edition of my best-selling book, *Taxation Without Representation,* I reported on the impact of illegal foreign nationals on the meat packing industry. It has gotten even worse.

Not many people know that in the 1980's the meat packing industry was primarily located in the big cities, and for whatever reason, much of the labor force were blacks, and they were unionized. Their wages were very good for the times but the work was really tough. Black or white, Hispanic or Asian, it did not matter, their hourly wage was $19.00 in 1980.

Over time, as big companies in this tough industry and other companies not so big, found little to no immigration enforcement at the workplace, they began to build new factories in small towns with names easy to forget.

They hired illegal foreign nationals with impunity and ignored unions and union wage rates in these new facilities. Little villages emerged around these plants, and few of the workers or residents of these new villages were American. They were interlopers from all over the world. For twenty years, nobody, including Congress, has seemed to care.

## Wage suppression; Americans hurting

As I was doing research for The Annual Guest Plan, I went to current sources that show what has happened since 1980. It has gotten worse, not better. The average wage in the meatpacking industry today is $9.00 per hour. This is less than half the wage of 1980, while prices for everything else has more than doubled.

That is about a 400% decline in earnings power. What caused such downward pressure on wages? You all know it was an abundance of supply of workers in illegal status who would work for peanuts.

Working conditions in U.S. meat and poultry plants have always been tough. Some say it should trouble the conscience of every American who eats beef, pork or chicken. Making food products from the nonstop tide of animals and birds on plant "kill floors" and "live hang" areas has always been hazardous and exhausting, and the reason workers were once paid so well is that conditions overall are disgusting.

The job of such employees is to take 1000-pound animals (or even six-pound birds) and to turn these once-live creatures into neat and tidy packages of meat for supermarkets or restaurants. It is simply a nasty business. Animals are dying all the time and the surroundings are full of blood and grease and the stench of death as a constant reminder of the carnage.

Few Americans want to work in such places without a decent wage. To show the impact on the industry of the new illegal foreign national workforce, you may remember the May Day strike from 2006.

## The big strike many remember

Known historically as "the Great American Strike," or "El Gran Paro Estadounidense," this was a one-day boycott of United States schools and businesses by immigrants in the United States.

Those who celebrated by striking were mostly of Latin American origin. They celebrated international workers day with this one day strike. The employee populations in the meat packing plants at the time were already mostly Hispanic, and most of the employees were in the country illegally.

They marched anyway and had their rally. Large meatpackers across the country had to shut down for the day as they had no workers to get the daily tasks done. Think about that.

And somehow, these thousands and thousands of illegal foreign nationals were unimpeded by law enforcement as they went to work the next day and the next and the next for barely livable wages. ICE officials were unmoved, and chose not to do their jobs by raiding the meat factories. Clearly they saw what we all saw.

This period from the 1980's until now showed a lot of change in the industry. Other industries have similar stories. The fact is this change was employer driven as unions had at one time been controlling the shots in big city plants. Employers are said to have had enough of the unions.

So, they transformed the meatpacking sector during the 1980s from one in which workers had secure organizations, bargaining on their behalf, to one where self-organization was a high-risk situation. It was like a gauntlet for workers.

## Objective: cheap labor—no matter how achieved.

Where companies could not relocate, they often shut down their plants and simply disposed of their long-time organized workers.

Then they did what they wanted, which in most cases involved finding a suitable plant or building one. They then reopened their business with a nonunion illegal immigrant workforce. And so, today employers in this industry hire exactly who they want and pay them as little as possible. Rarely do they find American employees willing to work in their plants for repressed wages. The downward pressure on wages continues right to the present day. Employers are emboldened knowing that Obama will do nothing.

The point of course is that the job market favors illegal aliens who will work for peanuts over Americans who are accustomed to work to earn a living. The Annual Guest Plan changes this dynamic in favor of Americans. Guests are permitted to work but not for sub-minimum wages as they may do today illegally.

With no enforcement, what does illegal actually mean? When a guest applies for a job and an American applies for a job, under the AGP, the American gets the job.

Just to demonstrate how uncaring our current administration is in regard to the advantage that interlopers have over Americans in the job market, they just recently made it even worse.

## Americans cast in a disadvantageous role

Since most scholars see the President's new amnesty as unlawful, we can still use the term illegal interloper to describe those recently amnestied by Obama. Whether he knows it or not, the president has given these interlopers a $3,000-per-employee advantage over Americans for similar jobs.

In other words, Businesses have an incentive to hire illegal immigrants over native-born workers because of what some are calling a "quirk" of Obamacare.

Many are unaware that President Obama's temporary amnesty, which lasts three years, declares as many as 5 million illegal immigrants to be lawfully in the country and therefore eligible for work permits to compete against American workers.

They are theoretically ineligible for public benefits such as buying subsidized insurance on Obamacare's health exchanges, and other benefits such as welfare. However, we know that through ID fraud, many illegals are collecting such benefits and will continue to do so until biometrics become the norm, not the exception.

Nothing will stop them from using their work permits when needed to work, and their fake ID's to get welfare benefits.

Under Obamacare, businesses that hire interlopers do not have to pay a penalty for not providing them health coverage. They must pay $3000 more to hire an American.

There is no Obamacare penalty for hiring an interloper. Native-born employees already have it tough but this makes it even tougher to compete to get a job.

Americans want an advantage and should rightfully expect it. The Annual Guest Plan provides the Jobs advantage to Americans.

# AGP favors Americans for jobs!

The following list summarizes the impact of The Annual Guest Plan on Jobs:

- Pre AGP --Favors Interloper; cheap wages
- Post AGP -- Favors Americans, not mean spirited
- AGP = Jobs much more available for Americans
- AGP = Guests may keep current jobs
- AGP = Citizens may bump guests, for new jobs

# Chapter 12   Tell me about the Advantages of the New Blue Card

## Citizenship

The AGP offers no path to citizenship. An annual guest is just a guest and never a citizen. They remain an annual guest through their entire lifetime as long as they abide by the program rules. The AGP offers no enhanced path or even a regular path to citizenship. This is not to say that an annual guest cannot enter into a program in their home country, like everybody else from that country, and get behind them all in line, and wait their turn for citizenship—like everybody else. In other words, there is no expedited path to citizenship. Citizenship rules are unchanged by the Annual Guest Plan.

## Permanent Resident (Green Card)

Besides the many, many visa types from critical worker visas to visitor visas from countries where a passport is not enough, the most desired type of resident status, other than citizenship, for a legal foreign national, is called permanent resident, or colloquially, green card status.

This is the immigration status of a person authorized to permanently live and work in the United States of America. Nothing other than citizenship is really permanent and so even permanent residents must renew their status. They hold status for ten years, and then they must renew or they are deported.

Foreigners in green card permanent resident status are not interlopers; though in their past history, they may have been.

To signify their status, they receive a United States Permanent Resident Card (USCIS Form I-551), formerly called Alien Registration Card or Alien Registration Receipt Card (INS Form I-151). Regular human beings call this a "green card."

It is simply an identification card attesting to the permanent resident status of an alien (foreign national with allegiance to another country) in the United States. The card was actually green in color from 1946 until 1964, and it reverted back to green May 11, 2010. Over time, the mere term green card began to refer to the entire immigration process of becoming a permanent resident.

Today, the green card serves as proof that its holder, a lawful permanent resident (LPR), has been officially granted immigration benefits, which include permission to reside and take employment in the United States. LPRs are also permitted to enjoy our lucrative welfare and education system if they have no jobs after five years on the program.  Annual Guests on the other hand are required to hold jobs in order to maintain their guest status, and are never able to collect any freebies on John or Jane Doe's back.

The green-card holder must maintain permanent resident status, and can be removed from the United States if certain conditions of this status are not met. Thus even a permanent resident, aka green card holder is not guaranteed a lifetime status.

## INS Broken into three by the Homeland Security Bill

Before the Department of Homeland Security was created in 2002, green cards were formerly issued by the Immigration and Naturalization Service (INS). The Homeland Security Act of 2002 eliminated INS and separated the former agency into three components within the Department of Homeland Security (DHS).

The first is called the United States Citizenship and Immigration Services (USCIS). it handles applications for immigration benefits. Two other agencies were created to oversee the INS' former functions of immigration enforcement: U.S. Immigration and Customs Enforcement (ICE) and U.S. Customs and Border Protection (CBP), respectively.

Permanent residents of the United States, who are eighteen years of age or older are required to carry their actual green card at all times. Think of this requirement if you hear anybody complaining about having to carry their AGP card, and an Annual Guest Plan Photo ID. Failing to carry the card is a violation of the Immigration and Nationality Act, carrying the possibility of a fine up to $100 and / or imprisonment for up to 30 days for each offense. Only the federal government can impose these penalties.

## Should US citizens pay benefits to "permanent residents?"

If you are not a citizen of the US, you should not receive any benefits, period. Not only would I recommend that an annual guest never be able to attain green card status, I would look to limiting substantially if not eliminating the green card completely. I would look to the creation of a blue card status that would not provide as much permanency or as many benefits as the green card status.

In fact, a new "permanent residence program" would look a lot like the AGP plan. The difference of course is that the AGP plan is designed to take care of the 20 to 60 million interlopers currently in the country v. any future program. A future plan to deal with green card abuse is not the focus of this book, but it does make sense to move to the AGP rules v the green card rules as it would save taxpayers a lot of dollars.

It does help to ask, "Why should permanent residents, with allegiance to foreign nations, take benefits that are paid by US citizens?" Good question! Our Representatives are too generous with our taxpayer dollars. It is a selfish act as they hope those in illegal status and legal green card status will remember them and reward them with a future vote. There are no such benefits with the AGP status.

## Congress should be arrested

This idea is simply unfair to Americans and it is a fraudulent scam for which our legislators should be arrested and prosecuted. If they are not voting for the causes of those who put them in office, they should be prosecuted for malfeasance?

## Blue card status helps America

With the enactment of the AGP (hopefully it will become legislation soon), the green card guest status can be adjusted under a new name, say, blue card status to denote guests that may be on a different time limit than one year. If you are in blue card status, you may get five years to become a citizen, and then you lose your status. There would be no green cards.

Right now, green cards are ten years in between renewals. Perhaps in the future a guest status similar to annual guest can be adopted with most if not all of the provisos of the AGP, and few, if any of the green card. Being an AGP blue card v a green card holder would prompt those who are lazy but love America to make the effort to become citizens.

This could give the option after a visa expires, that the individual apply for and become a temporary blue card guest, which would be a subset or another form of an annual guest. To become a blue card guest, like all guests, the receiver would have to promise they would take no benefits.

Most of us do not understand why our government sees a need to make a million immigrants per year permanent residents simply because they supposedly are irreplaceable in their jobs, or because of misinterpreted reunification provisions.

These guests, as all guests, and as all people in the world with visa legal status, have the option of going back to their home countries and applying for citizenship. But, there is little reason to continue a program that grants so many people permanent residency in the US without any oath of loyalty, especially with our employment picture so bleak.

# The Einstein card

I am not against the next Albert Einstein getting a special privilege to live in the US. But, I think there is only one Einstein. I would give ten Einstein slots per year to foreign nationals in a working visa status and if they win the Einstein Scholarship Test, they are in. Otherwise, I think the H-1B program is a sham designed to keep US college graduates from taking the highest paying jobs in the US. It would be hard to prove me wrong! Why do our legislators give our kids' jobs to foreigners?

In a future system above and beyond the AGP program, those, who under today's way too liberal rules, would have become green card holders, would become blue card holders, and they would agree to give up their benefits and freebies that they would receive as a permanent resident (green card holder) if the status were available as in the past.

# Blue card holders must hold jobs besides their cards

In other words, like you and I, they would have to earn a living by having a job, and as a prerequisite to blue card status, they would agree that they would never seek welfare or freebies of any kind, and they would apply for citizenship within five years or lose their status. Yes, of course, there would be a sixth year grace period before penalties set in.

Just as the Annual Guests, these blue-card temporary guests could remain out of the shadows for the duration of the agreed upon visa extension time, and when the time is up, they would agree to leave the country. Unlike the annual guest, there would be no renewal of a five year blue card that had not taken the opportunity to become a citizen under US terms.

Just as the Annual Guests will be asked to give up freebies, so also the new blue card, semi-permanent temporary residents. No freebies. And, so instead of having to be green card, permanent residents with benefits for ten years while preparing for citizenship, the blue-carders would agree to sign up to remain for five years with no benefits while they prepare for citizenship.

My proposal is not the blue-card program but it is a natural thought for anybody taking an honest look at how the US conducts its immigration "business."

I advocate for The Annual Guest Plan, not the blue card plan but since the green card program is so abused today, it would be nice to fix it while we are at it. I must say that I see few reasons for a green card plan, and none that I can think of as I write this line. Green carders are permitted after five years to take welfare benefits from the American taxpayer as foreign nationals who in many cases choose not to work.

So, looking at an America first plan, I stumbled upon how unfair the green card system of today is for taxpaying Americans. It would be my suggestion, if ever asked that we fit them all with a blue card. After all, a blue card program, just like the Annual Guest Plan costs taxpayers zero, and for taxpayers, that is a great number.

# Chapter 13   Americans Need Americans to Survive

## Any welfare today for Annual Guests?

First of all, in order for Annual Guests to become Annual Guests, they must swear off a lot of bad habits. A big one is that they must swear that they will never use their fake IDs again to gain welfare benefits. Benefits and freebies are specifically denied to an annual guest. Annual guest IDs will provide no benefits.

The reason we will ask Annual Guests to sign up agreeing to terms including no freebies is so that a Marxist progressive Congressman in the future cannot say that Annual Guests have a right to US citizen benefits. After all, our Congress perverted green-card status into another welfare class of legal foreign nationals.

Additionally, an annual guest must be employed in order to remain in the country. There will be hardship cases brought forth and I can see one, two, and three year forgiveness's in tough times. Additionally, for those who lose jobs, unemployment compensation will be available since this is an employer paid benefit. The terms of such compensation will not be different from the terms for citizens.

One more point. For those Annual Guests whose employer is not required to purchase health insurance, since there can be no uninsured Annual Guests, they must purchase their own policies. In the Annual Guest Plan, they would be made eligible for Obamacare if it still exists but, as a guest. In such status, they would be ineligible to receive subsidies. The AGP provides no freebies, and this includes welfare for guests and subsidies for healthcare.

No freebies are ever part of the AGP. In the event of emergency situations for well-behaved Annual Guests, USCIS agents may choose to permit other payable life-saving services to be charged to the annual guest's EAR.

## Annual Guest Plan saves taxpayer dollars

All of this debt will be tracked and payment will continually be requested and eventually demanded. The objective is no freebies, and so there is debt tracking in the ACCT DB. When a debt amount is large, the USCIS agent or the interviewer may establish affordable payback amounts. Under the current program illegals receive services illegally and never pay anything back, nor is it ever tracked. If the debt continually increases, and the taxpayer is accountable, it would signal a deportation action.

Contrasting the AGP with the Gang of Eight US Senate travesty from 2013, we have a great look into the future from the Senate Budget Committee Republican staff. Their report demonstrates that the Gang of Eight's "comprehensive" immigration reform bill would have cost taxpayers trillions of dollars by giving millions of amnestied aliens access to federal welfare benefits and poverty programs once they had become legal permanent residents (green card holders).

Additionally, the Gang of Eight has very generous family reunification provisions. Basically anybody who has ever been in the reunification queue would immediately have been granted green card status. From then the newly reunified families would have even more family members to be reunified and on and on with $billions up to several $trillion more in costs.

Analysts estimate 33 million new immigrants would be reunified and on a path to citizenship by the 11 million illegal foreign nationals. That's 22 million more people than the immigration activists admit are in the country illegally.

Again, these new green card holders—all 33 million of them, would be eligible for welfare and freebies of all sorts after five years. If Congress institutes the Annual Guests Program, those in AGP status would not qualify for any benefits. Americans should wise up and elect representatives to represent our interests, not the interests of foreign nationals. Having Donald Trump on our side will certainly help.

## Should foreigners vote in America?

Republicans and Democrats are clamoring to do as much as they can so that interlopers from all countries will love them more than the other Party.

Guests are guests and just like a guest in your house, they cannot get together with a few other guests and vote you out of your favorite chair. US Annual Guests under any program can never vote in any election—municipal or state, or federal.

Since citizens will not be required to have national ID cards, and guests will be required to have ID cards, and biometric data authenticating will prove who is who whenever needed, it will be much easier to assure that only American citizens vote in American elections.

## Will perpetrators continue attempting to subvert voting.

And, so a suggested modification to the state's voter ID laws, would hopefully recognize the AGP legislation. The Supreme

Court in 2013 declared that Indiana's way of voter ID verification passed the constitutional test. The AGP law would at best depend on the good will of the nation regarding ID laws that do not permit non-citizens to vote. That should not be an issue.

My recommendation is that everybody, citizen or non-citizen, have their index fingerprint checked at every voting site. Since only the immigration database would be searched, anybody with a hit in the database would be an annual guest, and thus they would be ineligible to vote.

The AGP database would be marked however that this annual guest tried to vote unlawfully in a US election. The annual guest will answer for that either before or during the next annual status renewal. Those voting with no hit in the DB, would be considered US citizens initially but would be required produce a driver's license or a special voter ID in order to vote.

Any outsider prompting Annual Guests to try to vote will be putting their status as annual guest in jeopardy. I am not suggesting the use of biometric ID's on citizens for privacy reasons. Data from citizens whose fingers are scanned at the polling booths will not be collected.

# Family reunification demand has always been a sham!

Family reunification is a recognized reason for immigration in many countries because of the presence of one or more family members in a certain country. Their mere presence can enable the rest of the family to immigrate to that country as well. Unfortunately, not everybody is honest and so a whole bunch of fake uncles and aunts and their children often come along with the full reunification package.

Reunification has become a major fraudulent activity in America. It is a trick being perpetrated on the US population by supposedly good-hearted officials to help assure that illegal interloper families can stay together after busting into America. And, of course all federal officials are looking for the vote of the recipients of good-will, rather than the approval of their home-town constituency.

Since home country records are not always well kept, just about anybody making a claim for reunification, even if the cousin records four times removed are no longer kept, becomes eligible for a green card very quickly. This undermines the purpose of the kindness extended by the American people.

This is a much abused system. Americans are such good eggs, we would rather forgive than fight for our rights. But, what if this act of giving beyond our means brings on the end of our country as we know it. What if our complacency is a signal that we are giving the new guys the implicit right to take over America? Who does that help?

There is no reunification in the US whatsoever under the Annual Guest Plan. However, the plan is very generous with cash payments, subsidies, and stipends to help reunifications occur in the home countries—not the United States.

You won't believe how much the AGP law would provide to assure reunification takes place—but not in America. Reunification of course should occur in the home country not the US. Why is the US involved at all in reunification of family members of foreign citizens?

It would be an act of charity for us to provide major stipends as assistance to aid reunification in the home countries, and it would benefit the US financially by not paying for their welfare for a lifetime.

## America would do fine with just Americans

After all; we are America! Perhaps I am one of the few who believe that America can do fine with just Americans as we had done for several hundred years before the Marxists recently took over our government.

Other parts of the proposed AGP legislation recommend providing various stipends to green card holders or anchor citizens or even citizens who earned their citizenship but who are not working. The idea is to pay such legal residents of today to leave the US and reunify with their families in their home country. The only way for them to come back to America would be with a short term-visa.

If reunification is as important as those who play at our heartstrings want us to believe, what is wrong with having the reunification occur with the interlopers going back home with a wad of cash so big, they would be the richest folks in their home towns, rather than our home towns.

I don't think anybody with a heart can see anything wrong with that. Each citizen reunified in their home country would in essence win a cash lottery to fund their home experience. I see nothing wrong with that? By the way, it is win-win.

The recommended stipends, shown in subsequent chapters, as you will see are substantial. And, so upon return to the home country there is an opportunity for a family to be fully reunited and have a nice nest-egg as well. They can begin a better life in their own country.

## Green card holders do not see citizenship as necessary

Since many of today's green card holders never choose citizenship as they would have to swear loyalty to the US, they can take advantage of cash to go home, and become successful. It surely would be tough to go from welfare to success in the US as easily as taking the boost given by US taxpayers. At the same time, they are never a burden again on the US taxpayer.

The cost borne by taxpayers to support interlopers in the US is so substantial that even with giving tons of cash to interlopers and those in specific categories, who opt to self-deport, and promise not to come back, the US would actually gain financially after five years or less for each person to whom a stipend or subsidy or cash payment is given.

Isn't reunification in the home country a better deal for interlopers and green card holders?

## United States should be the priority of Congress

US Officials need to begin worrying about the US before the immigration problem we have with illegal interlopers is exacerbated by legal "interlopers" from fraudulent, ongoing, never ending reunification. The precepts of paying interlopers to leave and for any of those in selected status to leave, helps save US all, and gives them a nest egg they can brag about..

With AGP, and hopefully as a change in US immigration law, reunification can only occur in the home country. If there is something wrong with that, as I examine it honestly, I do not see it. Considering the statistics, there are three times as many family members in the home country than the US. Why would the US be thee drop off point for reunification, when it can be spread to many countries.

To get closer to the dangers of an inviting, non-discriminating, all-inclusive immigration and reunification plan, which, by the way is not supported in the AGP, we have to look at some numbers.

# A look at the numbers

The US population is about 330 million. Exactly half of the population number (165 million) received nonimmigrant visas in 2012. These are not the same people, thankfully. A nonimmigrant visa is one in which a foreigner is either visiting or working temporarily in the US and it is all legal.

Many simply never choose to go home, and we most often have no idea whether they are terrorists or altruists. We do not have a system today that tracks whether they are still in the country. Can you believe that? Biometrics in the Trump position will change that.

In 2012, 700,000 of these temporary visas were given for those who would become employed by various companies in the US because there supposedly was not enough Americans to fill those jobs.

Their visas permitted them to hold these fine jobs for six years, and during their six years, their employers, because they work for less than American College Graduates, work with immigration officials to put them on a path to citizenship when their visas expire.

American corporations remove the waiting in line for these special foreigners who have taken our children's jobs and now want to renege on their promise to go home after being here the full six years permitted by their visas. Others simply do not go home. The hide from authorities, which has gotten quite easy recently, and they work from the shadows waiting for a big break.

Meanwhile our children, who graduated the same year as these foreigners, have lost the college edge. They are forced to resign themselves to the mundane, while trying to get McDonald's to raise their minimum wage to $15.00 per hour so they can pay off their college loans.

Please note that there are 92 million unemployed Americans in the US so the logic that there are not enough Americans to fill 700,000 high paying jobs each and every year for me is unconvincing.

## Why are citizens not working?

I have to keep saying it because parents sometimes think it is their kids' fault. It is not. It is our legislators' fault. Your kids and my kids, college graduates, and those with Masters Degrees, are sitting in our homes waiting for the economy to break in their favor. Each time it breaks, a congressman wants to up the number of work visas for foreigners. Why is that? I have my ideas but they are not part of the Annual Guest Plan.

Where interlopers siphon off the low-skill jobs, these worker visa folks siphon off the high paying jobs that your children and my children would have gotten when they graduated from college or graduate school. That's why 85% of new college graduates are forced to live at home after graduation. Does this help America and Americans?

And so the argument fails when it suggests that illegal and legal immigration does not add a lot of cheap labor to the marketplace. I know better. Your children and my children should work before any foreigner gets a job. Don't you think?

In addition to these, the US generously grants an additional million or more immigration visas (green cards). Most are purportedly for family reunification, but as noted, nobody is checking so there is a lot of fraud.

If you believe the current numbers, our immigration practices are so loose that more than a million reunifications are done each year. It is extremely significant. How can there ever be a job for an American when all of the created jobs are taken by the million or more reunified legally per year. They either take your kids' jobs or they go on welfare. At least if they go on welfare, your kids' jobs are not taken by them.

# Would US Senators lie?

In 2013, the Senate told us that they thought they had solved it. They lied. In their plan they offered generous incentives to those illegally here and those thinking about coming here illegally and legally.

Reasonable estimates suggest that the Gang of Eight bill would have brought another 33 million legal immigrants in the 1st decade after implementation. Senators and congressman appearing to these folks as their friendly representatives would gain by their vote, and so they chose to sacrifice their constituents for their own personal greed.

The Annual Guest Plan has no US reunification provisions. All reunifications occur in the home country

# Reunification has a bad history

The history of reunification is worse than bad, and its reputation is worse. Reagan's reunification, for example, suffered from major interloper abuse. In one case as an example, one amnestied family member found 97 others someplace and reunified them all with little checking. None of us are interested in taking every resident of Ireland, Mexico, Canada, Guatemala or even Bermuda, and emptying their countries of their people. So, that is why the AGP reunification is always in the home country and with appropriate incentive stipends.

How was Reagan's amnesty abused? We have already noted that in many countries, there is a loose administration of birth records, and besides in many cultures, bribing and accepting bribes are a part of the official landscape.

Thus, to repeat, anybody can get reunified, and US records show that anybody has been reunified over the years. Reunification simply is not a good deal for American citizens. Our Congress, if they cared for Americans more than foreigners, would make reunification a home country thing by law. It is a better idea and it would cost substantially less in US dollars than US reunification schemes.

# Chapter 14   Accountability for Interlopers

## Should not all loans require payback?

When a good friend asks for some money to help them through a crisis, if you are like me, you give them what they need to the extent you can afford it. After all, you too may be in the same situation in the future.  When you do this, do you simply withdraw from your account and add it to theirs? Is that the last time you expect to ever see the amount of the help even if the friend becomes the next Donald Trump? Have you no claim to what you have given? Or, do you and your friend know there is a debt due?

Other than for family matters, which are often unaccountable, most friends help friends as much as possible financially but the amounts given are expressed or implied loans, and both parties know a payback is expected if things get better. There are no huge gifts from one to another. Yes, eventually loans may be forgiven but by the choice of the lender not the borrower.

There is an old saying that is reflected in the song, Robinson Crusoe, sung by Al Jolson. When he described his pal, Friday, to show that he was a good man, in the song, Crusoe noted that "He did not borrow or lend." You remember in Shakespeare's Hamlet, 1602, Polonius said: "Neither a borrower nor a lender be..." Borrowing and lending are tricky deals among friends. In the big financial institutions, you know as a borrower, you pay every last penny plus interest.

How is it that the government sends huge amounts to citizens for their welfare – cash payments, rent subsidies, medical payments, and never even keeps track in any database anyplace, who actually receives the benefits?

## Can government actually give gifts?

Are they gifts from the government? Are they gifts from congresspersons? Are they gifts from the President? They are definitely gifts because nobody in the government, after the huge gifts are sent out every week, knows to whom the gifts were sent, or who received the gifts. Is this good for America?

And, so suppose just a day after a $2,500 gift goes to Joe Dokes, Mr. Dokes also receives a check from the Powerball Lottery for $7,300,000,000. Would Joe Dokes immediately send the government a check for the $2,500 "gift?" It is not likely, because Dokes always viewed checks from the government as gifts; not loans.

Likewise, the Big Six auditing firms checking the US Treasury accounts receivable would not find any entry indicating that Joe Dokes owes the government $2,500.00. Why? Because it was a gift! Now, if we chose to call these amounts helping loans instead of gifts, with no corresponding change in accounting (still no tracking), I would bet a small percentage, but at least a few people nonetheless, would pay back the government when extremely better times came about?

Why do we treat them as gifts? The recipient certainly did not earn a gift as in Social Security, Medicare, or Unemployment Compensation. I do not even want to know the answer. I am sure that it is tough enough being a great politician giving one taxpayer gift after another to one voter after another to ever suggest that the indebted voter might actually, ever, have to repay the gift!

# Who gets the gifts?

If the government does not know to whom they give the gifts, then collection is impossible. The givers of the gifts, the politicians, can never be blamed, since nobody will ever be asking and therefore, nobody will be asked for a loan repayment. Welfare and medical services and 118 other US benefits are simply free for the taking, and they are killing US. You be they are.

There is no accountability because Congress wants it that way. Congress wants to be duly recognized by the receivers of the largesse as the grand giver. They want people to feel indebted to them, though it is not them, it is you and I, the American taxpayers who fork out the dole received by interlopers and others with no accountability.

They get to buy votes with taxpayer dollars with no repayment required. No government "gift" should be an eternal gift. Government should not be permitted to give "gifts." Find gifts in any articles of the Constitution or the Bill of Rights, or even mention in the Federalist Papers. You won't! It was not how our country was founded.

Illegal foreign nationals and many others, with no hope of ever making a payback, get gifts from the taxpayers via Congress also. Who is being played for a fool here? Such interlopers are instructed by other interlopers to take the money and run, and don't worry...be happy! They know that the US will have no idea who they are.

The Annual Guest Plan solves this problem for good. We track immigrant / interloper / guest debts. That is why this plan will be hard to get introduced or passed in Congress without Americans getting involved. Congress loves giving away your money!

# Cost Accountability

Accountability for annual guest debt is a major feature of the Annual Guest Plan as introduced in 2015. However, it would help all of America if it became a part of all US welfare plans eventually. I am not talking about earned things like Social Security, Medicare, and Unemployment Compensation. Anything that helps anybody think that not working is the preferred action to assure benefits is on my target list. It should be on your target list also.

And, so with regard to the Annual Guest Plan, any aspirant who becomes a guest can stay in the US until asked to leave for some violation of the requirement to be well-behaved. They are on their own financially just like you and I. When Annual Guests who really try to keep up with their payments to taxpayers—run into issues in repayment, I would recommend that they should not be treated too harshly. As soon as they are back on top, they should be required to get back on the payment track as soon as possible.

Their financial transactions leading to debt to the US Treasury, under the plan, would all be captured in their EAR (Electronic Accountability Record) in the ACCT database. This database is the proof that there is no free lunch. There is no amnesty. There is no welfare state just for having been an interloper who became a guest. Those days are gone. Everything is accounted. Eventually, former interlopers would have to pay this back or figure out the best way to leave the country.

Keeping an accounting of interloper debt is as great a start for this program and for the United States as registering the 20 to 60 million interlopers for the first time. Once debt is accounted, it must be collected, even if it is piecemeal.

Attempts must be made that are not harassing to citizens or newly minted guests to assure payment or partial payments on a regular payment plan. Over a proper amount of time, Annual

Guests must pay back all accrued debt on their record and any future debt they may be permitted to accrue. Heirs and assigns should be required to pay some portion of an estate to reduce the debt balance of a deceased.

## Access to database records

Each record in the AGP database as well as the ACCT database will have multiple access keys. An ID #, which is like a social security number is appropriate. Of course the ID should not be a social security number. The AGP # will be encoded magnetically in the ID card in the same fashion as card numbers are recorded in charge cards.

A bar code, an RFID chip, fingerprint, retina, and facial scans will also be recorded from the interviews and they will be verifiable. They will come into play from the point of the registration process and the guest photo ID card. Any of these ID features will be able to be used to access data in the AGP or ACCT databases for those with authority to do so.

The data can be fetched therefore via biometrics or a verified guest number. As noted above, but repeated here for effect, I would advise that social security numbers not be used for Annual Guests. If an interloper or guest can be identified by a finger print, they can never snooker the US system into thinking they are a dead guy or somebody else whose ID they may have stolen.

## Americans do not want to be messed with!

Reality says that in a US in which most people do not want to deport the poor souls living in the shadows, how do we get the "shadow people" to begin paying US back for what they have taken? Americans are not happy about the authorized theft of taxpayer dollars in the form of gifts that have been granted by the POTUS and the Congress.

What if we came up with a standard way of paying back US taxpayers for those interlopers who eventually become Annual Guests? What would it look like? What would the standard required payback actually look like? Let's take a shot at building the scenario in simple terms:

The standard payback:

- Must pay 10% of debt or 10% of income each year
- Requirement to renew as a Guest.
- Can gain special repayment waivers during annual interviews.
- Additional processing cost- waivers added to EAR
- To repeat: No free lunch!

# Do Americans feel taken?

Americans are not dummies. We just have been lulled over a number of years of good government that such good government would continue. It has not continued. In fact, today's style of government is absolutely unacceptable for honest Americans. Who in the US can be pleased with this system of government given to us today by corrupt, arrogant, and greedy politicians?

In the notion of no freebies, as a requirement of the AGP, a corollary, is that every annual guest pays for everything. Let's honestly ask ourselves: "If not them, then whom?"

Place yourself in the role of an annual guest, recently freed from the shadow of deportation. If you are a guest, having once broken into the USA, and now having broken away from your days as an interloper, would you not be pleased?

If you are not pleased, should you expect that somebody who you have never met will step up and say they will pay all your expenses because you would like to live in America, expense free? Sorry, unless you find such a person, it would be best to appreciative your new freedom. Your expenses are on you, however—nobody else.

Government will not pay for you under the AGP. It may be tough to reconcile but the new plan says that any financial burden incurred by you will not be paid by US taxpayers— even if we once paid for those with fake ID's in the past, when many more people were in the shadows.

## Sunshine with no shadows

Celebrate the Sun. The Annual Guest Plan is a sunshine plan. Enjoy your tan. There are no shadows. Everything is in the open. Just do not ask American taxpayers to pay anything for your sustenance.

Charitable organizations such as the Salvation Army, Catholic Social Services, Jewish Charities of America, National Association of Free and Charitable Clinics. Shriners and St. Jude's Hospital to name a few, as well as many others are ready to help Americans or guests who need help with all types of issues. Government will not make payments to Annual Guests under the AGP. Period!

Here is a list of a few important notions that will help make this plan work for interloper and American taxpayer alike

- Guests live and work freely in the US
- Guests must be employed
- Guests must have healthcare
- Citizens will no longer pay for EMTALA
    - Emergency Medical Treatment & Active Labor Act

- AGP may use EMTALA as all US citizens but must pay for it, when billed, just as a citizen.
- EMTALA and all such emergency debt is added to the EAR
- Obamacare w/o subsidies if it still exists over time, must be made available for guests to purchase.
- Etc.

# Chapter 15 Speak English—even if you don't please!

## English and American

English and American are different languages. The English people dominated the colonies and so their language dominated the New World. American is very much like English and so Americans still say we speak English. I am of Irish descent, I speak English, not Gaelic, because English is the language of my country.

In colonial days, most of the citizens of the country chose to speak English as fluently as possible. Those, who did not speak the language of the country did not gain the great fortunes provided by the country. The same is true today. Learn English or stay behind and suffer until you can talk and understand the language.

Any citizen of the US with a few generations behind them knows that our grandparents may not have spoken English well, but they quickly learned the language to support their families in the New World. Only recently, when the notion that being a foreigner qualified for the mythical and politically correct positive notion of being diverse, did language become a stumbling block. Most regular Americans who are not part of the elite know this is pure bunkum.

## English cannot be optional

As I see it; it is not optional to know and speak English unless you want to be a failure in life. Not requiring English as our language is like Congress condemning those who receive the least remuneration for their work to stay in such jobs forever.

Not speaking English is like trying to program the internal parts of a computer using a spoken language when the machine understands only machine language. You will fail and those who try to speak foreign tongues in America will fail. It is a given. One would think that Congress does not want green card holders and guests to fail?

You cannot be a worthy American if you do not try to speak the language of our country. English, not Irish (Gaelic) nor Syrian, a language in which I know a few words, has been our language regardless of our native languages, and regardless of our countries of origin.

Everybody learned English and nobody complained as our nation gained its strength as the melting pot. We all needed to speak a common language so we knew what our conversation partners were talking about.

## Diversity divides; it does not unite

Americans were trained by the patriotic schools of our country that nation of origin did not matter because, after all, we were and are all Americans.

Diversity divides; it does not unite. We are the United States of America, and each and every one of us, who has spent some real time here in this country, along with the many who have researched our history, know that America, until the six Obama years in recent history has had its own unique culture. Diversity is a divider, and so it is a prized notion for those Marxists in control who clearly are pushing US down the path of failure.

The skin of America is red, white, yellow, brown, black and beautiful mixes of all colors. America has no national skin color. Skin color does not matter at all in America, especially as our nation has aged and matured.

Some Marxist progressives seem unhappy unless they can bring in new immigrants from Ireland and Syria and Norway, and Libya, and tell them they do not have to melt into anything. They encourage a diversity—not a unity of purpose for Americans and for our country. Not speaking English is another divider of people in the US.

Marxist progressive Democrats do not like American freedoms. Their ideas were not good in the 1600's and 1700's and they are not good today.

## Strength comes with unity

They are wrong! The strength of our country comes from all US citizens who at one time, way in the past, looked at each other in the melting pot and decided to melt for the sake of unity of purpose. Our strength does not come from those who choose to remain aligned with their past; their country of origin; or a divisive ideology. It comes from people choosing to be practicing Americans, and eventually real Americans.

That can work also when a person is in annual guest status. And, so English is our language and if you want to be part of this great country, learn English and speak English, especially when those who do not understand your foreign tongue are close by. That is respectful of America.

## English – the Language of America!

The Americans that I know are fully united in their support for an English language requirement as part of any immigration legislation. Newer polls suggest that nearly 76 percent of adults believe that illegal immigrants should speak and understand English before ever gaining a shred of legal status. The Pew Research / USA Today poll is the source.

Congress does not take this notion of a national language seriously enough as their main concern is always reelection. Borders, culture and language are important for America. Congress must put some notions on the table requiring new immigrants (no laws currently apply to interlopers other than deportation) to be proficient in English or at least be enrolled in a program to learn English.

The Pew poll also sheds light on a key fight between conservative Republicans and immigration reform supporters concerning whether or not the proposal should secure the border "first" before granting legal status to immigrants in the United States illegally.

The poll shows Americans are divided on the issue. Until Lou Barletta spoke up in a big way in the Halls of Congress recently, the membership had been completely ineffective on border security. Additionally, the President has done all he can to remove any border restrictions—even though the US cannot absorb all seven billion members of the world's population.

By the way, it is difficult to swear an oath of allegiance in the national language of a country if you cannot speak the language. And so in the Annual Guest Plan proposed legislation, English is designated as the official US language. It should have been done many years ago!

In summary, an annual guest must learn to speak some English in the first 3 months. It is OK to not speak the language at all during the registration period as long as a friend or relative attests to the registration data. A test will be given after the first year and each subsequent year as a guest until after the fifth year. At each renewal period, a test shall be given and at the end of the fifth year, the annual guest must pass a comprehensive English test; have annual guest status revoked; or pay for remedial English training classes.

## Oath of allegiance

The Annual Guest Plan includes the requirement of an Oath of Allegiance to the United States of America. Aspirants must swear a special oath of allegiance to the US before being granted status and then again after passing the 5 year English competency test.

The oath itself must be modeled after the US citizenship oath. It must be designed so as not to permit some smaller allegiance to home, but the language has to place US interests above all competing interests. It is the aspirant's choice as to whether to be an annual guest under the US terms and conditions.

Anybody who hates the US and expresses that view in any Annual Guest Plan interview or renewal must be deported immediately. Their families must then be scrutinized for potential terrorists. We do not want anybody who hates the US as a guest—ever!

The first question in the aspirant interview should ask if the aspirant hates the US. All who answer in the affirmative should not get one more minute in the country and should be deported right then from the interview station. It is not a joke!

## AGP solves a big problem for US and interlopers

The Annual Guest Plan solves the problem of 60,000,000 +/- interlopers illegally residing in the US. It favors Americans as opposed to foreigners and it assures that the immigration reform demands of Americans are met!

With so many human beings living in the shadows, and so many Americans being hurt by a lack of jobs and a lower standard of living due to the lack of enforcement of sound and solid immigration law, the problem begs for a real solution; not a series of tricks to attract illegal voters to one political party or another.

Nobody gets a green card or citizenship from participation in the Annual Guest Plan (AGP) but the interlopers here in an illegal status do get the opportunity to become real Annual Guests of the United States. This enables them to walk freely and work freely in America without the risk of deportation. That, my friends is a real big deal, and a generous act on the part of the American people for those who are in our country illegally.

## A guest is a guest

Wherever an advantage is to go to either an interloper; a registrant; an aspirant; a guest; or an American, the American always comes first in the Annual guest Pan. Let me repeat that as it is not the way it is today. All advantages must go to American citizens.

Moreover, a guest of the US is not a second class anything. They are guests—nothing more and nothing less. As a guest, they are not citizens or permanent residents and so they do not have the rights of US citizens. And, of course, in order to become a guest, they must agree and sign on the dotted line that they will abide by all stipulations of being a US annual guest.

No lawsuits will be accepted from any guest about the question of guest status. When an interloper signs on the dotted line during registration, they agree to abide by the rules of the process. When they sign to become an annual guest, they get only the rights in that document, other than natural rights, to which all human beings are entitled.

Consequently, a person in annual guest status, besides natural rights from God to life, liberty, and the pursuit of happiness, has only the specific rights as defined in the AGP law. Guests must play by strict US rules and they must support themselves & families since there are no freebies permitted in the plan. The full plan includes border security as defined by Congressman Barletta, with the additional notes added in this book.

Though we offer substantial thoughts on border security, the emphasis area in the Annual Guest Plan portrayed in this book is the millions of interlopers currently living in the shadows or operating under Obama's temporary amnesty.

# Chapter 16   Chain Migration: Anchor Babies and Reunification

## Citizenship of future anchor babies?

Babies that are born to illegal alien mothers within U.S. borders today are called anchor babies. Under the misapplied 1965 Immigration Act, these newborns act as an anchor that pulls the illegal alien mother, father, and eventually a host of other relatives into permanent U.S. residency in a process called family reunification. It is like winning the lottery; and many play it as a game in which America and Americans always lose.

It is so lucrative a deal for interlopers that a cottage industry has been born in which pregnant women are flown into the US from all over the world to have their babies free of charge in American hospitals and other specially designed birthing facilities. By law, pregnant women cannot be denied medical care based on their immigration status or ability to pay. The babies are then deemed automatic American citizens, regardless of the status of their parents. Though the custody parent(s) are by law to be deported, the law is not enforced.

That does not sound fair or right, does it? Over 400,000 anchor babies are born in the US each year, and they are immediately citizens with reunification rights coming when they become adults. However, the enforcement is weak and so family connected with the newborn are typically not deported.

Americans would never get this deal if in similar circumstance in the countries from which these pregnant women come.

# Taxpayers pay big time

Recently some people have been using the term Jackpot Babies to describe this phenomenon. As part of the jackpot, the US taxpayer also pays for the hospital bills of the interloper as she has her "American" child. Since the child is an American citizen by the misinterpretation of our laws, the taxpayers pay all expenses for the child until he or she is an adult.

The advantages of birthright citizenship are immense. The babies get Medicaid (including birth costs), Temporary Assistance to Needy Families and food stamps. Obviously, the baby shares his goodies with his family, even though they are in illegal status. The baby needs a place to live and to be nurtured, and this must be paid for by somebody. Uncle Sam (you and I) is the payer for all these services.

Though the mainstream corrupt press is derelict in presenting the real costs to American taxpayers of having so many people coming in to get on the public dole, the fact is that many of the legal and illegal residents in this country are simply takers, not givers. The US goes net minus simply by their living in our country. How many more can we afford? It seems the President will not be happy until the world's full population is settled between our two shores.

The Annual Guest Plan does more than simply create Annual Guests. It immediately takes people in illegal status off the dole. It also offers huge stipends for anchor citizens, reunified citizens, and green card holders to self deport, with both the deportees and the US gaining financially. Reunification occurs in the home country.

So, the Annual Guest Plan works for the legal immigrants in the US as well as the illegal aliens in the US. That is a lot of people.

# More anchor babies than even an AGP can handle

The problem even the AGP has today with anchor citizens is that even with the AGP assisting people to self deport, the spigot for new anchor citizens is not turned off, and the tub is actually overflowing. AGP is designed to take small buckets from the tub, but nothing will work if the tub is continually allowed to fill up and run over.

Andy Semotiuk of Forbes wrote this eye-opener in September, 2014:

*"There has been uproar in neighborhoods across Los Angeles county in recent months over a controversial industry called birth tourism. Wealthy foreign women [often Chinese] in the late stages of pregnancy fly to the United States and stay at special maternity hotels. The women stay just long enough to give birth and obtain U.S. birth certificates and passports for their newborns. These maternity hotels are often run out of single family homes in suburbia. Angry neighbors picketed outside a Chino Hills, California, maternity hotel until authorities shut it down for zoning and code violations in December, 2012. Birth tourism has also ignited outrage on Capitol Hill."*

## Blame Congress on this – Not POTUS!

How is it that Congress permits this to persist? Because the people do not complain and we reelect the same inept people to Congress time and time again. We get the government we deserve when we do not pay attention.

In the last decade, we all know that America lost over one million jobs. That means that there are 1 million wage earners from all countries who are no longer earning wages. Yet, there are at least 29 million more people in the United States, and they are not native born Americans.

This is largely due to immigration and births to immigrants, legal and illegal. One would think that a country that cannot find work for its own people would not be encouraging more births from the foreign sector?

## What are the numbers?

This book offers counter solutions to chain migrations such as reunifications and anchor babies. In 1999, there were about 250,000 legal reunifications of all kinds in the US, In 2009, there were 1,100,000, and the number is getting larger as each reunified person has left somebody in the home country that the US Congress think needs to be in America. On this issue, Congress is the problem, for sure.

Clearly we need to adjust our policies on anchor babies as noted in previous chapters. We need to tell the world that we have done so and we need to do more than discourage births of foreigners in our country. As part of this, we need to minimize the benefits illegal alien parents get for having their babies in the United States. At the very least, we need a policy that denies entrance to the several hundred thousand very pregnant women who come in as tourists or other border crossers, legally and illegally in order to create an instant citizen.

## Annual Guest Plan ends the chicanery

The US citizenry are being played for fools. Hard as it is to believe, after being burned by 29 million additional legal residents, we have no such policy to control our borders or the flow of pregnant women into the country at the moment.

Just as we need better border security, we need to stop this illogical system of people legally breaking the intentions of the law.

Under the Annual Guest Plan, the notion of an anchor baby or anchor citizen comes to an end. There will be no anchor citizens and as an added protection, the children of Annual Guests are automatically Annual Guests, not permanent residents and not citizens. Sure they can live in America but only as paying members of our society.

Nobody is suggesting that Annual Guests cannot have children. However, as guests with allegiance to a foreign country, their children are also part of the heritage of their home country. The best the US is willing to do in the Annual Guest Plan in this case is offer the child freedom as an annual guest in the US, never to become a citizen under the program.

Anchor citizenship is a bogus idea that officials, especially lawyers know has been executed differently from the intentions of the 14th Amendment. Its interpretation has hurt and continues to burden the country and needs to be rolled back 100%. Additionally, the US needs a way to roll-back the effects of anchor baby citizenship and reunification. This is very doable and it will cost taxpayers initially for stipends, but it will save taxpayers immense amounts of dollars over time—in as little as five years.

### Supporting interlopers for life is a ticket to bankruptcy

Whatever the up-front costs may be to solve a good part of the problem, it will not be as costly as keeping the effects of this travesty forever. Can you imagine paying 50 million people newly amnestied to live here with no need to work?

Can you imagine if the number is really 60 million plus the 33 million required by the Gang of Eight for reunification? What country can support such a plan without planning its death to be either being overrun or being overtaken by the new young interlopers coming in to get theirs share of what appears to many to be an unlimited grubstake.

It is well known that a person born in the United States under the current interpretation of the 14th amendment is that they are an automatic citizen regardless of the mother's or father's citizenship status. In most cases, there is no father involved because until the Obama years, the father would be deported if identified as an illegal alien.

The United States is unusual in its offer of citizenship to anyone born on U.S. soil. Only a few European countries still grant automatic citizenship at birth. The United Kingdom and Australia repealed their U.S. style policies in the 1980s after witnessing abuses similar to those plaguing the U.S. today.

Why does the United States continue to allow a practice subject to widespread fraud? Besides the dependency ideology of Marxist progressives being very much in play, the answer lies in how American jurisprudence has interpreted the 14th Amendment to the Constitution.

# Chapter 17   The Gross Misinterpretation of the 14th Amendment

## Former slaves did not have anchor babies

The 14th Amendment was added to the Constitution as part of the post-Civil War reforms aimed at addressing injustices to African-American slaves and other free blacks. It was a good amendment intended for a good purpose. That purpose has been bastardized into the perversion Congress considers its interpretation of the law today.

The amendment was not written to include anchor babies or any notion of opportunism. it was to right a wrong, and to insure no state ever put a former slave into an inferior status.

There were no anchor babies at the time this amendment passed the public scrutiny, and so there was not an ounce of thought given to a problem that began about 100 years afterwards. This amendment would not pass muster today in its current interpretation.

This historically great amendment was in many ways to say I am sorry to subjugated men and women who served as slaves in the South before the Civil War. Nobody was attempting to apologize to unborn babies of opportunistic mothers from all over the world.

# Slaves already were Americans

The idea was to help assimilate former slaves into the fabric of America—something that was well overdue from the founding for sure—in a just way. It was not intended to enable a fraudulent way for interlopers to skirt the American borders.

Section I of the amendment is the part that is operative regarding citizenship of those born in America who owe allegiance to America.

**14th Amendment Section I:**
*All persons born or naturalized in the United States, and subject to the jurisdiction thereof, are citizens of the United States and of the state wherein they reside. No state shall make or enforce any law which shall abridge the privileges or immunities of citizens of the United States; nor shall any state deprive any person of life, liberty, or property, without due process of law; nor deny to any person within its jurisdiction the equal protection of the laws.*

To give some justice to slaves, all of whom had suffered immeasurable harm, the Amendment states that "all persons born or naturalized in the United States and *subject to the jurisdiction thereof* are citizens of the United States."

It was crafted carefully so that US state governments could never deny citizenship to anyone born in the United States, who are subject to the jurisdiction of the US. Such was the status of all slaves at the time of passage. There were no anchor babies at the time. It meant all salves, no matter in which state they lived, were citizens of the United States— each and every state—period.

When the amendment was crafted, the United States had no immigration policy, and thus the authors saw no need to state explicitly what they believed was understood. The phrase "*subject to the jurisdiction thereof*" was intended to exclude from automatic citizenship American-born persons whose allegiance to the United States was not complete.

## US cannot claim foreigners as citizens of US

In the case of illegal aliens who are temporarily or unlawfully in the United States, because their native country has a claim of allegiance to the child, the completeness of their allegiance to the United States is impaired and logically precludes automatic citizenship.

Even people like myself, non-lawyers can read this as the intention. What the US policy does is bully the home country to whom these folks are still considered citizens, into giving up their own citizens or claiming them despite the US claim.

Who says the US can steal rightful citizens with due allegiance from other countries simply because of an accident of birth. Who are we kidding? What if other countries stole our babies when unexpectedly born in say Iran, or Russia, or Uzbekistan, or Mexico, or Ireland? It makes no sense.

The amendment, however, made perfect sense for former slaves to make their future plight much easier in the new slave-free US. Slaves, however, before and after the Civil War, whether 100% acknowledged or not, were always Americans. This amendment assured that if they lived in a state that withheld such status, it would not stand. I would expect that more descendants of US slaves would be speaking out against this reinterpretation of the amendment as it should not stand for opportunistic purposes.

# A few more ideas about Birthright Citizenship

As previously discussed, Birthright Citizenship is now what in 1965, a corrupt Congress decided to be the essence of the 14h Amendment. It has been continually misinterpreted by the courts. It is now interpreted as unrestricted citizenship obtained at birth, if such a notion is desirable or really possible in any country. Where has Congress been since 1965?

In historic teachings, no matter what we may think, there are only two types of birthright citizenship. One right is fair from a logical perspective and the other is quite frankly, ridiculous:

- Fair = jus sanguinis
- Latin for "right of blood"
- One of the parents was a citizen of the country at the time of child's birth
- Other nations embrace "right of blood"

Then of course:

- Ridiculous = jus soli
- Latin for "right of the soil"
- Child happens to be born in that territory
- Every European nation shuns "soil based right"

Jus soli is the interpretation of the US, as ridiculous as it may be for birthright citizenship?

It surely cannot be that we like the plan because 400,000 new citizens are born each year to illegal foreign nationals in the US in mostly a fraudulent circumstance.

The whole world sees the US system as ridiculous. They rightfully see US citizens as fools for permitting it in a democracy. We have become a people that cannot make our government do the right thing for us – we the people. Yet, theoretically under the Constitution, we own the government. Tell that to a government employee!

## Helping unborn babies be citizens can make you money

It is so absurd that, as previously noted, a new cottage industry brings in pregnant women from across the world for a jus soli birth. The US is being played for fools as our leadership does not seem to mind America looking "goofy" to the rest of the world and burdening US taxpayers with the care and feeding of over 400,000 new babies each year.

Why is Congress so blind? The answer is they are not; they simply choose not to represent Americans citizens in this battle. Most of the 114th Congress must not be permitted to have a next term. I can think of only a few Senators that seem to care an iota about the people.

I'd rather get rid of the whole Senate, and then send I'm sorry notes to those who would have been able to help if they had spoken up or voted against the majority. The people have to use dramatic tactics to regain the government. Forget about political parties. None represent the people., We need to reclaim the government.

## What must be done?

If Congress wants to survive the people's scrutiny; it must write a new anchor law that favors America and Americans and distance itself from the new cottage industry and its foreign beneficiaries.

Such new anchor baby legislation would properly interpret the 14th amendment so that it gets it right on the sticky allegiance point as jus soli children & parents have primary allegiance to their home country, not America.

Foreigners born on American soil cannot be given automatic citizenship because the country of origin has already claimed the newborn child as a citizen.

With a new interpretation of the 14th amendment, the system would be fairer to all and there would be substantial taxpayer relief. Service fees, hospital, and nurturing costs would be minimized. Congress must also be encouraged to write a new anchor law that fits in with the notion of stipends as defined in the AGP for anchor citizens currently living in the USA.

## Stipends for anchor citizens to downgrade status

For example, the custody parent or parents of current minor anchor babies must by law be given the right to gain stipends for minor children to change their citizenship status. Stipends would range from $30,000 to $50,000 for each anchor child born before passage of the AGP law in the U.S.

A stipend of $30,000 would be paid to either the custody parent of an anchor child citizen or to an adult anchor citizen if the anchor citizen changes legal status from citizen to annual guest. A stipend of $50,000 would be paid to either the custody parent of an anchor child citizen or to an adult anchor citizen if the anchor citizen changes legal status from citizen to self-deportee by returning to their home country.

This is a very generous program and it may help citizens of other countries now living in America in the shadows to build strong businesses in their home countries. It may be the best thing that ever happened or would happen to them in their whole loves. It is also a good deal for Americans. It would cost Americans far less than supporting such citizens for life. For children up to adult age, it would be the custody parent's decision choice. For anchor children over this age, it would be the anchor citizen's choice

# The 2009 Birthright Citizenship Act

The H.R.1868 Birthright Citizenship Act (BCA) of 2009 – was an honest attempt to change this law. It was not perfect, however. Below are some recommended changes—using strikeouts and add-ons.

The original sponsor was Rep Nathan Deal, [GA-9]. The bill was originally introduced on 4/2/2009 with 95 cosponsors. There are related bills that are good also, such as H.R. 5002 "No Sanctuary for Illegals Act 2010."

The BCA would amend the Immigration and Nationality Act to consider a person born in the United States "subject to the jurisdiction" of the United States for citizenship at birth if one of the person's parents is (1) a U.S. citizen. or ~~national; (2) a lawful permanent resident alien whose residence is in the United States; or (3) an alien performing active service in the U.S. Armed Forces.~~

Replacement clause: "(2) an alien who performs four years of active service in the US Armed Forces. Such a person  goes to the front of the citizenship line upon honorable discharge. Interim status would be "annual guest."

Children of Permanent Residents under the Annual Guest Plan may stay in the country as Annual Guests as an extension to the AGP.

The stipends and the notion in the Annual Guest Plan are all about making life better for Americans and for those who have never had to swear 100% allegiance to America, yet whose babies became citizens.

## Children of Green Card Holders

I am against # 2 crossed out above as noted because the preponderance of people in that category in recent years have opted not to become citizens, and I see no reason why a non-citizen, who has not sworn allegiance to the US, should be the birthright parent for an anchor child.

There are tons of green card status residents who choose not to be citizens. This is to their peril and their children should not be permitted to enjoy citizenship status when the parents rejected it. Their children can be Annual Guests for sure, but not anchor babies. Why? Because neither mom nor dad in green card status chose to pay allegiance to America by becoming citizens.

Like Teddy Roosevelt, I want citizens of America to become citizens for the right reasons. If Mom and Dad rejected citizenship then baby should not be an automatic citizen. Period.

## Recent Action in Senate on Anchor Citizenship

In mid-March 2015—in fact, the day I was writing this line in the initial version of this book, I received an email from Dan Stein of the Federation for American Immigration Reform (fairus.org). It was about birthright citizenship and It was written well. I am providing most of the email as written with slight modifications for capitalization, bolding, funding requests, grammar, and a few add-ons, etc.

*"Amidst the train wreck of the DHS "defunding amnesty" fight, we may have a chance to eliminate a loophole that hands citizenship to illegal alien and tourist offspring born on U.S. soil.*

*"Ending the birthright citizenship loophole removes one of the largest incentives to immigrate illegally and will save American taxpayers millions in providing social services to future citizen children of illegal immigrants. Meanwhile, untold numbers of wealthy foreigners will no longer be able to "game" this loophole by fraudulently obtaining tourist visas for the sole purpose of giving birth in the U.S".*

## Same flaw in this legislation

"Foreign nationals from around the world have every incentive to exploit this loophole. Just by giving birth in America, their offspring is handed citizenship and all the benefits that entails (social services, future voting rights, ability to sponsor relatives for green cards, to name a few)."

"Sen. David Vitter (R-La.) is pushing to end "birthright citizenship" in legislation aimed at combatting human trafficking. The serious-minded Senator Vitter has proposed an amendment that would clarify the 14th Amendment's birthright provision to only apply for children with at least one parent who is a U.S. citizen, legal permanent resident, or member of the armed services.

[As noted previously, I disagree deeply with the provision to permit a legal permanent resident to sponsor a citizen child because, I regret to say 60% of these folks are on welfare, and many of them came into the country because of the reunification provisions of the anchor citizen interpretation; but something is better than nothing. We can do better!]

Unfair [pro-foreigner; anti-American] opposition groups in the US are already up in arms about this potential change. Obama's executive amnesty has emboldened more illegal immigrants than ever to lobby OUR members of Congress for their personal gain. Their personal gain is not a gain for America. We must stop this.

# Chapter 18   Can US Taxpayers Afford Deportation?

## Deportation is current law—that is a fact!

Deportation is required under current law for any foreign interloper. Our former Constitutional Law Professor in Chief , Barack Obama has chosen to ignore this part of a duly enacted and authorized law of the US.

Those who would like to give America away to the lowest bidders have the notion that anybody who wants to be American should just show up and automatically be declared an American. They think the President is correct! They would settle for just showing up; being granted permanent resident status; and having the five-year waiting period for welfare benefits waived. New US citizens already get the full 120 load of US welfare benefits.

Many Americans do not realize that our taxpayer dollars are used to fund 120 unique welfare benefits from cash to aid for children to housing and medical care etc. for American citizens in need—at least theoretically in need. This is socialism, whether we like it or not. You can bet in our inefficient government that there is a lot of redundancy and duplication of services in the list of 120 different welfare benefits. You can also bet that before we see the list reduced to 119, it will reach 130. It is simply the nature of politicians.

# Marxist progressive want taxpayers to keep paying

Those practicing the Marxist progressive ideology, who today are mostly found in the leadership of the Democrat Party, want American taxpayers to continue to pay welfare to Americans in "need," as well as to pay for the support of the people who come illegally; work for peanuts; take the good jobs of many Americans, and suppress the hourly wage for others.

Marxists Democrats (I am a lifelong Democrat so I hear them) also encourage everybody, including our children to be in a needy situation and that it is OK to remain in it. Then, they will not have to work. After all, this is good because the bad, bad, rich guys will have to pay more and more in taxes to support them. Balderdash!

# Should our kids take the night off?

I don't know about you but I do not tell my kids to loaf and be laggards because I do not want them to die young with none of their own children which they can honestly support. I have always told my kids to work hard so that in this great country, they can become the rich guys.

Only lack of initiative puts anybody at the bottom forever. Nobody naturally picks the bottom; but many of us at one time or another have hit the bottom. My generation and my kids have been trained to pick themselves up whenever that happens; dust themselves off; and get back on the right track. That's how you have a winning life.

Of course then again, those trained by Marxists to take from the work of others, will stay nothings all their lives—no matter how sweet a deal cheap or even free beer seems to taste. If all rich guys are persecuted in the new world, can our kids do

OK? Do we want our kids persecuted if they succeed? You know the answer. Nobody likes paying for anybody else, and we want our kids to succeed.

# Maybe nobody should work?

These supposed altruist Marxists in the leadership ranks of the Democratic Party are always rubbing their fingers together as if to play a tune on the smallest violin in the world. The tune is usually "My heart cries for you."

They are very generous people with your money but they are very stingy with their own. They insist that government representatives in both parties craft intricate tax shelters for them when they get the power. Ironically, for such supposedly generous Marxists, their direct charity records are among the worst in the nation. They want others to pay for their extreme goodness.

Check out our President's giving record and while you are at it check out Dr. Jill and Vice President Joe Biden's charitable giving record to find out just how generous these millionaires actually are. You may find that when it is not their money in play, they have their most generous moments, as long as they never have to produce their wallets.

# Nagging Question Answered: Surprising Answer!

As you will see in the detailed analysis offered in this chapter—the answer to the question, "Can we afford deportation?" is clear. "Yes, indeed we can!" We can afford deportation and financially, the US would be much better off, regardless of what the Marxist progressives or the corrupt media has been telling you.

Remember the progressive agenda is to bring in more and more Democratic voters in waiting from whichever country they will come. Without a problem solver like The Annual Guest Plan, deportation is the only action that ends the problem for America and Americans. Deportation is in fact, the law! With AGP, deportation is not necessary, as the threats to America are handled within the plan.

Don't let anybody lie to you and tell you that our immigration systems and our immigration laws are broken. They are not broken. They are simply not enforced. We have already proven that in this book. Deportation to some seems like tough medicine but think of it as having been at your friend's house for days and almost weeks, and finally they ask you to leave.

Should you hide in the basement? We all would like a better option than making our unwanted guests go home penniless, but at least we are not asking them to go to somebody else's home

## Deportation may be the last resort; but very affordable

With the Annual Guest Plan, deportation is the last resort. I have to go back to the "our house" analogy. Think of the country as if it were your house. Would you ask the interloper to leave? Would you permit them to live in your house in perpetuity? That is what those in an illegal status are doing in America.

They live here in perpetuity without permission. It is not right for us or them, as their lives are miserable. Ask them. We cannot give them enough to make them happy and fulfilled.

They make such poor wages in many circumstances, and in others, they have to cheat using fake ID's so they can become dependent on the US welfare system. Nobody wants a life like that.

## Life in shadows is not a bowl of cherries

They surely did not run through the gauntlet and the Coyotege to get here so they could have an existence worse than in the home country or worse than their dangerous trip to the USA. Many believe that if the shadows could one day become sun-lit, life would be better. They are optimistic yet misinformed about reality. They left for the US without really knowing what life would be like here. For them, it is not good, and because of them it is getting worse for all people.

Remember, without the Annual guest Program, after the Obama illegal initiatives that are intentionally temporary, and after Obama's second term, deportation will come back to the US arsenal to assure that America can remain a sovereign country. We do not want to wake up and find that overnight, half the country are now Irish or Russian and we, the former citizens are now the minority.

Deportation is not only affordable for Americans, it is a price performer. It preserves our borders, language, and our culture. Check out the following proof of deportation affordability! You will see that you and I have been lied to all along by Marxist progressive propagandists in the administration and in the corrupt press. Can we afford deportation? Soon, you can answer this question yourself.

## The answer is clear on affordability of deportation

Ten years ago, Mac Johnson on discoverthenetworks.org proved with strong facts that "yes, we can more than afford deportation." Deportation is not only affordable; it puts cash into the US Treasury. US officials must have chosen to avoid these obvious facts to ever believe deportation was unaffordable.

How many US dollars does it take for a twenty-one year old illegal alien (US immigration nomenclature) with no job; to live to become an eighty-one year old illegal alien still without a job. Yes, we're talking about a man or woman, who for more than 60 years never held a job—ever. How much does 60 years of support cost?

Would the cost be different if the illegal alien were naturalized in his twenty-first year?  Surely the cost of US support for foreign interlopers is huge over a lifetime, and a substantial number, who by good fortune become green card holders and then citizens, remain on welfare. They trade in their fake ID's for real social security numbers, and they qualify for many of the 120 federal welfare benefits.

Deportation is current US law. The President has a temporary moratorium on deportations but they will begin again in several years, or when the courts strike down his unconstitutional temporary amnesty, or he leaves office.

## Self-deportation is the ideal

Self-deportation is clearly preferred in the US over coerced deportation. The Annual guest Program does help former interlopers to stay in America if they pay their own way! But this program is not yet in effect and in fact, it has not yet even been proposed as a law. Call your Representatives and tell them about The Annual Guest Plan.

Whether it is self-deportation or coerced deportation, deportation can provide major cost savings to the US taxpayer, with or without subsidies or stipends. It is that good of a deal for taxpayers. Subsidizing an interloper's life for five years or sixty years is not as good a deal.

# Deportation Analysis Iteration # 1 – Not affordable!

In this analysis, which was done by bleeding hearts to convince us without proof to get us all to give up on ever considering deporting anybody again—ever, we use the dollars as presented by CAP without change. These dollar figures were developed by the Center for American Progress (CAP), a liberal think tank. They were plucked from thin air and put forth to prove that the US cannot afford deportation. If you let their cursory analysis stand, CAP's conclusion is that we cannot afford deportation—case closed!

When you challenge the numbers as we do below; they prove the opposite. CAPs numbers say:

- Cost to deport all interlopers over 5 years
- CAP Est. $41 billion per year cost over 5 years
- CAP conclusion: "too high a cost for taxpayers"

CAP agrees these are its numbers but it justifies none of its conclusions.

Mac Johnson says CAP is Lying. His article is at
http://humanevents.com/2005/08/01/what-would-it-cost-to-deport-illegal-aliens/ .
Check it out!

# Johnson begins analysis with these words:

"Imagine that you came home tomorrow and found a stranger living in your home. Would you pay $148 to have him removed, or would you instead just legally adopt him and give him the run of the place to save the 148? The Center for American Progress, a liberal think tank in Washington, D.C., thinks the *practical* thing to do would be adopt the *undocumented family member* that broke into your home."

Mac goes on to quote the CAP analysis that it would cost $41 billion per year for five years to deport all illegal aliens. At the time this was just .34% of our GDP. In 2005, it was just 1.7% of 2005 tax revenue. The cost to American taxpayers for the support of illegal interlopers in America is substantially greater than CAP's estimated deportation cost of $41B per year. In other words, CAP was wrong.

It helps to consider that CAP is a Marxist progressive liberal think tank and so their numbers were made to be as high as possible and so their position is that we should never deport anybody because we simply cannot afford it. So, let's look at some facts to see how correct CAP's conclusions might be. Mac Johnson, by the way has done many analyses on the web for everybody's perusal.

## Net cost & savings of deportation – the facts

Let us first examine the agreed upon savings from multiple analyses. These are the lowest savings amounts if all illegals self-deport tomorrow:

- Direct savings to the Federal Government:  $12 Billion
- California -- provides huge services to illegals $10Billion
- Other states-- provide similar services to illegals $25 Billion
- Adds up to $47 billion in savings per year that does not get spent on support

# Savings total/year -- $47 Billion

So, with no further work, we can see that in Mac Johnson's analysis, by subtracting the CAP estimated deportation cost of $41 Billion from the Gross Savings of $47 billion from not providing welfare services and cash payments to interlopers, there is a net savings of $6 Billion per year. In other words, it not only costs us nothing if we deport everyone in illegal status, using CAP figures, the US gains $6 Billion each year, which goes directly into the US federal treasury.

CAP is wrong. Johnson is right. The US in this instance pockets $6B per year by deporting rather than keeping interlopers. Don't forget that these are 2005 numbers. Other considerations, not in Johnson's analysis, make the numbers even larger and the numbers are substantially better to support deportation today in 2015, ten years later.

# Criminal property seizures – income sent to home country

Let's consider that foreign interlopers are criminals. We all know that they either jumped our borders or they over-stayed their visas and simply did not leave. They may also have had to commit some petty crimes to sustain themselves while getting workable identification and settling in to a place in the shadows.

Marxist progressives may not buy that but the interlopers, all of them, did break our laws. More than likely, they broke more than one law. If an American breaks a law, they are a criminal. So should it also be said of interlopers.

The establishment corrupt press has been working overtime so that these people who broke our laws cannot be called criminals. However, the definition of a criminal fits about

100% of these border jumpers or visa over-stayers and ID card counterfeiters, don't you think? A criminal is"

> "a person who has committed a crime. A number of synonyms (words that mean the same as criminal) include the following: lawbreaker, offender, villain, delinquent, felon, convict, malefactor, wrongdoer, culprit, miscreant."

If any synonym fits, the definition proves that illegal foreign nationals are criminals, no matter how nice they seem to be at the checkout counters at Walmart.

Of course these are minor crimes perhaps but many other nations would consider illegal entry into a sovereign state a major crime. Try breaking into Iran.

## Can the US claim an illegal's assets?

When drug traffickers are caught, we have come to expect that their property, which was gained by their illicit trade, is most often confiscated. What if we confiscated the property of foreign nationals here illegally in the US? There would surely be a lot of complaints. The complaints would mostly come from advocates of the illegal activity of the illegals.

Do you think that interlopers in illegal status would have less reason to want to stay here if we were able to sell their assets gained in America to help pay back the system for the freebies they collected from the taxpayers during their visits. We can do this whether or not we deport an interloper; but it logically works better with deportation.

There is precedent in law to use criminal property seizures to defray the cost of services and the cost of deportation, making the deportation deal even sweeter financially for the US. Again we are not a charitable organization. The US is not Catholic Social Services; nor are we United Jewish Communities! Theoretically, the US is to operate on a balanced budget.

## The more you add, the better deal is deportation

Let's reflect about a few scenarios regarding criminal property seizures. Illegal aliens are criminals lest we forget.

Illegal aliens send an estimated $120 billion + home / year, according to the World Bank's estimates. Is this huge amount their just reward for taking US jobs and costing the US taxpayers many $billions in services to support them?

Their crime is illegal breaking and entering a sovereign state without a passport or visa. It is against the laws of all countries. Therefore, whether we choose to do it or not, the US has a right to seize dollars for those in criminal status as it is a big criminal enterprise with many tentacles.

The Central American governments are now doing what Mexico has been doing for years. They encourage high levels of emigration because it has become a major plus in bringing to their economy billions of dollars per year! It all comes from the U.S of A. while Americans pay for the support of the interlopers.

For every illegal alien that sneaks into the U.S. and remits money back home, the grand total remittance number to the home country only grows. The dollars spent by illegal foreign nationals are minimal as they send the proceeds back to their home countries.

If just one time officials were able to seize this yearly sum, and we apportioned it to each year within the five year analysis we are covering, it would double our deportation savings. It would add up to an additional $24 billion per year into the US treasury.

We also know that just by leaking the possible threat of asset seizure would cause more self-deportations, and we also know that self-deportations are unto themselves very positive financially for US Treasury.

## Criminal property seizures – Additional dollars

Since the US is already way ahead financially on the deportation analysis by Mac Johnson, in terms of affordability of deportation, let's use numbers that are very conservative as we know there would be more property than what we show and the property would be worth substantially more.

Let's say that each family has a car worth at least $4,000 & let's say that an interloper may have $1000 in other property including cash. Let's also lowball the number of people because some are children and many are below the age in which they would have major assets. How does this compute?

- $1000 + $4000 / 5 = $1000 per year additional per interloper over 5 years
- Let's use 5 million v 60 M as the # of interlopers & vehicles etc.
- Compute 5M X $5000 = $25 billion or $5 billion extra per year over 5 years.
- Yes, these #s would be much larger in 2015.

To compute how much extra cash for the US Treasury that there would be in this very conservative scenario, let's take the $5 billion per year for five years for cars etc. assuming there would be just one crack at such property, and add the $24B apportioned one-time cash seizure.

The total shows up as $29B/ year additional revenue for the US treasury. With property and cash seizures, the US treasury would receive an additional $29 Billion additional each year for the five years in this analysis. In addition to putting up border fences and all kinds of technology and more border guards, the very notion of property seizures would reduce interlopers substantially.

## Does deportation really cost less than zero?

And, so we can calculate a bottom line benefit of deportation for the US. It would not only be cost free; it would provide additional revenue for five years and then the cost for supporting interlopers would be almost zero. Let's look at the total of the numbers:

- Direct Cost to the Feds:  $12 Billion
- California -- services to illegals  $10 Billion
- Other states -- services to illegals $25 Billion
- Cash no longer going to home country -- $24 Billion/yr
- Asset Seizures -- $5 Billion/ yr
- Total/yr = $29 Billion plus $47 Billion before property seizures = $76 Billion.
- Now, subtract the deportation Cost of $41 Billion according to CAP
- $76 Billion minus $41 Billion=
- $35Billion to the good each year

## Can we stomach deportation?

The moral of this deportation story is that we can afford deportation if we can stomach it! We've got to believe these numbers as the deportation costs were put forth by an organization that is against deportation, and they still cannot make the argument with facts.

We are being lied to by the press and by the Marxist progressives continually into believing we are bad people. I cannot recall any time in my life when there were so many lies being told by so many people to so many people.

They tell us that we should not complain about supporting these good folks from other countries for as long as they have their hands out. I beg to differ; and so should you!

Donald Trump does not really want to deport good people who love America. Yet, he is right that it is the law and we can afford it for sure as they cost us so much. The Annual Guest Plan gives America the benefits of deportation in that bad guys will not become AGPs and will not want to be vetted yearly. Thus, by having them registered for free, we will know them, and we can deport them if they do not pass the vetting to become guests.

## Debunking Marxist analyses is good for Americans

Americans are good people. Our representatives, who for their own selfish reasons believe interloper and ethnic votes are more important than the welfare of US citizens, have purposely put us in this predicament. Americans are not bad people. The interlopers are not bad people either in most cases but they have violated our laws. We have a right to our country. They have a right to theirs.

My purpose in running through and debunking the CAP deportation analysis is to prove once and for all that we can deport everybody in America that is in an illegal status. We can do so if we choose and it would add dollars to our treasury. It would not cost us a penny.

We may get sick to our stomachs if we choose to do it because we are good people. However, when you think about a whole family being united in their own home country, it does feel lots better.

In other words, despite the lying analyses we see all the time on Network News and other Marxist progressive corrupt media sites, telling us that we cannot afford to enforce our own laws; there is no truth to their ranting. Additionally, there is no financial reason not to deport every interloper in an illegal status tomorrow.

Moreover, these numbers are low (conservatively estimated). Regardless of how financially lucrative the notion of deportation is for America, the best overall solution to the problem of 20 million to 60 million resident interlopers is The Annual Guest Plan.

## FAIR says deportation deal for Americans is even better

The Federation for American Immigration Reform (FAIR) has estimated that the cost to support illegal foreign nationals in the USs at the 11 million level is a staggering $113 Billion. Add the $29 billion for property seizures and the total cost savings / revenue if deportation is commenced is $142 Billion per year.

This would provide a net plus to the treasury of $101 billion each year. This could actually pay for the original Obamacare estimate. My recommendation would be to lower taxes and give it back to the Americans who have been taking it on the chin for supporting interlopers for too many years.

FAIR offers this quick analysis of deportation costs for those interested enough to check out their work: "The cost of harboring illegal immigrants in the United States is a staggering $113 billion a year -- an average of $1,117 for every "native-headed" household in America -- according to a study conducted by the organization. Check it out: http://www.fairus.org/

Please think this through and do not let anybody tell you that we cannot afford deportation. We may not be able to stomach it but we can not only afford it; we make up twice the cost in revenue.

# Chapter 19    Subsidizing Self-Deportation

## Americans are unfairly being punished

Americans have a big problem with foreigners competing for jobs using peanut level wages as their leverage, and then other foreigners taking from the freebies system when taxpayers are making less money than ever before. US employees, who are taxpayers are not only paying for interlopers; they are not keeping up with the huge inflation in food prices, and until recently, the huge increases in oil for heating and transportation.

Year after year, Americans are falling further behind. Consequently, at a gross level, it would be better for us to pay off those who take from our system so they can go back to their home countries one time as rich people rather than have them remain a burden year after year on US taxpayers.

We have already proven with conservative numbers that there is a big financial plus when interlopers go back to their home countries, and they no longer need or get US freebies.  If we analyze further, we would find that it is a much better deal to give them a really big wad of cash and wish them adieu than it is to pay many such interlopers every year to live free of charge on US!

# Annual Guest Plan offers huge taxpayer savings

You will be glad to know, that even without coerced deportation, such cost savings are part and parcel of the Annual Guest Plan. They are integral to the plan. Even if it cost us something in the first five years, the rest of the years are free of charge—zero cost to taxpayers. This plan may not enable you to keep your doctor or your insurance plan, but it will surely let you keep your money.

In the Annual Guest Plan, there is no taxpayer burden. The burden that would have been is eliminated. Any interloper that cannot make it on their own, will self deport or be deported, and we will be pleased to pay their expenses as they leave to go back home.

They are not going to Siberia. They are going home. We are being kind enough to pay them to go home, and to pay for their families to go with them for reunification in the home country. That is a deal. Their whole families can be reunified in their own countries, and US citizens will gladly pay their way.

Yes, they can be paid to go back home because we have awakened. We now know that we can not only pay expenses, we can afford some nice stipends for those on welfare and education credits as long as they agree not to come back. And, before we start paying anybody anything, ID systems, databases, and immigration IT infrastructure must be upgraded to never let them gain anything from our good will ever again.

## Some other deportation tidbits

When we decide to deport somebody, they too would receive a registration card on their way out if they do not have one under the AGP. Their card and the databases would be updated with their biometrics, and the cost of deportation stipends.

Once deported, there will be no easy comebacks. I am not sure what the correct fee would be if ever we find one of these self-deportees wanting to re-enter. I am thinking in terms of a $10,000 reentry fee plus a full payback of any stipends / subsidies used to prompt the self-deportation. Maybe it is good to let them back with a fine and maybe it is not. I will leave this tidbit for a later decision.

We already discussed the Gang of Eight bill and noted that it did not seem to give any consideration at all to American interests. For example, it permits deportees to come back into the country to receive amnesty and a path to citizenship. It is a very sweet deal but not for Americans. I keep asking who it was that the Gang of Eight were actually representing. The AGP provides no amnesty for deportees, and no easy way back, and no lifetime dole on the taxpayers.

One crime and you're out. Additionally, registrants, legal guests, green card holders, visa holders, if convicted and jailed, would receive an automatic & immediate deportation. If any law does not permit this, Congress must rewrite that law.

Those annual Guests who do not pay fees, fines, and debt would also be deported. As noted in the first part of this book, after a short grace period with counselling, they would receive their deportation notices. As discussed previously, counselling decisions may be appealed online in writing.

# You cannot hide from the Annual Guest Plan

This would be less expensive than a hearing. Hearings for appeals when necessary would be judged by American citizens in Administrative roles to make sure the processes are cost effective. Under no circumstances, should the federal bureaucracy grow to handle this program.

In the Annual guest Program, from the point of registration forward, the US will have the deportee's unchanging biometrics. In the AGP system, registrants and guests cannot get lost in US or when coming back! When service providers get their verification systems, as Congress Barletta says, they get one shot with one finger print scan. Never again after that do they get services and they will be much easier to capture and deport.

# Should we pay people to self deport?

Absolutely! We should definitely pay people to self deport as it helps us and saves treasury dollars in the long haul. A major objective of the AGP is to reduce American costs to zero for any interloper who chooses to become an annual guest. Those who choose not to be Annual Guests are automatically deported. Eventually we will have this 20 million to 60 million interloper mess cleaned up and America will be on its way.

The choices in the Annual guest Program are few and they all benefit the interloper and Americans alike. The dollars used for stipends to encourage self-deportation are because the cost of supporting foreign nationals is exceedingly high.

FAIR's estimates are low compared to other studies that calculate the cost at just about $340 billion per year in total, including suppressed wages. Using FAIR's analysis which is accepted by many scholars, and using 11 to 12 million interlopers as a starting point, it would cost $521 billion per year if the 60 million population were the proper estimate. Does it not make you wonder when interlopers can send $120 billion per year back to their home countries, how much of that is from our cash welfare system?

# No guest welfare / cash / medical / education benefits

The AGP is designed to be cost effective. In many instances it will provide a large stipend to interlopers and to prior reunifications who now stand in green card status and/or citizen status. In many cases there is no desire on the part of these people to be loyal Americans, and the dollar stipends, more than living in America, would be a deciding factor.

The AGP encourages actions that are beneficial to America. Self-deportation, with cash incentives is one such action. For example, giving a stipend to a permanent resident to surrender their green card or anchor citizen status would surely help the taxpayers. Additionally, the stipend dollars may be so attractive that the beneficiary can do much better in their home country than they ever could do in the US.

The stipends for anchor citizens, baby or otherwise will be huge to avoid a lifetime of major costs for American taxpayers. And the citizen who gets to go home to their own country goes back with a lot of cash in the bank and a lot of swagger in their walk.

So when we talk about deportation and guest subsidies what are we really saying. It would be great to have a lot of self-deportation today from interlopers who sponge off Americans. We can encourage such self-deportations by providing a stipend / subsidy to the former interloper or anchor citizen. It would cost a lot less than a lifetime of US support.

Non-citizens under this program would also get a chance for quick cash. It certainly would prompt a yes or no self-deportation decision. As noted many times in this book foreign nationals, legal and illegal in status, cost much more than even these generous subsidies and stipends.

# Here are some examples of favorable win-win scenarios:

### Adult Anchor Citizen

Suppose an adult anchor citizen likes America but would enjoy the $30,000 in cash more than she enjoys her US citizenship. She may choose to transition to Annual guest from citizen status. If she chooses to self-deport, she receives a stipend of $50,000. She would receive the payment directly.

### One Anchor Baby

If the anchor citizen is a child, and the custody parent or parents are in interloper status, each would receive a stipend of $5,000 plus a one-time payment to the custody parent of $30,000 for the child if they all transition to annual guest status. If they all choose to self-deport, the stipend would be $10,000 for each custody parent, and $50,000 for the anchor baby citizen. The parents would receive the child's stipend and would be paid directly for their own stipend. Parents and child would all have to self deport to receive the $10,000 and $50,000 stipends.

In these instances, cash from American taxpayers would be spent wisely for the good of America. And it would come back in a greater amount than the expense. The problem of 20 million to 60 million interlopers will not go away by wringing our hands and wishing things were not as they are.

### Five Anchor Babies

For a single custody parent of five anchor babies, the stipend to self deport would be a quarter million dollars, plus $10,000 for the custody parent. Yes, we can afford it for sure because there are six people involved that no longer will be on America's dime. We save a lot of tax dollars by not having to feed and clothe and house six people for a lifetime.

It may not seem right to pay somebody to go back to their home country. Our President says America and Americans are not exceptional. We are no better than any other country. I know that if somebody offered me $50,000 to come home from say, Ireland or Mexico, I would take it. If my kids and my wife were in there with me, the family would be more than a quarter of a million to the good. Can you imagine picking up more than a quarter million dollars in one transaction?

# Obama's Amnesty gives $35,000 for no US benefit

Yes, American can afford to fund a return to the home country of many, many interlopers. It is much less expensive than paying for them here. As you know, with the 5 million temporarily amnestied interlopers, somehow the Obama administration has come up with a way to fund $35,000 in tax credits to give to the families in his new program, and many will continue on welfare. I would suggest we throw in another $15,000 ($50,000 self-deportation fee) and get something real out of the deal that truly benefits America.

### *Interloper Parents of Anchor Children*

Let's look at another example. Suppose the male and female interloper parents of anchor babies decide they want to self deport . The US would again gains by offering a $10,000 stipend to each for effecting that act. Of course, they must take their anchor children to their home country to get their $10,000 subsidies and for this, they (the custody parents) would also receive a $50,000 subsidy for each child.

In this case, not only are the children's anchor status in play and collectible, the parents earn their own-- $10,000 each plus if there are non-citizen children involved and they deport along with the parents, the parent with custody can receive an additional $10,000 stipend for each non-citizen child. It is such a good deal that interlopers will no longer have to play the lottery as they just won it big time. They gain and American taxpayers gain.

### Additional subsidy / stipend examples

The dollars I have recommended are set at those levels to gain an action desirable to the US, and to make the offer attractive to interlopers. Please note we are not talking about going to Siberia here, unless of course an interloper is Russian. We are talking about going home in all cases.

The dollars paid over time would be subject to analysis and possible change but I see a great opportunity to save money and put many dollars into the pocket of a foreign national, who today is living in the shadows.

### Green card to annual guest or self-deportee status

Let's now examine the possibility of a green card transition to annual guest. I see this as a $30,000 stipend. Green card holders can collect all kinds of freebies whereas Annual Guests collect none. If a green card holder would choose to self deport, it should be worth $50,000 to them, and it would most certainly be worth $50,000 to the US treasury.

With an accountability database, we can also assure that all stipends are stored as fully repayable loans. They go on the EAR record in the ACCT Database but would remain non-collectible unless a deported individual decides to come back, and is granted permission.

In this example, permanent residents who would relinquish their green card status, would have picked up $30,000 to $50,000 in cash depending on whether they had become an annual guest or they self-deported. There is no return from annual guest to green card. It is a permanent change.

# Comeback Privileges?

However, regarding a self-deportation, depending on the number of requests, a self-deportee former green card holder may be able to pay back the $50,000, and pay a $10,000 fine to be permitted back in the US in annual guest status. In other words, if they are granted permission to come back, the debt in the ACCT EAR record, plus interest, plus the $10,000 fine must be paid before admission to the country is considered, and the annual guest interview processes would be commenced. It helps to recall that Annual Guests receive no benefits.

Other combinations may also be lucrative for taxpayers v unlawful US residents or anchor citizens on the taxpayers' dole. The objective is that US taxpayers pay nothing for interlopers. And, so, interlopers get themselves a nice cash bonus, and Americans no longer have to pay the expenses for life of a ton of interlopers. Whole families can get a nice nest-egg as an incentive to take action favorable to America. The nest-egg actually saves many taxpayer dollars.

# Summary of Benefits of AGP v Coerced Deportation

We have discussed this before but let's wrap it up as a bulleted list as we look at the Annual Guest Plan v Forced Deportation. We know that deportation is current law. Now we have all learned that the Annual Guest Plan is a much better option than deportation.

- **Amnesty:** No Amnesty – No forgiveness – Major fine
- **Voting:** No Guest Path to voting
- **Citizenship**: No Guest Path to Citizenship
- **Green Card**: No Guest Path to Green Card

- **<u>Jobs:</u>** Americans have priority on all jobs
- **<u>Benefits:</u>** No Welfare etc. for Guests
- **<u>Costs:</u>** Designed to cost taxpayers zero
- **<u>Renewal:</u>** Fee-based annual renewal
- **<u>Accountability</u>** EAR for fines / fees, services, & other debt
- **<u>Debt:</u>** Collection at annual renewal from ACCT status

## Self-deportees and Annual Guests get off welfare books

Once somebody self-deports, via the help of a subsidy or stipend, or on their own, they are no longer a burden on US society. Their crimes end and their ability to siphon dollars from US taxpayers ends. Can We Afford Deportation? We have already proven it is a winner. We gain from deportation. We have just made it easier for interlopers to self-deport.

We get all interlopers off the books. Not only can we afford coerced and voluntary deportation, the US Treasury gains. Thus American taxpayers gain. We can do all this and still provide huge stipends to interlopers to get them to help American objectives. The best part about the Annual Guest Plan with stipends for self-deportation is that interlopers gain again; but this time Americans also gain! We can call this win-win!

### Full anchor family return to USA?

As noted, the Gang of Eight plan permits deportees back into the country and onto to a path to citizenship. This is clearly ridiculous. Under the Annual Guest Plan, voluntary deportees may come back under special circumstances. In these hardship cases, the former interloper must pay a $10,000 fine and back all stipends which they received for self-deporting plus interest, as well as any balance on their Electronic Accountability Record before acceptance into the country.

Then, and only then would they be eligible to come back. At this time they would go through the same type of extensive interviews as part of the approval process for all Annual Guests.

Let's say that a parent with custody of three anchor children self-deports with a $10,000 stipend plus a stipend for each of the children. In order for the parent to come back, the stipend for the parent and three children, which is $150,000 plus interest besides their own $10,000 stipend with interest, plus a $10,000 fine, must be paid back before the annual guest approval process is undertaken. The children under no circumstances will be given citizenship status.

If the parent living in the home country has given up custody, there would be no natural way to repatriate. Other scenarios of course would need to be built. US objectives would be to move reunified or anchor citizens and green-hard holders, who today are eligible for social services and welfare, off the books forever.

Once off the books, under no circumstances would any in the individuals in these statuses be granted citizenship or green card status. However, depending on how USCIS makes its rules, it may be possible after paying fees, fines, and paybacks for such people to become Annual Guests.

# Chapter 20    What about Visa Over-Stayers (Blue Card)?

## Photo ID & biometrics get everybody—1 try

As part of Annual Guest Plan system design, all types of legal foreign nationals will carry a Photo ID card and have the same biometrics taken when they enter the country or when they are identified at a federal facility while still legal.

Congressman Barletta offers that such a biometric system gives an interloper one chance and just one chance before they are discovered. The second time they use their finger, they are caught. Let us not forget that Americans do want to catch law breakers regardless of what President Obama may think and regardless of the obstacles he places in front of law enforcement officials. Americans do not want to be the patsies of the world.

## IBM is best tech company in the world

Thus, the US needs an effective visa holder tracking system. It should use the same or a similar system to the Annual guest system software / biometrics. Rather than use a foreign company to implement the Annual Guest Plan software and infrastructure, I would recommend that it be designed, built, maintained, and in fact operated by a private firm.

I have suggested IBM as the design and implementation contractor in this for I know from first-hand experience that IBM means quality and IBM means service. Americans would prefer an American company; especially a company like IBM that is highly competent and highly respected. For a sound system project that includes design and implementation, also making IBM the operations contractor would provide a winning trifecta for America.

The software and the infrastructure must be put into place incrementally to capture registrant, guest, green card holder data ... all visa types. The devices would need to be available at airports, seaports, and every other border location.

Nobody in a deportee or illegal status would get in and those who get in legally would be duly identified and track-able. Such a system would assure that visa holders leave at the appropriate time. Biometrics would provide backup for the photo-id card with an indisputably proven identity. You may purposely lose your ID card, but you won't lose your fingerprints, retinas, or your face.

Nobody would want to endure another botched rollout like Obamacare so cronyism must not be a criteria in hiring a lead contractor for the job. IBM is number one and this is too important for number two. When Obamacare was first rolled out, the foreign company behind the dysfunctional HealthCare.gov system was unknown to the average American until the thing exploded in our faces.

The Obama administration had to know that this multibillion-dollar firm had a tainted history with other huge government contracts, and so it is a conundrum as to why they were selected.

The fact is that in major projects stretching from Canada to Hawaii, the parent company CGI Group and its subsidiaries ran into major issues and received many complaints about performance. This was well before being selected by the Obama Administration. As we now know, CGI Federal was paid hundreds of millions, along with other contractors, to create the Obamacare website and supporting software.

James Bagnola, a Texas-based corporate consultant who was hired by the Hawaii Department of Taxation in 2008, offered these thoughts in an interview with Fox News: "The morning I heard CGI was behind [Healthcare.gov], I said, my God, no wonder that thing doesn't work."

If we hire IBM, the project will work. That's why IBM is in business.

# Chapter 21   Out of the Shadows with Americans OK!

## Nobody thinks problem is solvable: I do!

The Annual Guest Plan is a stern and sane, pro-American, yet very compassionate plan that serves both citizens and interlopers alike. There is no denying that "we got a real problem," and it is not just in Houston.

We have become home to 20 million to 60 million interlopers from around the world. These are not necessarily bad people. They came to America for freedom and to fulfill their dreams. But, it was not the Promised Land to which they came. It was a far different and much less pleasant land.

US businesses lured them in to restrict the wages they paid Americans for doing the same work.  We cannot sugar coat it. They would not have come if American businesses had not promised them the world by their actions, and then delivered little to nothing.

Instead of dreams fulfilled; they found shadows and low paying jobs. Was it their fault for coming or our fault for permitting in our own way, for them to arrive and reside here and work in this country?

Americans are not to blame per se, but our representatives did us no service by permitting this to happen while bolstering their own political futures. If we can find just one honest broker of this travesty on America and Americans and on the interlopers themselves, would they have the courage to act? They have not done so yet!

This book is not about blame. It is about a solution that will work. The plan outlined in this book is a "next best" solution to actually enforcing our existing laws. Americans and interlopers alike are culpable for this huge issue in America today.

Interlopers broke our laws. Government leaders have failed to keep US secure. Republicans invited interlopers to take our jobs and to gain voters for their Party. Democrats invited interlopers to dilute the Republican vote. The result is that American taxpayers and job seekers lost the most.

We are at a point in which citizens are not suggesting anything. We are demanding a fix from those that benefitted the most from this. It is too bad the notion of shame is gone in the US for a lot of shameful people have a lot to account for when they meet their maker.

# Chapter 22   A Problem Studied Often

## Can an Annual Guest Plan Work?

All of Donald Trump's plans are to give Americans everything on an American first served priority. This plan is designed to make Americans pleased with the system. We do not have to settle by stiffing Americans and pleasing illegal foreign nationals. They seem to have little problem in our country pleasing themselves at our expense. Like it or not, it is the truth!

The plan does not permit illegal foreign nationals to have a role of any kind that is not permitted by the American people. Having an illegal foreign national holding your job is not in my plan. It has been in the Obama plan and it is in the Hillary plan. Their plans also grant the foreign national the right to outvote American citizens. How could anybody go for that?

Nothing can make our problem go away 100%! Just like in the post slavery years, there will always be some stains—some residue left from this travesty hoisted upon American citizens by those interloper gate crashers from around the world and a too permissive executive branch. All other plans have come up empty.

This plan will accomplish its objectives: 1. Make Americans Important, and 2. Assure that Illegal Foreign Nationals living in America are not unduly hurt when the program goes into force. There will be no deportations for those illegal foreign nationals that play by all the rules adopted by American citizens in the Annual Guest Plan.

This plan comes the closest to a real solution because it actually is designed to solve the problem; and it is fair to all parties. The big winners will lose something; and the big losers will gain something. If we can implement the Annual Guest Plan (AGP), unlike deportation being the only way out, we will all be able to stomach the solution.

When all is said and done, you are going to like the America and Americans-First Annual Guest Plan—if you permit you're burned out ears to "hear" it. Let's check out some great background thoughts on the subject before we hit the meat of the problem and the meat of the solution.

## US Commission on Immigration Reform— Summary

This US Commission, also known as the Jordan Commission for Barbara Jordan, its Chair, was put together to help Congress know what was needed regarding illegal immigration. As an aside, Barbara Jordan is one of my my personal heros. The more I find out about her, the more impressed I am. Her statements are the commission's statements and she is one smart lady. Her rulings are profound and need to be heeded.

The Commission agrees that the federal government should help alleviate these costs. The best way to do so is to reduce illegal immigration.... We recommend immediate reimbursement of criminal justice costs, because these conditions can now be met, but we urge further study of the costs of health care and education before impact aid is provided.

— Barbara Jordan —

AZ QUOTES

The commission's statements pretty well reflect the feelings of Americans who have not yet been lured into the notion of taking from the government and giving it all to foreigners.

## US National Interests First

This commission said that unlawful Immigration is unacceptable! They saw a big problem about employers hiring illegal foreign nationals without regard to Americans interested in the same jobs, and they had a big problem with there being no penalties to firms that hire illegal foreign nationals.

They concluded that there was another problem now besides lack of enforcement. That problem had to do with the tricks used by interlopers to falsify identification and appear as legal residents.

The commission concluded that employer sanctions can work with the proper ID technology.

This US government commission was deeply concerned that foreigners were not often coming to America for the right reasons. Moreover, they were concerned that when interlopers are granted citizenship for the wrong reasons, it hurts America and its taxpayers. And, so, they believe that all foreigners should become citizens for only the right reasons.

They were very critical of those who come to this country simply to get freebies: "Not to get food stamps, health care, job training, or their homes tested for lead." Is America about freebies or freedom?

The Commission concluded that deportation is crucial to a sovereign nation: "Those who should get in, get in; and those who should be kept out, are kept out, and those who should not be here, will be required to leave." They said that for our system to be credible, people must be deported and we should be deterring illegal crossings while facilitating legal ones.

## Immigration facts / amnesty Facts

Here are some facts directly from an analysis of the Commission's work. Former US Congresswoman Barbara Jordan from Texas (1973-1979) and Chair, U.S. Commission on Immigration Reform gave testimony on February 24, 1995, about twenty-two years ago, before the U.S. House of Representatives Committee on the Judiciary Subcommittee on Immigration and Claims.

This was nine years after President Reagan's unprecedented amnesty, which in such a short time was deemed to be a failure in US policy.

Even Reagan was upset that he had been sucked in so far as to approve it. Jordan's words still resonate, but the problem today has been quashed by our current President's dictatorial decrees, though we Americans still feel it. She stated:

" To make sense about the national interest in immigration, it is necessary to make distinctions between those who obey the law, and those who violate it. Therefore, we disagree, also, with those who label our efforts to control illegal immigration as somehow inherently anti-immigrant. Unlawful immigration is unacceptable…"

I recently spoke with Barbara Jordan of the U.S. Commission on Immigration Reform, and I increasingly believe we need a system to verify employment eligibility. The Commission's recommendation of a national registry may be the way to go.

— *William J. Clinton* —

"We believe that employer sanctions can work, but only with a reliable system for verifying authorization to work. Employers want to obey the law, but they are caught now between a rock and a hard place. The current system is based on documents. An employer must either accept those documents, knowing that they might be forged, and thus live with the vulnerability to employer sanctions for hiring someone presenting false identification."

"We on the Commission believe strongly that it is in the national interest for immigrants to become citizens for the right reasons, not the wrong ones. We want immigrants to be motivated to naturalize in order to vote, to be fully participating members of our polity—to become Americans. We don't want to motivate law-abiding aliens to naturalize just so that they can get food stamps, health care, job training, or their homes tested for lead."

"...deportation is crucial. Credibility in immigration policy can be summed up in one sentence: those who should get in, get in; those who should be kept out, are kept out; and those who should not be here will be required to leave. The top priorities for detention and removal, of course, are criminal aliens. But for the system to be credible, people actually have to be deported at the end of the process.

"... Finally, the Commission recommends better border management. Far more can and should be done to meet the twin goals of border management: deterring illegal crossings while facilitating legal ones. But we have to recognize both goals."

Twenty-two years later and what do we have?

*Lawlessness by Presidential Decree!*

# Chapter 23   Ideologies Prevent Enforcement

## Is it Democrats v Republicans?

The Commission agreed that ideologies and not the laws per se are preventing the enforcement of our written, passed, and signed immigration laws. Even members of Congress are cynics of the real intention of the government regarding enforcement. Read between the lines below:

## The Obvious Democrat Position

Being a Democrat for all my life, I hate finding reasons why Democrats have not been fair on any particular issue. But, being an honest man all my life, I see things as they are. The great shining hope of the American left is that a demographic transition through immigration and birthrates will finally make all those tiresome white people largely irrelevant in a new, post-American America.

I regret that means that if you are an American today, and you like America, your voice will not count in the new Marxist progressive Democrat America, which seems to prefer to make life easier for foreigners than Americans.

## The Obvious Republican Position

The great shining hope of the US business community which influences the Republican Party on the right, is that the same demographic transition through immigration and birthrates will finally provide enough fresh new people into the US; or enough people out of the shadows; who will agree to work for barely nothing. There is no need for a minimum wage when the employees are illegal. Heck; they work for peanuts! The Chamber of Commerce in America is against Americans and they use their resources to enhance the importation of low-wage foreigners to take our jobs. Greed is their major motivator.

## Do Republicans have same view on votes?

Many Americans are beginning to see that the Republican ideology is moving from a purely conservative position on this point (illegal immigration). Republicans want to prove they love illegal foreign nationals more than Democrats love them. And, so yes, elite Republicans within the establishment are trying to buy votes from these new entrants to America, as well as relatives and friends, mostly Hispanic—already citizens in the country. And, of course that is one of the reasons they all hat Donald trump.

Candidates for federal office on the Republican side, do not want to eliminate themselves from consideration among the new or the long-suffering interlopers. Conservatives, the only folks looking out for America as it was founded today, are 100% against the Republican posture in this regard. Conservatives have learned too well that they cannot trust Republicans to help Americans.

Few are being fooled in America as nothing has been done to solve the problem for the good of Americans. Our representatives have punted looking for the vote of non-Americans and non-citizens illegally. No major political party even claims to be pro-American! Think about that!

## The Voices of Reason

Alabama Republican Sen. Jeff Sessions is a major voice of reason in the debate. "I believe the interest that needs to be

protected is the national interest of the United States, and that
includes existing workers today, workers whose wages have
been pulled down, without doubt, by a large flow of... low-wage
labor into the country,"

Democrats & Republicans are failing America and Americans.
Nobody even talks about any part of the issue and so there is no
debate. Few in media, other than Rush Limbaugh of course,
who is another major voice of reason representing the cause of
all Americans, is speaking the pro-American conservative
language.

Limbaugh asks: "Where did the recent Measles outbreak come
from?" Nobody wants to say that it came from the 100,000
illegal unvaccinated "children" and adults permitted last year to
relocate by an unconstitutional Obama decree into any and all
parts of the US. Who knows whether you are down with the flu
or some disease that years ago had been eradicated in the US.

Teddy Roosevelt, often considered a conservative and just as
often considered a progressive, was a Rough Rider President
who loved to take a nip and a whistle wetter at the Menger Bar
across from the Alamo in San Antonio. He took the time to
stand pretty solid on immigration issues. There was no debate
about Roosevelt favoring Americans over illegal foreign
nationals.

With Roosevelt's policies in place, we would not be in today's
mess. Too bad our leaders since Roosevelt have failed us on
such an important issue for the country. Here is what Teddy
(TR) said:

"We should insist that if the immigrant who comes here does in
good faith become an American and assimilates himself to us,
he shall be treated on an exact equality with everyone else, for it
is an outrage to discriminate against any such man because of
creed or birth-place or origin."

"But this is predicated upon the man's becoming in very fact an American and nothing but an American. If he tries to keep segregated with men of his own origin and separated from the rest of America, then he isn't doing his part as an American. There can be no divided allegiance here. . . We have room for but one language here, and that is the English language, for we intend to see that the crucible turns our people out as Americans, of American nationality, and not as dwellers in a polyglot boarding-house; and we have room for but one soul loyalty, and that is loyalty to the American people."

**How would you answer this question about TR?**

Q: Could President TR have made himself any clearer that America is for Americans, not foreigners?

A: Not from where I am sitting, standing, walking, or riding!

# Chapter 24   The Morton Memos: Sneaky Way Around Constitution

## Much more powerful than a locomotive.

What if the President could break the Constitution without saying anything or telling anybody about it? Well, even before he had publicly declared amnesty in 2014, without a word, he had already declared amnesty years earlier. Perhaps he never would have announced it in 2014, if his supporters in the pro-amnesty ranks had not pushed him to do so. Amnesty was already being implemented.

We see that the people have finally caught on with the Hillary Email scandal that the President's standard response on "when he knew," though one time effective, simply cannot be true. No matter what the issue, we have heard many times that the president learned about it "from reading the news."

Eventually, even people that love you do not want to be duped, and so more Americans are noting that the chief executive of the strongest nation in the world must have at the very least one or two advisors, and he should not have to hear the news to learn about world events. Likewise, he does not have to read a newspaper to learn about what is happening in his administration. He is in all other respects the boss, and theoretically accountable.

# Can things be done without his pen and phone?

What if the president could put out an executive order without his pen and phone? What if he simply could whisper to staffers what he wanted; and without attribution to the President, they went ahead and got the job done for him. He could then break the Constitution and the press would be left with nothing else but to blame government staffers if they could even find out. The President would gain and he would get no blame. That's like a double win. The President learned about his own immigration orders from the mainstream press. Interesting theory!

So, he has a way to get things done outside of Congress, now in an unconstitutional fashion without anybody blaming him or any other Democrat? How about if he does not have to write and sign executive orders, and he simply endorses the authority for the memos of subordinates to have the same standing?

How about just a few memos written by a few inglorious bureaucrats? And, so, now that we have explored the Annual Guest Plan in reasonable detail, let's take a look at the pernicious way the recent pieces of the illegal Obama amnesty were born long before they were announced. Many of them are grouped under the term: Morton Memos. Our own Congress is mystified that Obama had been able to effect such drastic change in law without even having a fingerprint on the directives.

By the way, the DHS funding bill that passed in the House and for the longest time was stalled in the US Senate was supposed to repeal the Morton Memos. Unfortunately, they still stand as Republicans caved in their February attempt to repeal these within Section 579 - Defunding deferred action. In this bill, Congressman Lou Barletta from Northeastern PA, made sure that the infamous Morton Memos were in the Bill to be repealed.

Barletta offered this analysis on March 3, after the Republicans in the House caved in defeat on the defunding plan for the memos and the unconstitutional actions:

"Let us remember that it was the president himself who said at least 22 times that he did not have the authority to unilaterally grant amnesty to illegal immigrants. Despite our best efforts in the House, we simply were not able to break the logjam of Democrats in the Senate who insisted on funding the president's illegal actions as a prerequisite to an agreement on DHS appropriations.

"Requiring the funding of executive amnesty places illegal immigrants ahead of the national security concerns of the United States. I cannot understand the argument that providing work permits and federal benefits to those who have broken our laws is more important than funding the defense of our country. We have immigration laws for two basic reasons: to protect American jobs, and to preserve national security. The president's executive actions violate both of those principles.

"Fortunately, a federal judge in Texas has granted an injunction against the illegal executive amnesty while a lawsuit filed by 26 states proceeds. A federal appeals court will likely soon weigh in on that ruling. It seems it will now be left to the courts to determine if this president – or any other – is above the constitution or not."

This means the Morton memos have the same standing right now as law. They must be repealed. They are an affront to the Constitution. Let's take a good look at them right now.

238 The US Immigration Fix

## Status of the Memos in 2016

In June 2016, the uncertainty of the saga continues as even
after a court ruling the Obama team acts as if they have no
accountability. The June Supreme Court decision confirmed
what the president himself said at least 22 times: he does not
have the authority to take unilateral action on immigration.
This clearly is a court victory for the Constitution, and a
rebuke of the president's attempt to vastly expand his own
power at the expense of Congress and the will of the American
people. Now what?

Obama's team takes nothing sitting down. Near the end of
June 2016, the Obama administration said it is looking into
whether it can challenge the Supreme Court's decision to block
President Barack Obama's plan to spare millions of illegal
immigrants from deportation, according to U.S. Attorney
General Loretta Lynch. She said:

"We will be reviewing the case and seeing what, if anything
else, we need to do in court," For everybody else in America
when a ruling is upheld by the Supreme Court, it becomes the
law of the land.

Let's look at why these memos are so devastating to the
American people:

## The Infamous Morton Memos—the Short Scoop

These unlawful and unconstitutional memos have been very
damaging to an America that wants nothing to do with
amnesty for those in illegal status. In the darkness of night,
President Obama commissioned these memos long before he
gave his pen and phone speech. He made sure that he did not

have to use his pen or his phone to achieve the desired effect of
a de-facto amnesty.

Instead, he surreptitiously chose to defy the wishes of 66% of
Americans, and he set it up so he could not be blamed until he
was ready to take credit. That's what you can do when you
believe that you are more than a president has ever been, and
the Congress has promised not to impeach you for you
unlawful behavior.

## "Willful, Intentional, and Unconstitutional"

US Senator Jeff Sessions, R-AL, a pro-American advocate on
the subject of illegal immigration, and my favorites Senator,
has examined President Obama's lawless administration in
detail. Specifically, he looked at Obama's record on enforcing
immigration law (Obama's only duty in the matter).

Sessions created a timeline showing that the President's
shutdown of the immigration laws did not begin in the recent
past. It evolved over time; and it is willful, intentional, and
unconstitutional.

Sessions' insightful analysis is entitled: *Timeline: How The
Obama Administration Bypassed Congress To Dismantle
Immigration Enforcement*. It demonstrates with clarity how the
Department of Homeland Security (DHS, which is supposed
to play on the American side has taken an anti-American
position.

It is hard to believe; yet it is true, and the US Chief Executive
is the responsible party. DHS, on the President's orders has
backed away from its border security and interior enforcement
responsibilities required under the law. The president has no
such authority to relieve DHS of its duties and responsibilities.
Only Congress has such authority through legislation.

As noted previously, twenty-two times before he announced
amnesty, the president said he was not a dictator or an

emperor in public speeches. Yet, he has been making decrees with the force of congressional law as only an emperor would have authority to do. Even Republican lawmakers are fearful of challenging him. I wish for the sake of the country, they would get some guts.

# The Decline & Fall of the US Empire?

The Immigration and Customs Enforcement (ICE) Director at the time, John Morton wrote some clearly anti-American memos that at best are unconstitutional, and at worst are outright tyranny. They changed how ICE agents are to perform their duties. Neither Morton, nor the President had the power to create the new modus operandi for the immigration enforcement department. Only Congress can make laws.

Most of US never believed we needed to give so much attention to our government because we were able to trust that its actions were always for the good of America. Those days are long gone. Government is not for US any more. So, in the future we must pay more attention to things like John Morton's writings back in 2011 when these memos first surfaced.

Few things happen unintentionally. Having been nagged by the open borders lobby for a long time, the Department of Homeland Security (DHS) in early 2011 began to implement formal measures to unilaterally relax the enforcement of U.S. immigration laws. They had no power to do so.

Congress had made these laws and Congress was not consulted. The President if told about this would revert to the familiar. "He had learned about the issue just recently when he read the news."

Yet, through a series of memos issued by Immigration and Customs Enforcement (ICE) Director John Morton, without

power, they executed them anyway. Together, the series of
memos produced have become known as the Morton Memos.
They are bad policy and they are unlawful. They constitute
nothing less than the granting of administrative amnesty to
millions of illegal aliens currently in the United States.

Ben Stein, who sees life more clearly than most, once wrote:
"One of the great privileges that any literate man or woman or
transgender can have is to read Gibbon's Decline and Fall of
the Roman Empire. I had that privilege — at least to read it in
an abridged form — about thirty-five years ago when I was
confined to bed in Aspen, Colorado. The book, as witty and
sarcastic as it is learned, makes the point—among many
others—that Rome was doomed when its Emperors became
steadily more stupid, cowardly, self-obsessed, short sighted,
lazy, and grandiose."

Does this sounds like the US today! I regret that without
having an emperor instead of a president in charge, the US
could have remained the most powerful force for good in the
world. It also surely would have remained indestructible.
Today's President strikes fear into the hearts of Democrat and
Republican alike.

## Is the President on our side on immigration or anything?

On a different topic but in an attempt to better understand the
President's seeming lack of love for America, former
Ambassador to the UN, John Bolton commented on the letter
47 Republicans recently sent to Iran so the Ayatollah's all
knew America was not to be messed with.

In essence, Ambassador Bolton said that the deal carved out
Sunday March 8, 2015 was in effect a US surrender to Iran.
Bolton's words were: "Iran deal an 'abject surrender' for US."

Ironically with Iran on its way to the bomb thanks to our current surrender in the talks, it makes Thomas Sowell's confession of his greatest fear several months ago even more ominous, and more likely.

Sowell offered that his greatest fear was that the Iranians would get nukes and attack not Israel but the US, and take out a major US City, such as Chicago. His greatest fear is what would come after the attack. He has so little confidence in the President if he were still president when it happened, he sees Obama surrendering (giving up and crying uncle) this country to Iran. Period cased closed! Can you imagine US surrendering to Iran? Then what?

It took just one bomb to make Japan think twice. It took two bombs for unconditional surrender, back when atomic bombs were toys compared to the size and power they have today. Having to adapt to Sharia Law in this case for those who survive, would not be something that would come easy.

We all hope these interpretations about the inclinations of our president are wrong. After all, he is the President and it would help for him to really love Americans. Unfortunately, so far at least, he has not done much for thinking Americans to make us feel that he has our backs on the immigration stage and the world stage.

It seems that with the daily barrages of bad policy coming from the White House, we are being softened for a big bang of sorts, that changes America forever and not for good. It is an unsettling feeling. For the last six or seven years, it seems that our country has been and continues to be destroyed from within by the very government that was elected by the people to protect the country and make life better.

Nobody knew how radical the lessons in change would be as promised by campaign rhetoric in 2008. We have changed so much that many see little hope in our future. Many have given up.

# The infamous Morton Memos—the meat of the matter

Director Morton knew what he was doing with these memos, and so did all of DHS and so did the President. Obviously, Morton was commissioned by the President to write them and enforce them. The President is not stupid and so he not only knew without reading the news, he in fact directed the Director to write the memos and then direct their execution.

Quietly, yet in broad daylight, Morton created a number of memos so that when President Obama surreptitiously announced his fall 2014 amnesties with his pen and his phone, Morton's memos had already been in effect for some time, and our defenses regarding illegal aliens in the US had already been scuttled. The memos paved the way for quick implementation under the radar of US citizens.

These anti-American memos tell a story of deceit and hubris that must be told to all Americans. The good news is that people like Senator Jeff Sessions and Congressman Lou Barletta, R-PA are trying to repeal these country-killing directives as specified in the Morton Memos.

Please call your representative and Senators and insist these anti-American memos are repealed. Here are summaries of each of Morton's memos taken from Senator Jeff Sessions' above referenced analysis:

**March 2, 2011: Morton Memo #1-** ICE Director John Morton creates new administration enforcement "priorities"— convicted criminals, terrorists, gang members, recent illegal entrants, and fugitives (i.e., those who disappeared before their court date). The memo encourages ICE Agents to exercise prosecutorial discretion for illegal aliens who do not meet these priorities. It further directs ICE field office directors to not "expend detention resources" on them. In other words, it

244 The US Immigration Fix

permits run of the mill interlopers to go ahead and enjoy America.

**June 17, 2011: Morton Memo #2–** Directs ICE agents not to enforce the law against certain segments of the illegal alien population, including those who could qualify for the DREAM Act.

**June 17, 2011: Morton Memo #3–** Instructs ICE to refrain from arresting illegal aliens engaging in "protected activity" related to civil rights or other matters such as union organizing or public demonstrations. Democrats love unions and this seems to be a political payback.

**Nov. 7, 2011: USCIS memo without specific authorship** instructs attorneys to stop issuing "notices to appear" in court for non-priority cases. Shortly thereafter, the Justice Department announced a review of all cases on the docket for possible administrative closure.

Almost 20,000 qualified. This was a way of telling those who were probably were going to be deported, "Don't Worry! Be Happy!"

**Jan. 6, 2012: USCIS rule proposal without specific authorship** allows the relatives of citizens to apply for waivers to remain in the U.S. rather than first having to return home. That rule was finalized in Jan. 2013. Permits relatives of those who broke the law to be free from any punishment or deportation.

**June 15, 2012: USCIS without specific authorship announced** the Deferred Action for Childhood Arrivals (DACA) program, which uses prosecutorial discretion on an entire class of illegal aliens. It took effect 90 days later. So far, over 520,000 have received a two-year stay of deportation and a work permit. Only a small percentage were ever denied. Come on down!

**December 21, 2012: Morton Memo #4**– Prohibits ICE agents from detaining illegal aliens simply for illegal presence. A non-immigration crime must have been committed. This is a grievous assault on our laws and the Constitution but nobody in Washington cares about the people, so nobody complains.

If they did the same for enforcement of non-ticket holders at Disneyland, Americans at least would see some benefit.

**August 23, 2013: ICE policy without specific authorship** prohibits agents from detaining and/or deporting illegal alien parents, legal guardians, and "primary caretakers" of minor children. Eventually, all interlopers will have the excuse they need to stay and take your jobs.

**November 15, 2013:** USCIS memo without specific authorship offers parole in place (temporary-leading-to-permanent legal status) for illegal aliens who are the spouses, parents and children of American military members. One category after another and soon 60,000,000 are living in your home, enjoying your homemade Italian wine, while you are wondering if there will be ten more weeks of extended unemployment benefits.

**What does all this mean?** NumbersUSA provides the following analysis of the memos and it is right on the mark:

*"Memo by memo, and occasionally by rule, DHS management took away ICE Agents' discretion to intercept illegal aliens in the interior. In other words, blocked their ability to do their job as required by law. It's no wonder that ICE Agents (and those in the Border Patrol, for that matter) subjected their management to no-confidence votes on several occasions.*

*How can interior enforcement be further dismantled? The illegal-alien advocates' top priority is to extend "relief" provided under the Deferred Action for Childhood Arrivals program to, at a minimum, the parents of those with DACA status. Many want DACA status for all illegal aliens without major criminal backgrounds. However, the Administration has tentatively denied this option because they fear enlarging the program will force them to have to defend it in court.*

*An LA Times article said the Administration's review would effectively stop most deportations for those with no criminal convictions. One way to do that is to limit detentions under the Secure Communities Program to illegal aliens who have been convicted of major crimes. This would essentially set up a California TRUST Acts scenario. Another way is to remove fugitives and those reentering after removal from the Administration's "priority" list.*

*The Administration's review is being marketed in the media as something new but it actually started months ago. And DHS is getting advice from so-called "stakeholder groups." No, not NumbersUSA, just pro-amnesty groups like the National Immigration Law Center (NILC).*

*To assess which options might be on the table, it is useful to look at the options groups like NILC advocate. In December, 2013 NILC produced an analysis called How the Obama Administration Can Use Executive Authority to Stop Deportations. It says prosecutorial discretion powers would give DHS the ability to refrain from placing a deportable person in deportation proceedings; suspend or terminate a deportation proceeding; and postpone a deportation.*

*The tools for accomplishing these goals are forms of "administrative relief," such as deferred action. The Deferred Action for Childhood Arrivals program is one example of how deferred action can be used but that, apparently, is not the preferred option. But there are other forms of relief that provide a work permit – a top priority for advocates. According to NILC they include:*

- ***Deferred action departure**, which is like deferred action in that it's allegedly assessed on a case-by-*

case basis, but reserved for people from specific
countries with a natural disaster or armed conflict;
- **Temporary Protected Status**, which gives
temporary legal status and a work permit to anyone
from a country that is experiencing a natural disaster,
an armed conflict or an "extraordinary and temporary
condition;"
- **Parole in place**, which allows illegal aliens already in
the U.S.to remain (case-by case; provides work
permit) for a temporary period;
- **Administrative closure**, which temporarily stops
removal proceedings (case-by case) by removing
cases from the court docket; and
- **Stay of deportation or removal**, which temporarily
prevents ICE from deporting illegal aliens based on
human or foreign policy concerns."

## This ends NumbersUSA analysis of Morton Memos

In October, 2013, the National Immigration Law Center
(NILC) [not the good guys] produced What DHS Can Do
Right Now, a paper which offers three options for slowing
deportations.

**First, DHS must follow existing policies and promises.**
Ever since the first Morton memo, illegal-alien advocates have
complained that ICE Agents are not following executive
amnesty policy. They also argue these policies should apply
agency-wide because one branch may not follow the policies of
another. NILC wants Agents to be held accountable for not
following policies. That would have a further chilling effect on
enforcement.
**Second, NILC says** DHS must ensure due process and fairness
for illegal aliens. This includes advising illegal aliens of their
rights and refraining from conducting arrests in jurisdictions
that engage in racial profiling or pretextual arrests like traffic
stops.
**Third, NILC wants** DHS to "stop mischaracterizing and
criminalizing non-citizens as 'criminal aliens.'" This includes

not deporting a previously-removed illegal alien because of their "desire to rejoin" their family. It also includes ending the use of the Operation Streamline program, which conducts fast-track prosecutions in group hearings that process illegal aliens from arrest to jail — with sentences as long as six months — in as little as one day.

So expect the media-facilitated campaign to end "record deportations" to continue, perhaps supplemented by educational efforts on the 'humane' alternatives that are available to DHS. Whatever options the agency selects, you can rest assured they will manipulate our immigration laws to benefit those who broke them, not the citizens and legal immigrants they were designed to protect."

# This unlawful activity must be stopped

Being a Democrat who loves America, I have to ask how Democratic lawmakers find any of this good for their constituents. I am pleased that Senator Jeff Sessions and Congressman Lou Barletta feel the same as all Americans. So, at least there is hope that the conscience of the Congress can be re-awakened.

Senator Jeff Sessions and Congressman Lou Barletta are two of America's heroes on this subject. If this were a religious book, we might even call them patron saints for an America-first immigration policy. Instead we can call them patriots because they are both being ridiculed by the corrupt press for making a stand for America and Americans.

Unless you are looking for a rapid demise of America, follow these two patriots and examine their positions, and soon they will be your positions.

# Everybody should love Annual Guest Plan

The Annual Guest Plan makes all of the Obama amnesties moot as it takes illegal aliens off the dole and creates a no-freebies, Americans-win immigration policy. Nothing in life worth having is easy! But, the Annual guest Program is a No-Brainer for Americans.

The position our legislators has placed us all, is as beggars to the elite to do their jobs. Yet, they will not do their jobs for Americans unless we insist loudly. No more begging any of this cowardly lot. Americans must insist that our legislators do their jobs! When they don't; we must remember them on Election Day.

Americans, every one of us, win 100% with the Annual Guest Plan. The Obama plan, kept off paper so it cannot be traced, does not exist or it could be criticized. Judging by actions unfortunately, spoken or written in memos or directives, Obama's constabulary asks Americans to give up, and let foreigners take the best they can from America.

More and more analysts and historians suggest that the President does not like America or Americans enough to battle for us. What does Rudy Giuliani think? Is it not time for Americans to suffer a great come-uppance as others take our money; our jobs; and eventually our homes? Why not? Why should Americans keep having it so good? Senator Ted Cruz, a great American, has poignant thoughts on the matter:

**On March 23, 2015, U.S. Sen. Ted Cruz, R-Texas,** announced his run for President of the US. Conservative voices across America met his decision with great approval. In November, the Senator took a major pro-American stance on president Obama's unlawful amnesty attempt regarding funding proposals that were being considered by Republicans in the House:

"This November's election was a referendum on executive amnesty, and the American people overwhelmingly oppose President Obama's illegal amnesty. Republicans in Congress should use every tool at our disposal-our constitutional checks and balances-to stop President Obama's amnesty. The Senate should use its constitutional authority to halt confirmations for non-national security positions, until the President stops this illegal amnesty. And both Houses should use the power of the purse, which the Framers understood to be the most potent tool Congress has to rein in an out-of-control Executive.

"We should pass a short-term continuing resolution that includes language defunding the implementation of the President's executive action on amnesty.

"Nearly a dozen Senate Democrats have publicly expressed concerns about President Obama's executive amnesty. Support for the President's lawlessness decreases by the day, and House Republicans should provide Senate Democrats the opportunity to show voters whether or not they have heard the message the voters sent in the 2014 elections."

I have been reaching out to Senator Sessions and Senator Cruz for his adoption of The Annual Guest Plan for the good of all Americans. I have met with the Trump campaign during the Primary when they came to Clarks Summit, PA. I have provided them with Annual Guest Plan materials .

# Chapter 25   Does POTUS Have Power to Change Immigration Law?

## And the answer is:

This chapter begins by asking the question: "Does the President of the US have the power to unilaterally change US immigration law?" The answer is "No!" In fact, according to the Constitution, the President does not have the authority to change any law. The authority and the power of creating and changing laws rests with the Legislative Branch of the Government, which we call the Congress. Check out my new book, The Constitution 4 Dummmies at www.bookhawkers.com for further information

In this 2014 book, The Constitution 4 Dummmies! I would advise looking up separation of powers. The words are as clear as day. Our current President unfortunately is acting unlawfully, and the legislature (Congress) is not doing its job under the Constitution right now to take those usurped powers back. It is the duty of Congress when the President does not obey the Constitution to institute another constitutional prerogative action called impeachment. Impeachment is the only valid solution the Constitution gives for taming a tyrant. Just reading the litany of Obama Executive Actions would be enough to gain an indictment if our government were honest.

As you know from the title of this book, it is about a plan to grant an America-first annual guest status (not amnesty) to all of the illegal interlopers who can prove they are good people; will express loyalty to the US; will take no freebies; will pay back taxes; will pay a $2,000 fine on the installment plan; will never vote in a US election; will not ever become citizens; and will be second in line behind all Americans for new jobs.

## Why is the President against helpful action?

So, why is President Obama not in favor of a plan that can almost immediately bring as many as 60 million interlopers out of the shadows and place Americans in front of the line? Quite frankly, I do not know the answer to that. Rudy Giuliani has said that it is because the President does not like America and Americans. Rand Paul goes further and says it is because the President has chosen to ignore the US Constitution and he is comfortable being a lawless dictator.

Here it is in Rand Paul's exact words: "The president acts like he's a king. He ignores the Constitution. He arrogantly says, 'If Congress will not act, then I must.' These are not the words of a great leader. These are the words that sound more like the exclamations of an autocrat." The President has not helped the immigration issue. He has exacerbated the problem by siding with the foreign nationals against Americans.

On November 20, 2014, and quite frankly even before that, the Obama amnesty became official, though it was illegal. By executive fiat, the President announced his plans to grant amnesty to up to 5 million immigrants living illegally in the United States. We can safely bet that the rest of the interloper population will be right on their heels.

Though in more than 22 separate speeches, the President said that he could not, and would not take executive action on immigration, as he had no such power to act unilaterally, he violated his own posture on the matter. As a Constitutional Law Instructor, the President should know the Constitution. Knowing and following the Constitution, however, are not the same.

President Obama has justified his action by claiming that "Congress failed to act." This of course is not true. Congress did act. It chose not to grant amnesty. The President is grabbing more power now that Congress has told him it will not impeach him. This is not good for America. There are few tools the Congress can use to stop a lawless President. Any plan to help our immigration issue must pass Congress and then it must be signed into law by the president. Would the President sign the Annual guest Bill? Who knows? We cannot depend on Obama to help Americans over foreigners.

After being asked why he does not go it alone this Obama quote denying that he has the power to act on his own; is very telling in light of what he has already done:

"Actually, I don't." [have the authority to end deportations of illegal aliens.] "The notion that somehow I can just change the laws unilaterally is just not true." The only thing that changed was that he won his second term.

As distasteful as it is to say, this President is a great liar. He is not a prevaricator and teller of tall tales. He is simply a liar of convenience. From my observations of many of his lies, he either believes what he is saying, or he believes by his repeating untruths that he can make the people actually believe they are truths.

His inability to be able to distinguish truth from untruth is a dangerous quality in a President. The American people are paying the price every day, and Congress has already told the American people, that they will do nothing to stop him.

Now, with his most recent flip-flop, he said he actually can alter the immigration laws unilaterally. He was able to do so during the lame duck session because the 113th Congress was inept. His actions will stand now until this Congress is booted out because the 114th Congress is even more inept.

Why the big change in Obama's perspective? What changed in his life or in the Constitution that elevated our president to dictator or monarch status rather than a president? The law of the land is still the same. So, this change comes from the man himself. When it comes to the truth, inconvenient or otherwise, this President has been choosing to take on the side of personal convenience like no other politician that has ever preceded him.

He shrugs off the truth. He is impervious to the truth. He cares little about the truth. He chooses to do whatever he wants and then does not tell the truth about it if anybody is brave enough to call him out. He is the pure definition of a tyrant. Even before American law had become a victim of tyrannical acts by this President, the truth had to be minimized and finally eliminated as a constraint of his power.

As I try to put a finger on what it is about the President that causes him to bend the truth to suit his needs, I think of other officials in other countries at different times, who have done the same exact thing when trying to control the people. Germany, for example at one time had a position called Minister of Propaganda. What do you think he did for a living?

Let me take a crack at explaining why this president is comfortable when not in the company of the truth:

First of all, he is convinced we will believe his stories as he thinks we are not very smart and easy to be led to folly. Secondly, he is convinced we like him and want to believe all he says, since if we do not continue to believe him, how can we ever collect on all that hope and change? How can a trickster provide us with anything good?

Whether he intends to be so or not, his lack of focus on verity reminds many of some of the precepts of the one-time leader of the Third Reich. Here are a few insights from this mid-20th century master of mind manipulation:

✓ "Make the lie big, make it simple, keep saying it, and eventually they will believe it."

✓ "All propaganda has to be popular and has to accommodate itself to the comprehension of the least intelligent of those whom it seeks to reach."

✓ "How fortunate for governments that the people they administer don't think."

✓ "By the skillful and sustained use of propaganda, one can make a people see even heaven as hell or an extremely wretched life as paradise."

✓ "He alone, who owns the youth, gains the future."

I certainly am not comparing the Führer with our President but the coincidence in the apparent patterns of thought are very frightening.

Because so few people hear all that our President says, he has no problem contradicting himself, knowing he will get the benefit of the doubt—even eight years into term. This of course adds to a massive hypocrisy.

How many times regarding Obamacare have you heard the President and his minions defend the law: "If you like your doctor, you can keep your doctor. If you like your health plan, you can keep your health plan. Obamacare is not gonna affect you! You like your doctor, you like your plan, you keep it."

On November 20, 2014, Gregg Jarrett of Fox News wrote:

> *"In a book about immigration, we do not need other examples. If Obama ever finds himself in a court of law, he would surely be advised to invoke the Fifth Amendment. He is prone to contradiction and tends to be a good witness against himself.*
>
> *Consider his self-incriminating statements on immigration and executive powers. A year ago,*

*when asked if he had the authority to end
deportations of illegal aliens he said, "Actually, I
don't." Three years earlier, when pressed as to
why he could not act on his own on immigration he
said, "The notion that somehow I can just change
the laws unilaterally is just not true."*

*Well, now the president says it is true – he can
alter the laws unilaterally. Why the
metamorphosis? What changed? The law and the
Constitution are still the same. Which leaves
Obama. When it comes to the truth, inconvenient
or otherwise, he is a chameleon like no other
politician. He never hesitates to contradict* himself,
conjuring a new breadth of hypocrisy."

# How's that working out for the American people?

The President's job is to simply enforce the laws; yet this
President likes to make laws. Since nobody challenges him
today, he is the de-facto Supreme Leader. Republicans are
mum. Only Donald Trump calls it like it is.

The President gets a kick out of saying, "I'm president, I'm not
king." However, something has changed as he finds that not
having to ever run again for the presidency has freed him of the
yoke of answering to the people. Ironically, when asked about
his flip flop on whether he is a monarch, an emperor or
perhaps even a deity, the President, in patent Pinocchio style,
claims his position has never changed.

The facts are clear and the only distortions come from the
President and his minions in the White House and the
sycophants in the media. The President does not have the

authority to override Congress or the Courts. His power ends at faithfully enforcing the laws of the nation.

As I have said many times, I happen to be a JFK Democrat. As such, like JFK, I am a pro-American conservative. It displeases me as a Democrat that the President does not execute the office in a way that is beneficial to Americans. We are not citizens of the world. We are Americans. We may fight for the rest of the world when needed, but we are Americans first. I fear the President does not get this.

I have always had a concern that even before the Annual Guest Plan is debated in Congress, the President will have made all sixty million interlopers permanent residents of the US. Yes, I wish it would go away but I do have an unsettled feeling that by the next presidential election, an even bolder President will again choose to use his pen and his phone to create 60 million more citizen voters. Laws do not seem to matter to this president.

As you will see, the Annual guest Program gets us out of the deportation, amnesty, and freebie business for good. But, if the President insists on making every visitor a citizen, whether they come into the country legally or illegally, we may have a problem on our hands that even a change of power in Washington cannot solve.

The Annual Guest Plan is one of few hopes Americans have to solve the dilemma of 20 to 60 million interlopers, along with chain migrations, reunifications, and anchor citizens—in favor of America. We must pray that it is not scuttled by all interlopers being declared automatic citizens by the simple use of a pen and a phone.

# Chapter 26   Every Day It Gets Worse; Not Better

## Free tax credits for amnestied illegals

When I was working on this book for its original printing in 2015, just ten weeks into the new Congress, the Senate finished its engagement in a huge battle to get the 60 votes needed to pass the bill (H.R. 240) to defund Pres. Obamas Executive Amnesty. America lost as Republicans ultimately caved. Most conservatives believe that weak Republican leadership was looking for any excuse to give the President the right to act outside of Congress and the Constitution.

If there were an ounce of courage among the Republican leadership, it was invisible during the whole process. Republicans in most cases have ideas that can help the country but their big donors insist that illegal aliens keep the mills running to produce historic profits.  Soon, good conservative Americans will be forced to separate themselves from the weak, self-serving Fat-cat-serving, elite establishment contingent in the Republican Party.

It is even worse than before the turn of the year as progressives in the government have found a way to further reward each illegal alien who has been illegally amnestied by the president. The IRS (a personal tool of the President's) now says it is OK to give interlopers gifts of tens of thousands of dollars through IRS giveaways, contrivances, and credits, all paid by taxpayers.

All interlopers need to do to get the gift is file a tax return with no income and they get three to four years of retroactive tax credits... but it's not welfare! It may be $35,000 that was never earned, given to those who broke our laws—because they broke our laws—but we are told by Marxists in leadership roles that it is not welfare.

## Good Americans know this President is Wrong!

Before the Republicans lost the amnesty funding battle to the Democrats, as we wrapped up a chilly, nasty, snowy February 2015, and moved well into March, a federal judge issued a temporary injunction to block the start of issuing work papers for illegals and documents. Without the injunction, Obama's memos would have opened jobs and US benefits to illegal aliens.

The judge is concerned that if illegals already were receiving amnesty and the courts eventually found the memos and executive actions of the President to be unconstitutional, which they are, it would be hard to roll back the actions; and so he provided injunctive relief to halt the process until it is resolved. It would be too late to stop the unconstitutional act, once the first taste of benefits were distributed.

Until the Senate Bill failed, many Americans had been complaining about this but the complaints fell on deaf ears as Democratic Senators—that's spelled Bob Casey in Pennsylvania—still are unexplainably hell-bent on giving our tax dollars to foreigners. It is clearly a better deal than a lottery win for many newly amnestied interlopers.

It is too late for Americans to continue to pressure the Senate (Bob Casey in PA) to pass the Bill, which would have stopped amnesty and the giveaways of tax dollars to buy votes. But, it is not too late to remember which Senators voted for foreigners, and which voted for Americans.

## Republicans cave, as usual

Democrats proved again that they are the most powerful force in Congress. As sad as it is for a conservative to say, Boehner and McConnell have developed a love affair with Obama that transcends their obligation to their constituents.

Even though conservatives gave Republicans the power as elections blew-out Democrats across the country, many Republicans have begun to have second thoughts on what they promised their voters. And, so the saying, "Why not just vote Democrat?" is becoming one of my sayings. At least Democrats are predictable.

Republicans were out-toughed by steadfast Democrats. They caved and delivered far more power to Democrats than that which they had earned in the last election. Republicans decided that even though they owned the votes in both chambers of Congress, Obama's plans had to be funded.

It was no accident, it was by plan. Conservatives were duped again by Republicans. Republicans chose to double-cross their constituents. That is what I call malfeasance. One courageous judge took issue with Obama though when our weak Congress would not. Right now, this judge's actions are all that give us hope in this matter.

Immediately after the federal court judge's decision, an angry President—because he did not get his way—along with his administration began shopping for a better judge at the Appeals Court level to get his giveaways of taxpayer dollars back on track for the newly amnestied.

We all know the Obama Administration will use all of its powers to surely find a Marxist progressive judge to reverse this ruling. So, most conservatives believe that the best way to have had this amnesty reversed was for the representatives of the people –US Senate to pass the DHS bill that was before it. It did not happen.

Republicans cower at the notion of Obama and eventually Obama beat the House and the US Senate and now he is the Ayatollah of America as he is even above our Congress.

I regret to say that it sure seems that conservatives would do just as well with no Republicans in Congress. Then, at least we could beg Democrats for alms. Maybe every now and then we would get some alms because Republicans in recent years offer nothing.

I credit Democrats with a lot of moxie and the power of persistence. I do not admire their goals for sure. But, they sure know how to whip weak Republicans to a pulp. Conservatives have to elect more people such as Congressman Barletta and Senator Sessions.

I do expect the White House to find their judge and at any moment, an Appeals Court someplace is more than likely to overturn the first judge's opinion. But a court cannot overturn specific and recent legislation passed by Congress that leaves no doubt what it wants. But, again there is no chance of this until October 2015.

Every day it gets worse, not better, as Republicans stand still in terror, and let the lawlessness continue. Now, the Obama administration is attempting to clear the way for illegals in Obama amnesty status to vote in national elections. I can see why Democratic Senators might be against Americans on this vote. Few are willing to cut their own throats even if it is in the country's best interests.

For America's sake, hopefully enough Democratic Senators will eventually break with the White House on this vote if it comes up again in October along with any other great bills such as The Annual Guest Plan.

Unfortunately, there is rightful concern among conservatives that Republican leaders have sent a signal that it is OK for them to take long vacations as they do no good for America when they are in Washington. Democrats can manage by themselves. Republicans no longer even show wimpy resistance to Obama though conservatives have given them a majority in both houses.

Besides being unconstitutional and giving the President unilateral dictatorial powers in the US, why is it that the President's amnesty must be stopped?

1.  The American people will pay for three to four years of the legalized aliens back-tax credits. Yes, you read that right. Last week, IRS Commissioner John Koskinen testified before Congress and stated that President Obama's Executive Amnesty allows for the newly legalized illegal aliens to qualify for the generous Earned Income Tax Credit (EITC). They will also be allowed to claim retroactive credits for up to three years once they are issued a social security number -- even if they didn't file or pay taxes at the time! This is criminal. Yet, the payoff for a family of four interlopers will be as high as $35,000, all paid for by US taxpayers

2.  Illegal aliens will more easily be able to vote in elections. Work permits aren't the only thing that illegal aliens will receive under the Executive Amnesty. Rather, they'll be granted drivers licenses by states and Social Security numbers, too. Various state election officials testified before Congress in the last few weeks that they lack the tools to be able to detect such a massive number of potentially fraudulent voter registrations generated by state DMVs.

3. American workers will be even harder hit in the labor force. The Center for Immigration Studies (CIS) just released a study with a shocking finding over the past decade, for every new job created, the U.S. has imported 2 new immigrants. Since 2000, 18 million new immigrants have arrived in the U.S., but only 9.3 million new jobs have been created. Now that H-1B spouses can get Social Security cards, this will make it even worse. Our best jobs that should be going to our children graduating from US universities will be going to foreigners.

The assault on Americans never stops. The U.S. Department of Homeland Security announced on February 24, a major immigration "reform". This "reform" allows spouses of individuals on the H-1B visa (known as H-4 dependent spouses) to apply for work permits. The new unconstitutional rules go into effect on May 26, 2015. This is another unlawful overreach by the President and as noted is patently not constitutional.

# Chapter 27  Our Immigration System Is Not Broken

## Only propagandists say the immigration system is broken

Americans who have taken time to understand our immigration laws, know that the system is not broken. It was carefully designed and well-constructed to protect US citizens from outsiders trying to disrupt our nation upon entry. Until recently, it worked quite well.

But, a prerequisite to any federal law functioning as intended is that our Congress and our President must be honest in their enforcement of the laws. Yet, for their own distorted reasons, which they will never divulge, the Congress and the POTUS recently decided to simply ignore our immigration laws and declare that the system is broken. It is not broken; Congress and the POTUS are broken.

Many of these laws have been working fine since the founding of the country—well over 200 years. These laws are not broken. Check out your history. Congress and the POTUS are broken for sure.

We might just as well call the whole thing off and begin with a new Constitutional Convention for how perverted these elitists have made our system of laws. I fear, however, that if we were to start over, without Madison, Jefferson, Hamilton, and Pennsylvania's own Ben Franklin, we would get more of the same. Who would ever care enough to create a system that was designed for the people and not for the politicians?

The bogus claim that the immigration system is broken is as true as Dan Rather in 2004, when he made up a story that a skilled pilot in the Air National Guard, George W. Bush was really not in the Guard.

It is as true as NBC Nightly News anchor Brian Williams' bragging over the years about being in a helicopter that came under rocket-propelled grenade fire in Iraq in 2003.

It is as true as Hillary Clinton claiming to have arrived in Tuzla, Bosnia under sniper fire in 1996, when coverage of her visit at the time showed her being greeted leisurely by an 8-year-old with a welcoming poem.

The immigration system is not broken. Those entrusted to enforce the system have committed malfeasance in office. They all should be prosecuted.

Those who want to destroy America's ability to defend its borders claim the system itself is broken for their own distorted purposes. Their reasons are self-serving and untrue.

Their claims of a broken system do nothing for the public good. Yet, their outright lies that are believed and assimilated into the fabric of the low-information American media hounds by a corrupt press do help their cause long after the shock value has gone away.

Unfortunately without video proof, words are all we have to express ourselves, and we have a POTUS today better skilled with the gift of delivering words than any of us. But, time has proven those words cannot always be trusted.

As the propaganda minister in Nazi Germany, Joseph Goebbels said, "If you repeat a lie often enough, people will believe it, and you will even come to believe it yourself." There's a big lesson for US leaders to be learned, and the notion that our immigration system is broken is a lie that has been spread by deliberate and continual communication of this false message.

## Can we all be good guys?

People become what they are by constantly being exposed to various stimuli. If you constantly read, watch and listen to positive messages, odds are that you will naturally become a positive person. And it works vice versa as well. If you are exposed to lies all the time, you begin to believe the lies— especially if you are already inclined to believe.

Strong people would like to think that they are thinking independently of their environment, but the truth is that most of us think, act and believe in a certain way as a result of several unconscious cues that we get from our environment. If the media continually talks about the President helping to fix our broken immigration system we are inclined to believe the system is broken. It is not true, but we believe it anyway.

What has happened is that today's major media has become an arm of the government. Without being paid by the government, because they sport the same ideology as Joseph Goebbels, they have no problem engaging in the same type of propaganda as Joseph Goebbels, intentionally. It feeds their ideology. And so, the narrative of our POTUS that our immigration laws are broken is repeated, and repeated until many think it is actually true. A free and independent press as the founders envisioned would be sure to help America today in its quest for the truth.

In 2015, as I write this book, it is not the immigration system that is broken, it is the Obama Administration enforcement that is broken. The laws are fine!

If your job were to make a round piece of chocolate each time a mixture came your way, and one day, you decided to make some triangles or squares or rectangles, would the system be broken or would your part in the system be broken?

Clearly the latter would be the case. A system is *a group of interrelated parts working together as a whole.* When one part of a system collapses intentionally or unintentionally, the whole system collapses.

So also with the President's job regarding immigration laws. If the President has decided to make rectangles or triangles instead of circles, he is destroying a system that would not be broken without his decision to break a critical part of the process.

Like it or not, President Obama signed an oath to enforce US laws. He never signed an oath to make laws or change laws as that is illegal. And, so it is the President's job at the top of the executive branch to enforce immigration laws as well as all other laws passed by Congress, the only legitimate lawmakers in the country. When the POTUS chooses to do otherwise, he is violating his oath, and thus, he is breaking the law.

Our POTUS, like him or not, has decided not to enforce immigration laws. He has ignored a functioning system. The system is not broken.

## What is the extent of the problem?

There are 20 million to 60 million interlopers in America today. I dare you to prove me wrong on 60,000,000 as the proper number. Do you believe that the government would admit to the 60 million number if they knew the number exactly?

The Annual Guest Plan begins with registration and within six months of implementation, Americans would know the actual number of interlopers within the country. And, none-to-few interlopers would be deported.

Congress and the POTUS do not seem to care about the impact on Americans as their focus is on future voters and future employees from other countries.

Meanwhile the cost to support this illegal migration is staggering. Mexico and many other countries are dumping their poor, their helpless, and their dependent people on American taxpayers and we are simply paying the bill, rather than firing our President and most of the Congress.

FAIR estimates that at less than 20M interlopers, it is costing the US $113 billion per year but they admit if the number is really 60 million interlopers, the tax on Americans to support the population of interlopers and the recently almost amnestied, reaches three times that amount per year.

## The Annual Guest Plan solves the problem!

The Annual Guest Plan (AGP) is the newest and best solution to solving this problem. Do Mrs. Clinton, the POTUS, Mr. Biden, or Mr. Durbin really want a solution? Does Mitch McConnell or John Boehner? It sure seems they are happy that they can declare the system broken, though intentionally unenforced would be a better term.

The AGP takes the cost to Americans for the largesse doled out to foreigners, and reduces it to zero while it puts smiles on the faces of interlopers and Americans alike. That is a lot of savings to pay for real enforcement if we have the stomach to enforce our laws. If we choose to permit our laws to remain unenforced; why do we need a Congress at all?

Unfortunately, nobody in government appears ready or willing to enforce our existing laws. Moreover, there is no reason to believe that if new laws which this POTUS did not like, even if he were pressured to sign them, and did sign them; he would break them de facto by maintaining his no enforcement policy decrees.

We are a kind nation. Even though illegal foreign nationals hurt our incomes and our lifestyles, and gangs threaten our very existence, for very perverted reasons. As a nation, we are suffering from the bad choices of our legislators and the President. Many believe it cannot get better until we clean house.

# Chapter 28   Interlopers Are Destroying America!

## Should we give them a place at the table?

The crux of any effective immigration policy is deportation. If interlopers think all they need to do is arrive in order to stay, why would the world not descend upon the US as we are the most generous nation on earth? Would there not be 7 billion more people here in the next few days if all you had to do is arrive? This is the greatest country on earth.

We have used the term interloper in this book without defining it. Let's define the term now. An interloper is: "One who intrudes in a place, situation, or activity." That is it. It is not insulting to call something what it is and it is not insulting to label the players in an act using the most descriptive term. Those who intrude (without invitation is the implication) into the United States of America; into our welfare system; and into our employment scenario are undoubtedly interlopers.

This is a simple definition that explains just who these uninvited and unwanted visitors actually are. They may not be illegal but they are in an illegal status. It's just the way it is. Would all of us not prefer that Aunt Martha spend the holidays with us rather than having to support an unknown and unwelcome interloper in our home instead?

Sometimes we choose not to understand simple terms which annoy us. Think about this: When was the last time you invited an intruder to have a Turkey or Christmas day dinner with your family, simply because they broke into your home?

Would it matter to you if the intruder had no intention to harm or steal? Say, they just wanted their way in your place because they learned from others that you were generous?

If an unwanted guest of questionable character was found on the sofa in the rectory, and insisted on being fed and watered and housed, would the rector think that was the right way to introduce oneself?. I would expect the choice of answers to be "never" and "no." This would be the norm as you and I and the guy next door, and even the rector, naturally think that guests should be invited?

Would it be OK to send them back to their home state of say Ohio—if it were possible? Would Ohio take them back? Maybe Ohio is bad [Sorry Ohio—just making a point] since these particular interlopers may have come from Ohio? Maybe they would not even want to go back to Ohio? Then what? Why is it your problem when people take advantage of people?

## Why can't there be enough for everybody?

What if there is hardly enough for you? Can there possibly be enough for both you and your "new guest interloper?" I think the parable of the loaves and the fishes was a one-time deal.

Please do not go blaming the rich again for even Bill Gates, the richest man in America, cannot pay for all the illegals that gain benefits in the US of A. How do I know this? I calculated the needs and I calculated the most Gates can offer, and even he falls short. When you have the time take on the math yourself to prove me wrong or right!

Whether the President says it or not, when you go to the store and milk is 80c and then a few months later it is at 130c, how did that happen? It happened because you are paying for others from other countries. If nobody ever told you that and you did not figure it out yourself, please consider it because I just told you.

Even good programs such as food stamps, and welfare dollars and hard earned cash dollars are gamed by interlopers. "Gamed" means they cheat Americans and nobody tells them that cheating Americans is not OK. It is not only not right, for those claiming to be religious, it is a sin. Do they ever pay anything back? They take from a system to which they have never contributed, and never pay back.

Shouldn't churches, and non-governmental social service agencies, who take our dollars on the charity plain, be the ones helping the needy, legal and illegal, and the not the government. Government is far too generous with our tax dollars and that is why America is broke.

Americans take it on the chin every day because lawmakers choose not to represent us. Lawmakers from the POTUS on down, will not enforce the laws. American citizens cannot even apply for many jobs. Too many companies are held harmless when they hire non-Americans in illegal status, who will work for less than peanuts.

Companies have figured out how to separate you from your job so they can pay interlopers peanuts rather than pay you a livable wage. Interlopers often take less than the minimum wage that liberal progressives claim is necessary. Yet the same bleeding heart progressives do not insist that interlopers receive the same pay as Americans.

## The Annual Guest Plan - designed to work

Government is the problem in most cases not the solution. Government Marxists choose to use their social engineering skills to take from those whose heads are barely above water, and give to those who lie about how well they are doing in the underworld economy.

274 The US Immigration Fix

So, is there a way to redirect the efforts of government to something that works better for Americans and interlopers alike rather than the status quo or a POTUS amnesty? I think there is, but it has to be spelled out in capital letters for our leaders to understand.

The Annual Guest Plan (AGP) is a solution that turns worthy illegal foreign nationals into Annual Guests, instead of keeping them in lifetime shadows. Yes, it admits they did wrong by violating our sovereignty and our borders. Like a dog that eats your teeth the night after a great party, it does no good to spank the dog when the crime is finished and the act of punishment will not help matters. Maybe we should just figure out a way to live with 60 million interlopers on our terms. Right now, we the people, seem to be living on their terms!

## Guests don't have rights; just privileges granted by citizens.

The AGP is good for interlopers, and it is good for us. But, we must realize these folks are never brought to our level. They are guests and they must always behave as guests. What is a guest? The most simplistic, yet very strict definition of a guest is as follows:

" A guest is a person who is invited to visit the home or office or country or take part in a function organized by another."

We tend to differentiate invited guests with uninvited guests. However, in reality, there are no guests who are uninvited. Guests are intrinsically those who have an invitation, so *invited, as an adjective* is redundant. An Interloper can be defined as the opposite of a guest.

The term, *uninvited visitor* does make sense and we have lots of them in America, but they are hardly guests. We do not have

to treat them as guests, no matter what Brian Williams tells us!
Yet, we may choose to make them guests if overall, it helps
Americans.

## Guests are guests and nothing more.

In the Annual Guest Plan, guests have no intrinsic "rights!"
The plan provides the granted privilege of residency, which is a
big deal, and it provides protection by law enforcement.
Annual Guests, when approved, are guests; not citizens.

The landlord (citizens of the US) or the home-owner makes the
rules for guests and there are no involuntary freebies of any
kind. In other words, a lord of the manor may choose to give,
but a guest is verboten to take.

## Origin of the Annual Guest Plan

The AGP began several years ago as the Kelly Plan of 2012.
My name is Kelly. At the time, I devised a solution for the 60
million interlopers that government said could not be deported.
I called it a comprehensible & sane immigration remake. AGP,
The Annual Guest Plan is just that! It was its spawn.

There is no need for a comprehensive immigration plan that
gives away American sovereignty because the laws already
prescribe what we need to remain sovereign. It is our POTUS
who chooses to ignore these laws, though they worked for
centuries before he came upon the scene.

## I have been analyzing this for a long time!

Some of you may know that I wrote a book in 2012 titled,
*Americans Need Not Apply!* In the book, I spelled out how
60,000,000 new employees (OK, not all work but many do)

made it tough for Americans to hold jobs or to be able to keep jobs at normal wages.

I watched, researched and learned that nobody in government seemed to care about Americans and they were willing to give equality of rights to illegal foreign nationals, who simply decided to break our laws and show up in the never-ending benefit line. Quite often the rights of the illegal community exceed those of American citizens.

And, so in 2013, I wrote a second book that reflected that. Additionally, I sketched out in detail a plan similar to the Annual Guest Plan called the Kelly Plan. It was my first cut at a plan to solve the problem once and for all, and admittedly, it was rough. The book title is *No Amnesty! No Way!* I spent a lot of quiet time thinking before I began to write. I think you will like the details of this plan.

# Chapter 29   Are Illegal Immigrants More Employed Than U.S. Men?

## Current US immigration policy punishes Americans

Just for the record, if male US citizens cannot get work because of illegal foreign nationals, then it follows that US women, who typically have a more difficult time than men in competing with men to find work, are also affected and more than likely the impact is greater. By the time a woman shows up for work, a foreign national already has the job and the US male who thought it was his for the taking is just as disappointed and disgusted.

Americans are concerned that their jobs have been taken away and nobody in government cares as long as a new voter from another country is available to vote (somehow) in their stead. It is a good bet that the new guy will not only vote but will vote for those who helped them get the job. That is what I call corruption, plain and simple. And, it is Americans who get hurt. It is not fate, it is a plan by the Democrat Party to assure they get elected in perpetuity.  If you feel you are being messed with by your government, you have the right feeling.

After writing three other books that complained about this circumstance (Taxation Without Representation; Americans Need Not Apply; and No Amnesty! No Way!, I felt that I was one of the only ones who recognized it. I was willing to call it by its name—corruption). I decided rather than proving that the problem existed, which I did each time I wrote a new book,

I would try to do something about the problem. The Annual Guest Plan is my serious attempt at solving it!

In this regard, I built a simple but multi-faceted plan that put Americans first. It did not require the deportation of illegal foreign nationals who were not subversives. With Illegal aliens being last on my list, I had no problem doing what need be to put Americans first in this plan.

Sorry if this offends anybody. I know that I am last on San Salvador's list. I am also last on China's list. I expect to be last on every other country's list. However, in America, I expect to number 1. Like you, I expect to be one of the first on the list with all the other American citizens. Let the citizens of other countries build their own lists.

In my plan, all Americans are ahead of all people from foreign countries legal or illegal. Any questions? Despite putting Americans first, the Annual Guest Plan deports nobody who chooses not be deported. Yet, it offers Americans the opportunity for a better living in the front of the line. Every American citizen comes before every foreign national. Any questions?

On March 30, 2015, the Fix This Nation Blog wrote this powerful essay about the importance of voting a pro-American President into office in 2016. Americans are the ones being left behind in this not so successful economy. Illegal foreign nationals have never had it so good. This piece in many ways tells you why you must finish reading this whole book:

> "According to representatives from the Pew Research Center, illegal immigrant males are more likely to hold gainful employment in the United States than their citizen counterparts. Demographer Jeffrey Passel told Congress that as of 2012 – the most recent year for which statistics are available – 91 percent of illegal immigrant men were in the workforce as compared to only 79 percent of U.S.-born men.

"Unauthorized immigrant men of working age are considerably more likely to be in the workforce than U.S.-born men," Passel wrote in his official testimony before the Senate Homeland Security & Government Affairs Committee. He went on to explain that "unauthorized immigrants are more likely than the overall U.S. population to be of working age and less likely to be young or older. That is one reason that the unauthorized immigrant share of the labor force is higher than its share of the population overall."

"Of course, given his use of the word "unauthorized" to describe these immigrants, one can surmise Passel's political bent. Seeing him make demographical excuses for what is an "inexcusable" situation is therefore no surprise.

"And what is the nature of that high employment rate? Well, according to a new report done by Pew, more illegals than ever have moved into the white collar field. Since the recession, 180,000 more illegals have taken on management or professional jobs. The study confirmed that 13 percent of illegal immigrants were working in these better-paying jobs as of 2012. Passel attributed this to an overall shift in the American marketplace as well as the Dream Act, qualifiers of which mostly went to college.

"These numbers, of course, will only continue to swell once the president's 2014 executive actions are implemented. Unless stopped by the 26-state lawsuit against the administration, those actions will provide illegals with Social Security numbers, work permits, and protection from deportation. Employers will no longer have to hire them on the down-low, and because they will not be subject to Obamacare's employer mandate, they will have plenty of reasons to favor them over U.S.-born workers. It doesn't take a wizard to see how this will turn out.

"This is all the more reason to elect an anti-illegal immigration, pro-American president in 2016, an outcome that seems less likely by the day. So paralyzed by the fear that they will drive away Hispanic voters, the GOP seems unwilling to throw their support behind a hardline candidate. Of course, the sanctity of our borders has absolutely nothing to do with race. The left, unfortunately, has managed to shape the conversation in such a way that Americans who oppose amnesty are accused of xenophobia and "jealous hoarding," as one NY Times writer put it.

"As long as they're able to paint this as a moral issue rather than an economic and cultural imperative, they'll win every time. It's up to us to find candidates and representatives who can explain that there's nothing morally objectionable about enforcing the law."

# Chapter 30   Fees & Fines for Annual Guests & Employers

## Interlopers & Employers declared GUILTY!

Interlopers could not have lasted more than a week or two in the US without getting jobs someplace. The risk that employers took in hiring them under the minimum wage, especially in the 1980's and 1990's was huge. Therefore, a rational thinking being must conclude that the rewards of hiring employees in illegal status, at times when punishment was an option, were significant. Employers made a killing having illegal employees working for them for peanuts.

And, so in this chapter, we make suggestions about the types of crimes that require punishment of a sort (fines) for both interlopers, who got to enjoy America's freedoms and protections and many other benefits; and for employers who made a killing off their backs. It is now time to pay the piper.

I suggest that Americans feel no guilt or shame about getting something back into the treasury for all the years we have been whooped by interlopers and employers, with the willing hand of our elected representatives, who assured we Americans would lose at every turn.

# Fees and fines will pay for implementation

All of the numbers in the following charts are estimates based on facts. They are designed to be reasonable. America should be able to collect these fees and fines with no problem over time.

When fines cannot be paid immediately, USCIS agents will have the option to permit the debt to be carried in the interloper's EAR in the ACCT (debt database). The EAR record is created at registration and completed during the aspirant interview. From then on, it is updated with appropriate charges, fines, and fees.

The following fines are proposed to be assessed upon interlopers for crimes and misdemeanors against the American people. There is no amnesty.

| Type of Fine | Amount of Fine |
| --- | --- |
| Interloper one time fine | $2,000 |
| Fake ID fine | $500 |
| Medical services fine | $200 |
| Job Fine (Have Job) | $100 |
| Driver's license fine | $100 |
| Not carrying ID | $100 |
| Demographic not updated | $200 |
| Reentry after deportation | $10000 |
| New Interloper post-date | $10000 to $50000 |
| Failure to register | $5000 |
| Failure to apply for AGP | $1000 |
| Failure to renew | $1000 |

For those who fail to register and are discovered and apprehended, they may pay a $5,000 fine immediately, and engage in the registration and annual guest sign-up process.

Or, they may sign up for an all-expenses paid trip to their home country with the costs added to their EAR.

The annual guest or deportee pays all processing fees for any special considerations. American taxpayers pay nothing.

# Employer fines

Without complicit employers in this major perpetration brought on the American people, there would be no such interloper problem in America today. The greed of businesses for increased profits brought big and small companies alike to the point where they felt it worth the risk to their business to hire interlopers in illegal status for peanuts rather than hire Americans for a proper wage.

Therefore, in terms of paying back the United States, the companies of America that have employed foreign nationals in illegal status need to pay their fair share back to America for the years and years of profits they gained on the backs of Americans and the poor souls they employed.

Americans have either lost good paying jobs or have been forced to take substantially lower paying jobs as companies fattened their bottom lines. I am a tried and true capitalist but this perpetration on foreign nationals and on Americans did not have to be. It was pure greed.

It was the answer that US based companies had to those of their peers who were able to offshore work. It is almost impossible to offshore services or production jobs that require immediate employee intervention or access to perishable material. But, the Turkish phrase captures what they did: " If the mountain won't come to you, you must go to the mountain."

Just as we permit the Annual Guests to put some of their debt into an EAR for tracking, the AGP program will provide a similar means of tracking for the debt owed by the companies who have gained for far too many years as Americans and even interlopers suffered from their greed.

And so, a substantial employer fine is recommended to be imposed if as little as one and as many as a company-full of interloper employees / contractors have ever been used by the organization since the Reagan amnesty of 1986. The fine would be added first to the Employer Electronic Accountability Record, another form of the EAR that we can refer to as the EEAR in the ACCT database.

The fine amount per company is to be determined at the company interview/audit. In addition to the fine, companies will pay for the time expended in the audit. Additional levies / penalties will be executed if the employers choose not to tell the whole truth.

Please note, this fine will not punish innocent companies. Any company that hired as few as one interloper is guilty so most businesses in the US today are guilty, plain and simple. Companies may appeal the guilty verdict by proving beyond speculation that their policy and their results were 100% in compliance with the AGP plan—in other words, not one interloper was employed for any length of time from 1986 on.

Companies that are guilty will all be punished at the same rate per active employee in any immigration status. They will be fined proportionately to their employee base. If zero employees have been in an illegal status from 1986 through 2015, then the employer will not be fined at all.

However, if one or more employees were in interloper status, the fine amount itself is based on the number of employees working for the company as of 2015, not the year of the infraction(s).

To repeat, the rule for whether a company is fined or not is simple: "If one employee in the company or in any of the bought–out or derivative companies in the organization, was in an illegal status over the thirty-year period, the company is fined."

What are the employer **fines** and terms of payment?

- Fine -- $2000 per current active employee
- Six Months to Pay Fine
- Late Payment (10% per month)
- No Payment – 4X Fine
- Company may request a good-faith payment plan

## Fair employer fines raise substantial revenue

Category ranges and estimated potential revenue totals to pay back Americans for this travesty are shown in the Employer Fines / Fees summary after a few more charts. First let's summarize the AGP fees and fines again and then show the employer fees and fines. The overriding goal is that this plan should cost the taxpayers zero. Corporations have been paying zero while the taxpayers have been carrying the load for far too long.

Americans with some background in corporate finance as well as adept investors know that U.S. companies have more than $2 trillion overseas. This is according to an analysis that paints a bleak picture of whether that money will ever make its way to the US. The study also suggests that there would be limited economic impact even if it does.

I can see some good plans being built to bring some of that capital back to help pay the debt that will be owed by corporations for having once hired illegal foreign nationals.

There is lots of money overseas. If it were brought back to pay fines and fees, I would suspect a mutually beneficial deal could be worked out.

**Fees: Annual Guest Plan** — **Fees**
- Registration 1st 3 months — Free
- Registration months 3 to 6 — $50
- Registration in grace period — $500
- Annual guest application — $100
- One time IRS Interview (if back taxes) — $100
- Each appeal of denied application—min. $250
- Annual renewal — $100

**Fees: Employers who used 1 interloper within 30 years**
*All employers in this status must pay first year's fees*

- Company registration (mostly online) — $1000
- Reg. Interview per location 1 time — $5000
- Verification hardware per loc. / year — $1000
- Online Connection per location / year — $1000
- Annual renewal incl. 1st year per loc. — $1000
- IRS Interview One Time — $5000
- Total first time fees per location — **$14000**

- Employers who choose to go all American pay $0.00
  - In fees in future years

$14,000 is the proper employer amount as noted above. The full employer analysis is shown in subsequent pages.

# Sample revenue chart from employer fees and fines

The summary charts below demonstrate potential total US revenue from employer fines and fees. It presupposes that at some point, every employer has hired at least one interloper. The government is not about to determine how many interlopers over a thirty year period were hired. One interloper hired indicates guilt.

Thus, one hired interloper means a business pays the fine at their level of involvement, which is based on # of potential interloper employees (i.e. their current employee count). They may pay all hearing costs to prove they never hired an interloper and they will be exonerated if found not guilty

## Estimated Employer Fines & Fees.

Let's see how much this would cost businesses that have enjoyed unfettered access to workers in an illegal status for as many as thirty years. That is another way of saying that they made untold millions of dollars by choosing not to hire Americans for American work. Do not feel sorry for their huge fines. There are an estimated 6 million employers in the US

### Employer Fees Summary – all employers (US Revenue)

# Employers in US—approximately 5,809,833
Initial Fees ($14000) X 5809833 = $81,337,662,000
Annual Fees ($2000) X 5809833 = $11,619,666,000

- $81,337,662,000  one-time fees
- $11,619,666,000 annual fees
    - If company chooses to continue to use Annual Guests
    - 

## This is a Big Deal and a Big Fine

The following charts summarizes potential total revenue from employer fines. If an employer never hired an interloper, there

288 The US Immigration Fix

is no fine, and also, none of the fees above for 1st time apply. To give us an idea of the fines, we have assumed in the calculations that within a thirty year window, all employers hired interlopers. If a business hired interlopers and it is now out of business, the prior owners are deemed harmless. It's obligations have been assumed by the new business owner if the business still exists in any form.

- Total fines = $320 Billion from all employers combined
- Employers have received benefits well beyond $2,000 per illegal immigrant.
- If one illegal immigrant is declared, the full fine is in effect.
- Add to this about 92 $Billion in fees from above

Total first year employer fees and fines = $413,057,328,000.00
- **413 + $Billion**

**Estimated employer fines & fees (shown at substantially lower rate)**

| Category Range | Appx Mean# Employees in Category Range | # of US Employers in Category Range | # of US Employees in Category Range | Fine perEmp. $2000.00 | Fees -- Reg IRS Tools, etc |
|---|---|---|---|---|---|
| | | | | Fine per category | |
| 1 to 10 | 3 | 4,600,000 | 13,800,000 | $27,600,000,000 | |
| 11 to 100 | 30 | 1,100,000 | 33,000,000 | $66,000,000,000 | |
| 101 to 500 | 200 | 90,000 | 18,000,000 | $36,000,000,000 | |
| 501 to 5000 | 1,250 | 18,000 | 22,500,000 | $45,000,000,000 | |
| 5001 to 100000 | 37,000 | 1,800 | 66,600,000 | $133,200,000,000 | |
| 100,001 to 250,000 | 125,000 | 18 | 2,250,000 | $4,500,000,000 | |
| 250,001 to 2,000,000 | 260,000 | 15 | 3,900,000 | $7,800,000,000 | |
| | | | | | |
| Totals | | | 160,050,000 | $320,100,000,000 | |
| Total US Labor Force | 160,000,000 | | | | |
| | | | | | |
| Total # US Businesses | | | | 5,809,833 | $14,000 |
| Total Reg & IRS Fee | | | | $81,337,662,000.00 | |
| Annual Business Fees | | | | $11,619,666,000.00 | |
| Total Fees 1st year | | | | $92,957,328,000.00 | |
| | | | | | |
| Total Fees/Fines YR 1 | | | | $413,057,328,000.00 | |

# Chapter 31   Other Employer Implications

## Employer Options

These fines and fees for employers will go a long way in paying the front-end stipends for self-deportees and those downgrading their status. Businesses deserve the fines they get for taking a chance on the government cracking down on their illegal hiring. So, I have no remorse—none at all—for them. Unlike deportations, we should all have the stomach to punish the companies that created the only reason that illegal foreign nationals came to America—to get a good job and live well.

Neither have happened to the foreign nationals who remained in illegal status; nor has any good come to Americans for their being here. American businesses, however, made a financial killing.

Though it would not at all be part of the fees or fines, these companies, who profited from the backs of poor trusting souls, should be encouraged set up foundations to help the interlopers who go back to their home countries. Why not sponsor a village or a small city and create a small industrial zone to help assure that those sent who self deport can make it when the cash runs out.

We know who benefitted. It was US homeland based businesses. They drew employees from other countries to their workforce to save dollars and increase profits. In so doing, they collectively messed up America. The Annual Guest Plan is the best approach to solve the problem for good. The fines and fees will help but the cost is far more substantial than the fines.

## Some business restrictions

Once businesses pay their fees and fines, and by the way, they would not be permitted to summarily, without cause, fire an annual guest, they can conduct business as usual in a new business as usual scenario. No new interlopers can be employed in the US workforce, ever again, period! Owners and executives will personally be fined in the future for violations.

Registrants and Annual Guests are OK to work immediately, and they are OK to be hired. Any business so inclined after paying the one-time fees may hire a registrant, aspirant or an annual guest with just one caveat. The must pay certain fees outlined above annually for equipment and connections to verify their workforce. If an American citizen wants an advertised job for which they qualify, the American citizen gets the job and must be employed for at least three months before being dismissed.

Businesses need to register to hire or to keep former interlopers or Annual Guests for a number of reasons. They need a legal status to obtain the verify hardware / software or to be able to use the software at any post office or state agency.

For such services, the government agencies will charge a fee, independent of the fees noted above. When businesses hire Annual Guests, they must provide equal healthcare options to the options provided to American citizens.

# To hire Annual Guests – employers must...

To hire Annual Guests, businesses must register their intentions with state governments, who are in charge of the affairs in their own states. The process must be led by state governments, which choose to participate. State & federal computer systems would need to be programmed to interact regarding annual guest employees. Such programming should be done one time at the federal level by IBM or another company, and the software made available for free to the states.

With IBM in charge of design and implementation, I would feel comfortable assuring guest or citizen status. The process would be e-verify-like but better as e-verify has political overhead which it is forced to carry. AGP cannot be a political football. It favors no political party.

# Employer tools for verification

An employer must verify the status of any potential employee or contractor or be accountable for not having taken appropriate action in the hiring process. I would suggest that the enforcing agency examine contractors especially those who formerly supplied those in illegal status.

There should be an enforced ratio of contractors to employees for those contractors that once supplied interlopers and now may supply Annual Guests to work environments. Since these contractors were quasi employers over the last thirty years, they must also pay the fines that other employers must pay.

Nobody is interested in being snookered by the contractor v employee notion ever again. In plain English, I would suggest that no more than 5% of an employer's workforce can be supplied by contractors without exceptional scrutiny.

Paper verification methods should be permitted for perhaps six months of this program as IBM or another chosen vendor gets up to speed in assuring that electronic verification works and works well in all areas from employer locations to the border and to service providers.

I think that as long as the penalties are enforced and are stiff, businesses will make their plans well known even if the paper used for the first six months is Marcal Facial Quality or Charmin. No employer will want to be caught in the web cast by a government program intended to help run of the mill Americans.

If paper employee verification is enabled via forms and if paper verification is submitted (not suggested), the business would agree to pay a substantially higher processing fee, because taxpayers in this program agree to pay nothing.

## Are there exempt industries?

What if we asked: "Which industries must verify new employee hires?" Perhaps the answer should simply be *all industries*. Surely government at a time that so many employees are unemployed would not hire foreigners who have sworn only partial allegiance to our country. Yet, Annual Guests may compete for those jobs.

However, the education and medical industries—service providers and manufacturers, as well as all private industry firms, such as large and small corporations, must have the tools to verify employment. Nobody wants the wrath of enforcement to fall upon them.

Annual Guests may be hired but Americans are preferred until all Americans that want to work are working. That should be clear by now. Nobody wants Annual Guests to starve, and that is why there is an EAR, and generous stipends to self-deport, when the annual guest, after repeated attempts cannot find suitable employment.

## Employee verification techniques

Whichever the employer, they must be enabled to verify / update the state / federal annual guest database as well as the guest accountability DB, ACCT through the supplied software systems. They can gain verification most simply by it being triggered by a Photo-ID Card, though all employers should be able to also verify using basic biometrics such as a fingerprint scan as a double check.

However, better systems must be developed for the AGP so that the photo in the database is flashed back for even more positive authentication and verification, as well as the call for a fingerprint or other biometric scan, which can then be compared, verified, and / or authenticated.

In all cases, if there is no authorized verification, the perpetrator is deemed as a fraudulent interloper. ICE should be called and the interloper seized and questioned by local police while at the station for service.  And, so, biometric backup verification must be enabled for any annual guest, aspirant, or registrant who may be looking for a job in America.

Here are some considerations regarding employers who may have paid fines; but who do not want to sign up to be able to hire Annual Guests for their companies.  These are presented in bulletized form below. Those employers who do want to employ former interlopers must follow these directions to a "T."

# Employer Tools for Verification

- Year 1: Employer may rent space from state for verify of potential employees. They may also be verified at state / federal offices
- Year 1: Verify can also be performed at federal locations. Public Post Offices would be ideal locations. Welfare offices would also be great state venues.
- Year 2: All verification done on employer site with proper hardware and software tools.

# Employers' Employee Verification

The following bulleted list shows what can be done:
- Technology enables perfect employee verification
- E-Verify s/b not used—instead AGP software / system
- Simple to do – less difficult than Accts Payable
- Contractors must register if guests as employees
- Contractors cannot hire unregistered interlopers.
- Employers cannot use unregistered contractor employees.
- Employers cannot use unregistered contractors with Guests.
- Contractors must report on all contracted workers provided.
- No illegal foreign nationals in US workforce, period.
- Unlike today, employers will be fined and prosecuted for using unlawful interlopers.
- Caution: do not try to break this law intentionally.

# Employers & Healthcare Insurance

Free healthcare in 2015 / 2016 is not part of current interloper benefits. However, with fake IDs and other contrivances, many interlopers are receiving health benefits illegally.

Right now, Obamacare subsidies is not legally a benefit to an interloper. This is good because the government would want to offer it with huge subsidies so that the foreign nationals would pay lots less than Americans. This is verboten in both Obamacare and the Annual Guest Plan. Americans have the advantage under AGP.

Today, in the first half of 2015, with no Annual Guest Plan in force, employers are incented to hire interlopers in illegal status since they would not have to pay $3000 for Obamacare for the interlopers. This puts Americans at a disadvantage. The AGP permits no situation as its guiding rule, in which Americans have less favor in US law as interlopers or non-citizens.

To even out this discrepancy, though Obamacare is a bad system and it costs way too much for all, as long as it is law, it must be made available to Annual Guests from their employers or from the government. Let's summarize desirable healthcare options for Annual Guests:

- All Guests & all Visa Holders must have health insurance
- It may be employer supplied or self-supplied via Obamacare
- No subsidies for Annual Guests or visa holders of all kinds (no freebies)
- No healthcare expenses borne by taxpayers
- No Medicaid for Annual Guests!

It helps to recall the objectives of the Annual Guest Plan so we continue to realize that it is pro-America and pro-American.

Any public service, material or welfare cash received by an annual guest, including EMTALA & healthcare, under the plan, approved by an USCIS agent would be added to the EAR record, and eventually paid back..

There is no free lunch. AGP is America first. More and more Americans are waking up sick of paying through the nose for foreigners who choose to take rather than give.

## Summarization of Employer Hiring / Healthcare Factors

- Employers may hire Annual Guests
- They must give Americans that apply first priority
- Employers may not hire illegal contractors
    - Fine imposed / worker
- Guests may keep current job positions
- Same healthcare must be provided for Annual Guests & citizens
- Eliminates cost advantage of hiring interlopers v citizens
- Part time citizens & guests treated the same on job.
- If part time, support can be proportional—not different
- Insurance companies must provide acceptable, affordable policies
- Policies may be purchased by businesses or by Annual Guests
- Each guest must have health coverage– including children

Sometimes US citizens think that our government is at odds with our thinking. We have reason to think so as our President often chooses to act as a dictator, in which there is no US Constitution. Perhaps even worse than that, our Congress pretends that it has no power.

I have proven in this short analysis in book form that interlopers cost the US big time in many more ways than can be analyzed quickly for regular Americans. Citizens continue to have lost jobs; wages suppressed; and then they are forced to pay for benefits for foreigners in greater measure than their own needs.

A logical rational being dropped in the middle of all this would conclude that good representatives would have called this asininity off at the pass. But, they have not. And unfortunately, too many Americans still believe our 114th Congress, the worst in US history is doing its best. If they are, then the charge would not be malfeasance, but instead, incompetence, and the penalty should be to never again occupy a seat in our national legislature.

The fact is: "Congress and the President are AWOL on what is best for Americans" It's time we changed things. Don't you think? I keep hoping we will all wake up at the same time, like yesterday,  and we say, "ENOUGH ALREADY! "

# Chapter 32   Immigration Fix Summary

## Misguided Love

The US government executed a policy since 1986 that has hurt its own citizens and decreased the opportunities for all Americans in America. Along with powerful corporations, and Republican And Democratic big business donors, It has also lured many innocent people to America to live in shadows and to work for peanuts. We could have done much better if we followed proper ethical principles, instead of greed as the modus operandi.

The Annual Guest Plan attempts to make up for our poor leadership and the greed of our captains of industry. May God have mercy on those who inflicted such misery on the interlopers and the citizens who have endured this pain for so long. The perpetrators will need God's mercy in the end.

The Annual Guest Plan is the best correction that anybody could find to this dilemma. Only greed or obstinate behavior will keep our leaders eyes from being opened at the promise this plan offers.

# Get on the phone with your legislators today!

Americans should not wait a minute more to put this plan on our leadership's doorsteps. If they do not see its value, then we are charged with the awesome responsibility of replacing them. If the wealthy among the conservative ranks are for maintaining this perpetration against humanity, they are not conservatives. They should be shunned by all clear thinking people.

We have well demonstrated in this book that It would cost substantially more in future government payments to citizens in anchor or reunified status as well as green card holders and those who remain as interlopers in the shadows, than to implement the Annual Guest Plan.

In essence, lump sum stipends are a better financial deal for Americans over the long term. Additionally, one might view this whole scenario of paying for desired results as a compensatory payment for a very bad US policy that was motivated by greed and multiple levels of thinking.

As you have witnessed in examining the notions brought forth in this book, the Annual Guest Plan is sane and comprehensible. Most of all, it is designed specifically for the benefit of Americans. It does respect the fact that illegal foreign nationals are human beings, but it is unquestionably for Americans first.

Besides being the right thing to do, this plan also provides the prospects for raising revenues and it will substantially reduce and finally eliminate the expenses Americans are now shouldering on behalf of our "uninvited guests." Additionally, employers with big checkbooks will need to make restitution, and that too can help their spirits and the reality of the situation here in America.

# For the good of America

In summary, the plan collects fines and back taxes and so it is not an amnesty. It offers no citizenship, and no voting. There is no welfare cash; no food stamps; no free medical, and no free education. New jobs go to Americans first.

Additionally, deportation is the last, not the first resort. The small fees associated with the Annual Guest Plan are a small price to pay to be in America for a lifetime. Americans will no longer pay any of their way. The fees collected from Annual Guests will fund all costs.

An accountability database assures the country gets paid back what is due, while a demographic / biometric database assures we know who is who. In order to put teeth into the plan, deportation is an option for any bad guys.

The Annual Guest Plan is a great solution. It cares about interlopers and American citizens. No plan does as much to help all parties. The plan solves the immigration dilemma of 20,000,000 to 60,000,000 interlopers, which exists today. It also limits America's future liability for those who are already collecting welfare benefits based on their anchor citizenship, reunification citizenship, or green card status.

Despite US kindness, many green card holders never have chosen to swear allegiance to the US or take the first step towards citizenship, though they certainly could have done so and I sure wish they had. Now, that is a real shame!

Overall, our problem here in the US is with leadership. It is long overdue that our leaders put forth a plan designed by Americans for Americans! That plan is known as The Annual Guest Plan, and it needs to be law much sooner than later.

# Appendix A   The Power of Technology – RFID

## Technology can really help enforcement

Once registered, former interlopers in registrant or annual guest status can easily be located. RFID or similar technology within the card can help locate any interloper or a legally registered guest.

To help you understand the power of RFID, let me digress a bit and explain the technology. It is here today, and available for use with ID cards, regardless of how much Republican elites may choose to punt and declare that seven years is the best that can be done with any technology. Not so! Republicans who say that are not being truthful.

## RFID Wireless Identification Technology

RFID chips can be made part of the registrant and / or annual guest ID card, and the same type of cards should be used by visa holders per HR 399. The ID component of HR 399 can be done before the legislation passes if we have the guts as a country.

RFID stands for Radio Frequency Identification. This is groundbreaking technology today because it costs less than 30c and the price is getting lower and lower as time goes by. It is all about a transmitter smaller than a dime that can be embedded in everything from a T-shirt to human or animal skin, communicating data over a short distance to a reading device. In the AGP case, we would want RFID on the Photo-ID cards

When RFID chips are a few pennies a piece, they will replace barcode on retail product packaging. You won't believe how many things can be done.

Let's say you pick up about 20 items and put them in your cart at Sam's. Today, you would empty your cart on the checkout conveyor and the cashier would scan each item after first scanning your Sam's ID card. In the selfie Aisles at Sam's you do the work but the process is the same.

Then, when the checkout is done, you pay the amount with cash or debit card or credit card today; receive a printed receipt and leave the register. Then, to get out of the store without major harassment, you stop at a checker, who assures there was no chicanery in your cart or your receipt, as they look over your cart and receipt. Then, they give you the OK sign so you can leave the store.

You then go to your car and put your items in. Then, you go home, take them out and put them where they need to go. It is not a bad process. RFID is not involved. When it is, it makes the whole process spooky efficient.

In the near future, your standard way of paying –Visa, Sam's Credit, cash, etc. may be imbedded in your Sam's Store Card. As you approach the non-cash self-checkout ( no people required) you would leave the items in your cart, When scanned by the RFID scanner, your Sam's ID card sitting in your wallet or purse would scream out its ID and other information in the same way as if a clerk had scanned the card.

Meanwhile, the products in your cart, with their own paper-like one-time-use three-penny RFID chips are screaming out their IDs and anything else necessary for a clean checkout, all items at once. The scanner sorts it all out then it instantaneously sends the cart data to the transaction database, and the receipt program, in the same fashion as it occurs today, all necessary databases are updated, and all authorizations are approved for the order total, and a printed receipt may or may not be printed. It may instead be sent to your smart phone.

All of this action is linked to customer, credit card, and product databases for customers and products. By the time you move your cart full of products through what once was a checkout line, the checkout is complete. You may choose to wait while your receipt is being printed, or you may go directly to the exit scanner at the door which will green light your cart, and you are out the door and off to your car without having to see a checker.

By the way, the order checkers never run out of ink, and they have to go through specialized boring job training taught by ex-Maytag Repair-men (humor).

A scanner at the exit open or closes the door based on whether you paid for everything in your cart. It is actually an exciting future in store for us at Sam's Club, where this technology is already used for their in-house warehousing. I give you this information so that you can know just how powerful and all-encompassing RFID technology can be when used properly.

RFID is also very effective today in helping identify missing pets, monitor vehicle traffic, track livestock to help prevent disease outbreaks, and even follow pharmaceuticals to fight counterfeit drugs. The technology is also employed today to help us start our cars using RFID chips embedded in the ignition key and for EZ-Pass on the highways.

When you add an RFID chip to the new ID card of a former interloper, they are effectively broadcasting who they are to anyone within range whenever scanned. Unless a registrant or a guest tosses their ID card, which would of course be a punishable offense under the law that would lead to a fine and perhaps deportation; there simply would be no place to hide. US Citizens of course should never carry such ID cards issued by government to avoid the "Big Brother" effect.

Technology is clearly neither good nor evil. It is simply a tool to help us do things better. Bad people with guns, knives, or bows and arrows do bad things. RFID and biometric technology of all kinds can be used by bad people for bad things. That's why we have law enforcement so we can catch those bad guys. Our use of technology must be better than the bad guys'.

How many want reading this chapter right now want to give up their iPhone or their web browser simply because it might be hacked and their data may be compromised? Not many! Instead, we ask for it all to be made safer, rather than for us all to go back to the days when everyone had a mallet, a chisel and some stone to record our communication.

We all know how productive the Internet makes us individually, and we know how easy it now is to use such technology to conduct business. RFID, smart cards, fingerprinting and other technology employed to disrupt the flow of interlopers, and to interdict them is a good thing. It will bring tremendous benefits to citizens and to businesses. Of course the system must be designed to maximize the benefits and limit the opportunity for abuses. Seven years is far too long to wait for anything!

# LETS GO PUBLISH! Books by Brian Kelly: (sold at www.bookhawkers.com etc.).

**LETS GO PUBLISH!** is proud to announce that more AS/400 and Power i books are becoming available to help you inexpensively address your AS/400 and Power i education and training needs: Our general titles precede specific AS/400 and other technology books.

**Take the Train to Myrtle Beach The Trump Way**
The Trump plan to reestablish passenger rail and build high speed rail in the US

**RRRRRR The Trump Way -- Reduce, Repeal, Reindustrialize, Raise, Revitalize, Remember—Reduce taxes Reduce immigration Reduce regulations Reduce spending Repeal Obamacare  Reindustrialize America Reduce offshoring Raise tariffs Revitalize energy Reduce redistribution Reduce & eliminate lying Reduce government Remember mistakes**

**Healthcare & Welfare Accountability The Trump Way**
Donald Trump's businesses are all accountable and he knows how to bring accountability back to the US government.

**The Trump Plan Solves the Student Debt Crisis**
Solution for new student debt and the existing $1.3 Trillion debt accumulation

**101 Secrets How to be a High Information Voter**
You do not have to be a low-information voter.

**Why Trump?**
You Already Know… But, this book will tell you anyway

**Saving America The Trump Way!**
A book that tells you how President Donald Trump will help Americans wind up on top

**Jobs! Jobs! Jobs! The Trump Way**
Donald Trump has many ways planned to solve the US Jobs Crisis.

**The US Immigration Fix**
It's all in here.  You won't want to put it down

**I had a Dream IBM Could be #1 Again**
The title is self-explanatory

**Whatever Happened to the IBM AS/400?**
The question is answered in this nee book.

**Great Moments in Penn State Football** Check out the particulars of this great book at bookhawkers.com.

**Great Moments in Notre Dame Football** Check out the particulars of this great book at bookhawkers.com or www.notredamebooks.com

**WineDiets.Com Presents The Wine Diet** Learn how to lose weight while having fun. Four specific diets and some great anecdotes fill this book with fun and the opportunity to lose weight in the process.

**Wilkes-Barre, PA; Return to Glory** Wilkes-Barre City's return to glory begins with dreams and ideas. Along with plans and actions, this equals leadership.

**The Lifetime Guest Plan**. This is a plan which if deployed today would immediately solve the problem of 60 million illegal aliens in the United States.

**Geoffrey Parsons' Epoch... The Land of Fair Play** Better than the original. The greatest re-mastering of the greatest book ever written on American Civics. It was built for all Americans as the best govt. design in the history of the world.

**The Bill of Rights 4 Dummmies!** This is the best book to learn about your rights. Be the first, to have a "Rights Fest" on your block. You will win for sure!

**Sol Bloom's Epoch ...Story of the Constitution** This work by Sol Bloom was written to commemorate the Sesquicentennial celebration of the Constitution. It has been remastered by Lets Go Publish! – An excellent read!

**The Constitution 4 Dummmies!** This is the best book to learn about the Constitution. Learn all about the fundamental laws of America.

**America for Dummmies!**
All Americans should read to learn about this great country.

**Just Say No to Chris Christie for President two editions – I & II**
Discusses the reasons why Chris Christie is a poor choice for US President

**The Federalist Papers by Hamilton, Jay, Madison w/ intro by Brian Kelly**
Complete unabridged, easier to read version of the original Federalist Papers

**Companion to Federalist Papers by Hamilton, Jay, Madison w/ intro by B. Kelly**
This small, inexpensive book will help you navigate the Federalist Papers

**Kill the Republican Party! (2013 edition and edition #2)**
Demonstrates why the Republican Party must be abandoned by conservatives

**Bring On the American Party!**
Demonstrates how conservatives can be free from the party of wimps by starting its own national party called the American Party.

**No Amnesty! No Way!**
In addition to describing the issue in detail, this book also offers a real solution.

**Saving America**
This how-to book is about saving our country using strong mercantilist principles. These same principles that helped the country from its founding.

**RRR:**
A unique plan for economic recovery and job creation

**Kill the EPA**
The EPA seems to hate mankind and love nature. They are also making it tough for asthmatics to breathe and for those with malaria to live. It's time they go.

**Obama's Seven Deadly Sins.**
In the Obama Presidency, there are many concerns about the long-term prospects and sustainability of the country. We examine each of the President's seven deadliest sins in detail, offering warnings and a number of solutions. Be careful. Book may nudge you to move to Canada or Europe.

**Taxation Without Representation Second Edition**
At the time of the Boston Tea Party, there was no representation. Now, there is no representation again but there are "representatives."

**Healthcare Accountability**
Who should pay for your healthcare? Whose healthcare should you pay for? Is it a lifetime free ride on others or should those once in need of help have to pay it back when their lives improve?

**Jobs! Jobs! Jobs! Original Book from 2010**
Where have all the American Jobs gone and how can we get them back?

# *Other IBM I Technical Books*

**The All Everything Operating System:**
Story about IBM's finest operating system; its facilities; how it came to be.

**The All-Everything Machine**
Story about IBM's finest computer server.

**Chip Wars**
The story of ongoing wars between Intel and AMD and upcoming wars between Intel and IBM. Book may cause you to buy / sell somebody's stock.

**Can the AS/400 Survive IBM?**
Exciting book about the AS/400 in a System i5 World.

**The IBM i Pocket SQL Guide.**
Complete Pocket Guide to SQL as implemented on System i5. A must have for SQL developers new to System i5. It is very compact yet very comprehensive and it is example driven. Written in a part tutorial and part reference style, Tons of SQL coding samples, from the simple to the sublime.

**The IBM i Pocket Query Guide.**
If you have been spending money for years educating your Query users, and you find you are still spending, or you've given up, this book is right for you. This one QuikCourse covers all Query options.

**The IBM I Pocket RPG & RPG IV Guide.**
Comprehensive RPG & RPGIV Textbook -- Over 900 pages. This is the one RPG book to have if you are not having more than one. All areas of the language covered smartly in a convenient sized book Annotated PowerPoint's available for self-study (extra fee for self-study package)

**The IBM I RPG Tutorial and Lab Guide – Recently Revised.**
Your guide to a hands-on Lab experience. Contains CD with Lab exercises and PowerPoint's. Great companion to the above textbook or can be used as a standalone for student Labs or tutorial purposes

**The IBM i Pocket Developers' Guide.**
Comprehensive Pocket Guide to all of the AS/400 and System i5 development tools - DFU, SDA, etc. You'll also get a big bonus with chapters on Architecture, Work Management, and Subfile Coding.

**The IBM i Pocket Database Guide.**
Complete Pocket Guide to System i5 integrated relational database (DB2/400) – physical and logical files and DB operations - Union, Projection, Join, etc. Written in a part tutorial and part reference style. Tons of DDS coding samples.

**Getting Started with The WebSphere Development Studio Client for System i5 (WDSc).** Focus is on client server and the Web. Includes CODE/400, VisualAge RPG, CGI, WebFacing, and WebSphere Studio. Case study continues from the Interactive Book.

**The System i5 Pocket WebFacing Primer.**
This book gets you started immediately with WebFacing. A sample case study is used as the basis for a conversion to WebFacing. Interactive 5250 application is WebFaced in a case study form before your eyes.

**Getting Started with WebSphere Express Server for IBM i Step-by-Step Guide for Setting up Express Servers**
A comprehensive guide to setting up and using WebSphere Express. It is filled with examples, and structured in a tutorial fashion for easy learning.

**The WebFacing Application Design & Development Guide:**
Step by Step Guide to designing green screen IBM i apps for the Web. Both a systems design guide and a developers guide. Book helps you understand how to design and develop Web applications using regular RPG or COBOL programs.

**The System i5 Express Web Implementer's Guide.** Your one stop guide to ordering, installing, fixing, configuring, and using WebSphere Express, Apache, WebFacing, System i5 Access for Web, and HATS/LE.

# *Joomla! Technical Books*

**Best Damn Joomla Tutorial Ever**
Learn Joomla! By example.

**Best Damn Joomla Intranet Tutorial Ever**
This book is the only book that shows you how to use Joomla on a corporate intranet.

**Best Damn Joomla Template Tutorial Ever**
This book teaches you step-by step how to work with templates in Joomla!

**Best Damn Joomla Installation Guide Ever**
Teaches you how to install Joomla! On all major platforms besides IBM i.

**Best Damn Blueprint for Building Your Own Corporate Intranet.**
This excellent timeless book helps you design a corporate intranet for any platform while using Joomla as its basis.
4
**IBM i PHP & MySQL Installation & Operations Guide**
How to install and operate Joomla! on the IBM i Platform

**IBM i PHP & MySQL Programmers Guide**
How to write SQL programs for IBM i

www.ingramcontent.com/pod-product-compliance
Lightning Source LLC
Chambersburg PA
CBHW072111270326
41931CB00010B/1517